Collected Plays of Daniel Curzon

Volume I

(1977-1982)

IGNA Books / San Francisco
Telephone: 415-585-3410

Distributed by BookSurge.com

Library of Congress cataloging-in-publication data

Curzon, Daniel

Collected Plays of
Daniel Curzon (Vol. I)

I. Title

Front cover photo of Danny Brown, St. Rose of Lima, Detroit, Michigan.

Back cover photo of author by A. Deriev

ISBN 0-930650-07-7

Printed in the United States of America

CONTENTS

Dedicated to all the kids in Detroit who attended the plays the author put on in his boyhood – but not to the bullies who spoiled things.

SEX SHOW, 1977

SEX SHOW:
Comedy Madness

Performance Note

Best performed with five actors of the same sex, dressed in red T-shirts and Levi's, using a few props to suggest different characters, with a few simple platforms and screens.

At rise, each actor enters and claps twice. They gradually form a pyramid on the platforms, then all clap twice together and say *Sex Show* as one.

Add music, especially between skits.

Nominated for Best Script,
San Francisco Bay Area Theatre Critics Circle (1977)

"One of the best pieces of theater entertainment running in the Bay Area."
– *San Francisco Bay Guardian*

"Often funny, always irreverent, exceptionally well presented."
– *Bay Area Reporter*

"Well directed, actors lively and engaging."
– *San Francisco Chronicle*

"Highly recommended." – *The Sentinel*

FAMILY PORNOGRAPHY

CHARACTERS:
MOTHER, in a string of pearls and rhinestone glasses
FATHER, with a clip-on necktie
SON, twelve, in a baseball cap
DAUGHTER, eleven, with a pink ribbon

(MOTHER, FATHER, SON, DAUGHTER enter and take their places in four chairs facing the audience. All are eating popcorn and drinking Coca Cola out of paper cups.)

MOTHER — Don't eat that popcorn so fast.

SON — (Still eating too fast) It's real good!

MOTHER — (as DAUGHTER starts to go into the row in front of her) Jenny! (to SON) You'll get indigestion.

SON — No, I won't.

FATHER Listen to your mother, son.

SON (Sulks a bit, then slides down in his seat, where he gobbles popcorn.)

DAUGHTER Mom, Billy's eating his popcorn real fast again!

MOTHER Billy, what did I tell you?

SON (punching sister) You old tattletale!

FATHER Now enough of that, you two.

DAUGHTER (Pinches her brother, who yelps.)

FATHER Now you two be quiet! The movie's about to start, and I don't want to hear another peep out of either of you. You understand?

(SON and DAUGHTER settle down but

manage some surreptitious pinches.)

MOTHER (as the film begins) Oh, I just love these Walt Disney movies!

FATHER (patting her hand) Yes, it's nice to know there are still some things you can take the whole family to.

DAUGHTER I didn't like the last one we saw.

SON Me neither. It was dumb.

FATHER Shhhh!

SON Well, it *was* dumb!

FATHER It wasn't dumb. It was family entertainment!

MOTHER It's the sort of picture we're not embarrassed to take you to.

SON (under his breath) It was dumb.

DAUGHTER (jumping up) Hey look! It's got David Cassidy in it! Oh, I just love David!

MOTHER Yes, I've always liked David Cassidy. He seems like such a nice boy.

FATHER He's the grandson of Hopalong Cassidy, did you know that?

DAUGHTER Hey look! It's got the Osmond Brothers too! All five of 'em!

FATHER Clean-cut kids, every one of them.

MOTHER I think it's so nice the way Donnie and Marie sing those lovely songs together — not like some brothers and sisters I could name who're always fighting.

(MOTHER looks over at her children.)

FATHER — Yes, why can't you two sing together instead of always pinching each other?

(DAUGHTER and SON look over at each other. Then on cue they burst into "Tits and Ass.")

FATHER — That’s enough now! Sit down!

SON — (points) Hey, who’s Helen Hayes?

MOTHER — (finger aloft, a maxim) She’s the First Lady of the American Stage — or was.

SON — What’s she doing in a Disney movie then?

MOTHER — Shhhh. She’s a great dramatic actress.

SON — I never heard of her. And who’s Cae-sar Rome-a-roe? (Mispronounces it Rome-a-roe on purpose throughout.)

FATHER (correcting) Caesar Ro*mer*o is a long-time star. Or was.

SON Was he a spic? He's got a spic name.

FATHER (looking around to see if they've been overheard) Caesar Romero is one of America's finest (pause) Chicano actors, and don't you ever forget it, Billy.

DAUGHTER This better be good! (Spills some Coke on MOTHER's leg by accident.)

MOTHER Jenny, be careful! You're getting pop all over everything!

SON Make her get down and lick it up!

DAUGHTER	Shut up, you fag!
FATHER	Now enough of that kind of language, young lady! Sit down!

(He pulls her into her seat.)

MOTHER	Where do you pick up language like that anyway!
FATHER	Why do you think we bring you to these Walt Disney movies — so you'll talk like a little guttersnipe?
DAUGHTER	(Sulks, but mouths "You fag!" at her brother. Again spills some Coke on him.)
SON	(jumping up, making a fuss) Jenny spilled pop on me! (He tries to hit his sister but is stopped by FATHER.)
FATHER	Sit down, both of you, and behave yourselves!

	Do you hear me!
MOTHER	If you don't behave, we're not going to bring you with us the next time we come!
SON	We don't care!
MOTHER	You do too care. You love these movies, and you know it.
SON	I hate 'em.
DAUGHTER	Yeah, they stink. I never liked Helen Hayes.
MOTHER	(scandalized) What do you mean! Of course you like Helen Hayes! She's the First Lady of the American Stage!
SON	I hate her.
MOTHER	Listen here, young man, you do not hate *Helen Hayes*! She gave the

best years of her life
up there on the screen to
entertain you in these
wholesome movies, and
you'd better appreciate
what she's done for
you!

SON (under his breath) I hate Helen Hayes.

FATHER (to SON) Do you want some more popcorn?

SON No.

FATHER Coke?

SON No.

FATHER Well then, sit still.

DAUGHTER (watching the screen) Hey, why is Helen Hayes taking her clothes off?

MOTHER (at a loss at first, but then she finds an explanation) It must be part of the plot.

SON	Caesar Rome-a-roe's taking all his clothes off too!
FATHER	They're probably going swimming.
SON	No, they're not! He's kissing Helen Hayes's belly button!
DAUGHTER	Look! Caesar Rome-a-roe's unbuckling Helen Hayes's bra!
MOTHER	Shhhh! I'm sure it has something to do with the story. Sit still and behave.
SON	They're all wrinkled!
MOTHER	They're in love with each other and that's why they're kissing.
FATHER	Mr. Disney has never let us down yet, and you can be sure he knows what he's doing now.

SON	Look! Caesar Rome-a-roe's taking Helen Hayes's panties off — and ripping 'em!
MOTHER	Well, he's doing it a very (pause) tasteful way, you can see that right off.
FATHER	Caesar Romero is one of our finest Chicano actors.
DAUGHTER	Look! He's got his thing out! Look how big it is!
MOTHER	I'm sure it's all part of the . . .
DAUGHTER	Now he's making Helen Hayes bend over.
MOTHER	(now knowing quite what to say) Well, yes, he is. But don't you see how graceful she is. And she's over seventy.
SON	He's really giving it to

her, isn't he?

MOTHER Well, it's in Technicolor!

FATHER Mr. Disney has never let us down yet.

DAUGHTER And now she's got his thing in her mouth!

MOTHER But they're in love, and (patting hubby's hand) he's certainly going to marry her at the end.

FATHER This whole sequence is a dream, and they're going to wake up and we're going to see that it didn't really happen.

SON Caesar Rome-a-roe just shot all over Helen Hayes's leg!

MOTHER Well, yes he did. But you saw how well photographed it was, and not a pubic hair in sight!

FATHER	Maybe this is a wildlife picture, by mistake.
SON	Looks like a porno film to me.
MOTHER	Now you close your mouth, young man. We won't have any talk like that.
FATHER	We certainly won't. You sit down and watch this picture. I'm sure Mr. Disney knows what's he's doing.
SON	Now look! David Cassidy is on top of Helen Hayes!
DAUGHTER	Oh, I just love David Cassidy!
FATHER	He's the grandson of Hopalong Cassidy?
SON	He's coming all over her face!
DAUGHTER	(jumping on the chair)

Wow! Is this movie every *dirty*!

MOTHER — It's not dirty, and you sit down! I didn't see anything on Miss Hayes's face.

DAUGHTER — Look! Look! Now Helen Hayes is doing it with Caesar Rome-a-roe again. And David Cassidy is *watching*. Oh, isn't he dreamy!

FATHER — (quietly) I don't understand this movie.

MOTHER — It must all have something to do with . . . symbolism!

DAUGHTER — Mom and Dad, look! Now there's a Great Dane in a Volkswagen!

SON — And now the Osmond Brothers are there! And they're all doing it together in the

	Volkswagen!
FATHER	It's really quite interesting, isn't it?
MOTHER	Well, I don't know . . .
FATHER	Mr. Disney has never let us down yet, we know that, right?
MOTHER	That's true, and they did advertise this movie in *Family Circle* magazine.
FATHER	Well, let's make a family circle then.

(Places his arm around MOTHER.)

MOTHER	Are you sure, dear?
FATHER	Sure! Come on! (wickedly) Slip down your panties!
MOTHER	(Mimes folding her skirt neatly, then slipping

down her panties,
then kicking them off
with one foot) Are you
sure this was a G-for-
General Audiences?

FATHER All I know is that Mr. Disney is somebody we can always trust!

(Sticks his popcorn box between MOTHER's legs.)

MOTHER (after a hesitation) Now, children, do it tastefully, like Mr. Disney!

(FATHER picks up his popcorn box, and all four hold their boxes above their heads in a toast. After two beats, they toss the boxes behind them. All their legs come up and cross in a scissors pattern as their hands come down slowly toward their crotches.)

ALL Whoopee!

BLACKOUT

WHAT DID THEY DO IN GOMORRAH?

CHARACTERS:
FIRST , with a staff
SECOND
A SHEEP

(Two SHEPHERDS are sitting back to back.)

FIRST See that smoke over there?

SECOND What is it? (Looks over his shoulder.

FIRST All that's left of that place.

SECOND What place was that?

FIRST Gomorrah.

SECOND Had a fire, huh?

FIRST A bad one.

SECOND (Getting up to look) Is that that place on the suburbs of Sodom?

FIRST Same place.

SECOND (shading eyes) I can't see a stone left upon a stone.

FIRST (gesturing with his staff toward the sky) *He* did it.

SECOND Yeah? What pissed Him off?

FIRST Well, He got mad at Sodom first. You know what they were doing over there!

SECOND So I heard. Disgusting, wasn't it!

FIRST Sure was. They had it coming.

SECOND But what were they doing in Gomorrah? How come *they* got it?

FIRST They were perverts too.

SECOND No kidding? What kind?

FIRST I really wouldn't want to say.

SECOND Come on, you can tell me.

FIRST (after a brief hesitation) Well, the way I heard it they were fornicating with fish.

SECOND They were what?

FIRST Fucking fish.

SECOND Fish fuckers, huh? Why were they doing that?

FIRST How do I know! They were perverts, that's why.

SECOND And He got pissed off at 'em for it, huh?

FIRST You don't see nothing but smoke, do you?

SECOND (thinking about it) How do you suppose you do it with fish?

FIRST Wouldn't know. Not into fish myself.

SECOND You suppose you take 'em

	to bed? (Puckers up mouth as though about to kiss a fish.)
FIRST	There was talk of orgies with small-mouth bass.
SECOND	Small-mouth, huh? Pretty kinky!
FIRST	They started out with just small fry, sardines, you know, but then they got into the real heavy stuff.
SECOND	How heavy?
FIRST	Sharks!
SECOND	Oh! Yeah? How big?
FIRST	Big mothers! They weren't satisfied with the small ones anymore.
SECOND	Did they ever get into whales?
FIRST	Probably. They seemed like the type.

SECOND Any crabs?

FIRST More than likely.

SECOND How disgusting!

FIRST I know.

SECOND So that's what they were doing in Gomorrah, huh? (Looks back at it.)

FIRST Don't look over there too long, or you'll turn into a pillar of salt.

SECOND (jumping back) Ah, I wouldn't want to look at that nasty place anyhow! Fish fuckers! What's the world coming to!

(He sits back down with his back to the other.)

(A SHEEP enters, grazes.)

SECOND Sheep are quiet today.

(Pokes FIRST with his elbow.)

FIRST Sure are.

SECOND That one over there,
beside the olive tree,
is sort of cute, isn't she?

FIRST A real doll.

SECOND Want to go over and
give her a good time?

FIRST Sure, got nothing else
to do.

(They sing "Merzy Doats" as they amble over to the SHEEP. One bends down and lifts its head as the other places the crook of the staff around its neck and pulls the head up from the grazing.)

SECOND Hope she hasn't got
no fleas!

(The SHEEP goes "Baa" as one starts to mount her.)

BLACKOUT

VD

CHARACTERS:

NARRATOR, who reads from a big book like a Bible

PLAYERS (4), who play multiple parts

(All the sex acts in the following should be simulated in a stylized, exaggerated, comic way.)

NARRATOR And on the sixth day God created the Earth. (Points to center stage.) And on this Earth God created Adam.

(Adam appears center stage, arms crossed.)

NARRATOR And God took one of Adam's ribs (Adam reacts.) and created Eve.

(Adam half sits, half lies on stage as a second Player appears center stage, looking winsome.)

NARRATOR And then God created VD.

(He produces a red bean bag shaped like a heart, hands it to Adam like God in the Sistine Chapel painting.)

(Adam takes the bean bag on his crotch, examines it, grimaces.)

NARRATOR And there was no cure for this VD because God had (Pause.) fucked up.

(Adam shakes his fist at the heavens.)

NARRATOR And that very day Adam gave the VD to his wife, Eve.

(Eve lowers her crotch to Adam on the ground, looks at the audience, and says, "ut, oh!" She stands with the bean bag against her crotch, facing the audience.)

NARRATOR And then Eve gave the VD to her boyfriend.

(A Player wriggles in as a hissing snake, comes up from behind, between Eve's legs, and takes the bean bag in his mouth. Eve makes a Mae West sound and strolls off.)

NARRATOR — And there came a Great Flood upon the Earth, and Eve's boyfriend took refuge in a great boat with other creatures.

(Three Players line up as occupants of a great boat, on their hands and knees in a line.)

NARRATOR — And during the forty days and forty nights (The three Players and the snake rock back and forth in unison.) Eve's boyfriend gave his VD to many.

(The snake hands the bean bag to a Player (a pig, who oinks), and the pig hands it to another Player (a cat, who meows), the cat hands it on to another Player (a cow, who moos).

(The first Player now gets up and goes to the end of the line and becomes Noah and enters the cow from behind.)

NARRATOR — And thus the cow gave it to Noah.

(Louder, surprised "moo" from the cow, who's being entered.)

NARRATOR And Noah gave it to his daughters.

(Noah, drunk, slaps the bean bag against the crotch of his two daughters, who make delighted sounds.)

NARRATOR And Noah's daughter gave it to Moses. (One daughter hands the bean bag to Moses, who was the cow.) Who gave it to his concubines.

(The other three Players line up like three chorus girls, one leg up, a hand on the shoulder of the next.)

NARRATOR And the concubines gave it to David.

(The last concubine in the chorus line hands it to the fourth Player.)

NARRATOR And sometime later David gave VD to Jonathan.

(David sodomizes Jonathan, who sighs in pleasure.)

NARRATOR Earlier David had tried to give it to Goliath, but had been turned down. (Goliath is made of two Players-one on the other's shoulders. They turn down the thumbs of their free hands.) And so he settled for other methods. (David uses his slingshot. The rock topples Goliath, who breaks into two Players as they fall on their knees and face the audience.)

NARRATOR And Jonathan gave VD to no one, because he touched no other and pined away for love of David.

(Jonathan sighs, then fades away as David runs his finger down his cheek.)

NARRATOR But no need to worry — for King David was

giving VD to all his wives.

(David tosses the bean bag to the farthest wife. The three wives are on their knees, waving like cheerleaders.)

NARRATOR And one of King David's wives gave it to Samson, who went blind.

(Samson gets the bean bag, touches it to his eyes. Then he makes a revolving millstone (another Player) go around twice, with Samson bent over. Two other Players form pillars and collapse on top of Sampson's back.)

NARRATOR In the meantime of course Samson had given VD to Delilah, who gave it to anybody who asked.

(Delilah gets the bean bag from Samson as the millstone turns.)

(Delilah saunters across the stage, touching the hips of two other Players who were the pillars.)

NARRATOR And one of these was St. Paul.

(Delilah slaps St. Paul's rear end with the bean bag. The former Samson, now St. Paul, blesses himself and takes the bean bag.)

NARRATOR And St. Paul gave it to the Corinthians, or was it an Ephesian?

(He starts to give it to one of the Players, changes his mind, starts to give it to another.)

Who gave it to Nero.

(He places the bean bag on a Player's head. It falls off into another Player's hand.) Who gave it to his mother and his sister and his pet Pekingese.

(The Player touches the bean bag to the breasts of two other Players who are striking feminine poses. He comes up behind the pet Pekingese, enters it. The dog barks in an asthmatic way, then shakes the bean bag in its mouth.)

NARRATOR And Nero's Pekingese

gave it to the next emperor, who gave it to the next emperor, who gave it to the last emperor, who gave it to the first monk.

(The Players form a Rube Goldberg-like line, starting from one emperor to the next and then starting back with the monk, who gets it in the rear.)

NARRATOR And the monk gave it to a nun.

(A Player on his knees grabs the bean bag from behind, through the crotch of the one playing the monk.)

NARRATOR And the good sister gave it to a choirboy.

(The nun moves on her knees to the choirboy, who is singing in a high voice. As soon as the bean bag touches his crotch, his voice gets much lower.)

NARRATOR And the choirboy later gave it to two prostitutes.

(Two Players stroll past the choirboy as though swinging their purses. They bend, forming a single unit with their rear ends touching. The Choirboy places the bean bag on their joined butts.)

NARRATOR And the prostitutes gave it to all who followed — Charlemagne, Richard the III, Frederick the Puny, Frederick the Fascist, Frederick the Fool, Margaret of Anjou, Elizabeth of Tunisia, Mary, Queen of Scots, Gwendolyn of Aphrodisia, Anne of Austria, Anne of Cleves, Anne of Cloves, Anne of Cinnamon, Anne of Sugar and Spice and Everything Nice!

(The four Players make a square and toss the bean bag as if it's a hot potato. On the line about "Anne of Austria," one Player moves center stage, gets on his knees, hands the bean bag behind him to the next Player. Then each Player passes back over his head until it all climaxes in "and Everything Nice.")

NARRATOR And Anne of Sugar and Spice and Everything Nice gave VD to Queen Edgar of Fire Island.

(Queen Edgar places his groin on the hip of another Player.)

NARRATOR And Queen Edgar of Fire Island gave VD to a real estate agent from Cedar Rapids, Iowa.

(Edgar hurries over the agent. From behind he gives a quick, surprising thrust to the agent.)

NARRATOR And the real estate agent gave it to a lawyer in Bermuda.

(The agent moves over, drops the bean bag on the back of a Player who is on hands and knees.)

And the lawyer passed it on to (grandly) the Duchess of Windsor!

(He hands the bean bag to her in an elegant arc. The Duchess takes it and extends her pinkie.)

And the Duchess gave it to Harry Truman, who gave it to Bess Truman, who gave it to the Prime Minister of Great Britain!

(Harry Truman is old and quivery, as is Bess Truman. Two Players form an ocean. Bess Truman tosses the bean bag over the "waves" to the Prime Minister, who makes a monocle with his fingers.)

NARRATOR And the Prime Minister gave it to Pat Nixon.

(Pat Nixon takes it, very squeamishly.)

And naturally Pat Nixon gave it to Richard Nixon.

(She hands it to Richard with pinched, fussy fingers.)

Who passed it on to Gerald Ford.

(Nixon sticks it under Ford's armpit.)

NARRATOR And Gerald Ford gave it to Shirley Temple Black. (She tap dances downstage.) and Angela Davis. (Angela moves downstage too, with an upraised arm.) — in a three-way! And Angela gave it to a convict in Soledad Prison.

(Angela turns and fist-fucks another Player.)

While Shirley passed it on to Arthur Godfrey.

(Angela Davis holds the bean bag to a prisoner's rear end, Arthur Godfrey strums his ukulele as Shirley grins.)

NARRATOR And the convict in Soledad passed the VD on by raping a "fag" in Cellblock 12.

(The convict rapes the "fag" from behind. Two other convicts come up to get their share. The bean bag is passed along against the "fag's" rear end. The "fag" bends over, then falls to his hands, collapsing with each succeeding rape.)

NARRATOR A short while later the convict escaped from prison and tried to rape a temperamental transsexual.

(The convict sneaks up on another Player, rubs his crotch against the transsexual's. He gets a chop to the neck and falls down. Transsexual says, "Well!")

NARRATOR And then somebody said —"Why in the world doesn't everybody use tetracycline! *Everybody*! At the same time!

(The raped "fag" and the convict sit up to say this line with the Narrator — from "Why in the world" on.)

(Transsexual takes out imaginary pills, walks over and hands one to each of the other Players, including the Narrator. In unison all five take the pills.)

NARRATOR And it cam to pass that it *didn't* come to pass.

(The transsexual hands the bean bag to the Narrator. The Narrator drops the bean bag in front of himself.)

And no one gave VD to anybody else ever again, and the world was the way God should have made it in the first place!

(The four Players assume positions with two of on their backs and the other two grasping their legs from above. The top two say "Hallelujah!" Then the two on the floor say "Hallelujah!" even louder.)

NARRATOR (Smiles at audience.) Amen!

BLACKOUT

LEGEND

CHARACTERS:
NARRATOR, with large book
FIRST MIME
SECOND MIME

NARRATOR — Once upon a time, the Almighty gave a wonderful gift to mankind.

(First Mme, kneeling center sage, discovers an imaginary gift, unwraps it.)

NARRATOR — And mankind was overjoyed at the marvelous gift from God.

(First Mime gets up, tries on an imaginary garment, with his back to the audience, feeling the material.)

NARRATOR — And the name of this wondrous gift was SEX.

(First Mime turns toward the audience

and opens his mouth in a parody of lust.)

NARRATOR And the Almighty found it good and thus gave it to all His people.

(First Mime continues to stroke the garment, rocking back and forth.)

NARRATOR Mankind was very happy with God's gift and he wore it everywhere. He wore it to parties. (First Mime comes by, waving it to the Narrator.) He wore it through big fields of flowers. (First Mime picks up an imaginary flower, then leaps and clicks his heels.

He even wore it to his job, because without SEX mankind's job was quite tedious.

(First pantomimes assembly-line work, but strokes his garment to show his contentment.)

NARRATOR — Mankind's life was richer and more delightful and full of much goodness because he had SEX.

NARRATOR — But then one day!

SECOND MIME — (leaps in from stage left, dressed in a bishop's vestments)

NARRATOR — An Old Fart noticed that mankind was using SEX, and the Old Fart fell into a great rage.

(Using a cane, Second Mime leans in toward the garment, then stamps and turns in a circle.)

NARRATOR — The Old Fart went up to mankind's SEX and stared at it and reacted.

SECOND MIME (Looks closely, makes disgusted noises, turns away violently.)

NARRATOR You see, the Old Fart was neurotic and tried to take SEX away from mankind.

(Second Mime comes back behind First Mime and rips the garment off his back, but the Second Mime hangs on to it, and the two have a tug of war.)

NARRATOR But finally the Old Fart, who was very strong, began to win out.

(Second Mime hits the back of the legs of the First Mime with his cane, sending him to his knees.)

And he tried and tried to tear mankind's SEX because he thought that people should be spiritual.

(He forces First into prayer posture.)

NARRATOR He told mankind he must pray instead of thinking about SEX, and to beat himself with whips, to chastise his body until it was under submission.

(Second Mime hands the First Mime the cane so that he can whack himself with it several times. The Second Mime stops him when he sees that the First Mime is enjoying it.)

NARRATOR The Old Fart told mankind he must never think about SEX, never, ever!

(Second comes up behind the First and places his hands over the eyes, ears, and mouth in a see-no-evil, etc. gesture, ending with a forceful push to First's head on "never, ever," so that First winds up with his forehead on the stage.)

NARRATOR Instead he should be "pure of heart" and hide it.

(Second Mime bangs his cane twice as a warning and then exits.)

(First Mime, in reacting to the warning, he scurries to stage right and hides the garment under an imaginary rug, then looks over his shoulder at where the Old Fart exited, nervous.)

NARRATOR — The Old Fart kept threatening to punish mankind if he didn't give up his SEX altogether, but mankind kept digging it up out of its hiding place and wearing it in secret.

(First Mime digs up the coat, sneaks upstage, puts on the garment, then hugs himself with his back to the audience, as though someone else's hands are going up and down his body. Eventually his hand comes down to his crotch, where the audience can see it groping.)

NARRATOR — Then one day the Old Fart discovered mankind wearing his SEX, and he was exceedingly angry. He grabbed mankind by the ear and flung him on the ground! (Second does so.) Then he called mankind vile names.(Second Mime shakes his cane and mouths vile names at First.) Until mankind cowered in a corner.

(First rolls over and over until he's back in a corner.)

NARRATOR Then he knew he would have to teach mankind a lesson for his own good, whether he agreed or not. So he grabbed mankind's SEX and *besmirched* it!

(Second takes the garment from First, wipes his rear end with it, then blows his nose on it, then tramples on it, then bangs it with the cane.) (First starts to leave, makes Second think he has given up, but Second catches him anyway and bangs the cane loudly. Only when convinced that the SEX won't be touched any more does the Second Mime hobble off.)

NARRATOR And from that day to this, mankind has thought of it his wonderful gift of SEX the way the Old Fart wants him to.

(First slowly picks up the dirtied SEX, holding it with two pinched fingers on each hand, then looks up at the audience with a grimace on his face.)

BLACKOUT

TRIBAL RITE

CHARACTERS:

BEAVER, a kid with baseball cap, ball, and mitt
DAD, with clip-on tie
MOM, with apron and duster

BEAVER (to audience before curtain) With special thanks to the Keraki tribe of New Guinea, who do it like *this*!

(DAD is sitting on a chair. BEAVER is spread out on the bed. Three chairs covered with a blanket can serve as the bed. To keep this skit light, add business with DAD and BEAVER playing catch, bouncing the ball, etc.)

DAD But you've got to go, Beaver!

BEAVER (adolescent voice) But *why*, Dad?

DAD If you don't do this, you won't grow up to be a man.

	Didn't you study your Boy Scout manual?
BEAVER	All I have to do is lie across this hide-a-bed with my pants down, is that right?
DAD	How else do you think your voice will get deep, Beave?
BEAVER	Ah, my voice is okay! (It cracks.)
DAD	And if the Elders don't fertilize you, how will you ever grow a beard?
BEAVER	Did *you* do it?
DAD	(with a chuckle) Of course I did it, Beaver.
BEAVER	Golly honest?
DAD	Golly honest I did! (Twirls his mustache.)
BEAVER	Did Wally do it?
DAD	Yes, your brother did it too. That's why he's a grown

man now, with a wife and a mortgage and car payments and everything.

BEAVER Some of the kids at school say it's just a custom.

DAD Your little friends at school are quite, quite wrong. Everybody in our town has to do it or he'll lack manliness when he grows up. You wouldn't want to lack *manliness*, would you?

BEAVER (moving away) Well, I went to the Eighth Grade Prom like you told me, didn't I? And I went to Scout camp last summer, even though I didn't want to go.

DAD And didn't those things make you a better boy?

BEAVER I didn't think the Prom was any fun. The boys stood on one side and the girls on the other, and then Mr. Atkinson made us all do the Bunny Hop!

DAD But you like the Bunny Hop, Beaver!

BEAVER I think we all looked stupid, hoppin' around all over!

(He hops the Bunny Hop.)

DAD I worry about you, Beaver. Most boys *like* to hop. Is there something the matter?

BEAVER No, but I met this boy at Scout camp last year who said *they* don't get fertilized by their Elders!

DAD Probably from some strange little village, where they don't even have TV.

BEAVER His name's Tommy. He said when boys in his town get to my age they fuck girls!

DAD Watch your language, Beaver.

MOM (peeking in, then coming in)

Watch your language, young man! Filthy-talking boys grow up to be dirty old men, exposing themselves in parks.

BEAVER I'm sorry, Mom and Dad.

(MOM exits.)

DAD You're going to be even sorrier, son, if you don't take down your trousers and lie across this hide- a-bed real soon!

BEAVER But Tommy said —

DAD And I'll bet you all the so-called men in Tommy's town are weak, sissified sillies! Who can't even hunt!

BEAVER Well, I saw Tommy's dad and he wasn't a weak, sissified silly.

DAD Do you think your mom and me would steer you wrong, Beaver?

BEAVER (squirming) Golly, I don't think so, Dad.

MOM (coming in again) Would any of your friends and family and teachers and priests and coaches and government officials steer you wrong, Beaver?

BEAVER Golly gee, Mom, I don't think you would, but . . .

DAD Just bend over, Beaver, and you'll see. . . . Are the Elders still waiting, dear?

MOM Yes, they're in the family room, still waiting. They've been so patient.

DAD Shall I have the Elders come up now, son?

BEAVER Will it hurt?

DAD Only the first one. By the time the thirteenth has placed his seed in you, you'll find it quite *nice*.

BEAVER	You *sure* they did this to you, Dad?
DAD	How do you think I became an adult?
BEAVER	(Moves away.) Isn't there any other way to get to be a man?
DAD	No, this is the right way. We've been doing it generation after generation.
MOM	Don't you trust your own mom and dad, Beaver?
BEAVER	Thirteen times?
DAD	One for each year of your age. You've been to the Prom and to Scout camp and you've got your own motor bike and transistor radio. Now all you have to do is get fertilized by the Elders and you'll be a full-grown member of the community.

BEAVER Will they use some grease?

DAD (shocked) You know grease is not permitted, Beaver!

MOM (Hands on her cheeks.) Oh, this boy, what's going to become of him!

BEAVER Will I be a real, true man when it's over? You promise?

DAD (putting an arm around his son's shoulder) Son, there are good customs and there are bad customs in this world. (Beckons MOM down beside their boy.) But would *we* have bad customs?

MOM Your brother Wally never objected the way you're doing, Beaver.

BEAVER What about Eddie Haskell?

DAD If you won't go through

with this, you might as well pack up and leave this town, don't you realize that? Nobody will have you here, and that's final!

MOM (coming to the other side) We love you, Beaver, and just want you to get penetrated.

BEAVER Well . . .

(BEAVER hands his cap to DAD, then the mitt and ball to MOM. He takes a deep breath. DAD turns BEAVER around, pushes his head down so that BEAVER's rear end is in an "available" position. MOM gives a sob as her little boy prepares to become a man.)

DAD (touching MOM's arm) Tell the Elders to come up now, honey, would you?

MOM (Gives a big final sob.)

BLACKOUT

HOW SIN AFFECTS THE WEATHER

CHARACTERS:
NARRATOR, with a large book
BRUCE
TWO FAIRIES, played by one person in a two-headed costume, with a wand
TWO CITIZENS

NARRATOR And there came two Fairies to Bakersfield in the evening.

(The Fairies enter in the two-headed costume.)

And Bruce, a fruit-picker, rose up to meet them.

(The Fairies goose Bruce with a wand from behind.)

And he said, "Behold now, my friends, turn in, and tarry with me all night, and then, later, ye shall rise up early and go on your way."

(The Narrator reads these words as Bruce mouths them.)

And the two Fairies said, “Nay, but we will abide in the street all night.”

(The Fairies mouth these words too, and drop both arms of the costume to indicate their reluctance. Mime the words throughout except where lines are expressly designated.)

And he pressed upon them greatly.

(Bruce rubs his crotch against the Fairies, beckons hard.)

And he did go out for Colonel Sanders’ Kentucky Fried Chicken and Dari Delite in like manner, and they did eat.

(The previous actions are pantomimed.)

But before they lay down, the Citizens of

this city, the very
populace of Bakersfield,
compassed the house
round, both old and
young, all the people
from every quarter.

(The Citizens jump in and make a semi-circle. Bruce and the Fairies act afraid.)

And they called unto
Bruce, and said, "Where
are the two Fairies
which came into these
this night? Bring them
out unto us, that we
may jail them!" And
Bruce went out at his
door unto them, and
shut the door after him.

(He does so, closing the door behind him with his foot.)

And said, "I pray you,
brethren, do not so
wickedly! Behold now,
I have an ex-lover
which lives further
along this street. Do ye

to *him* anything as is good in your eyes. Only unto these men do nothing, for came they under the shadow of my roof."

And the Citizens of Bakersfield said, "Stand back!" And they said again, "This one fellow came in to sojourn in our wonderful city of Bakersfield, and this pervert will needs judge of us! Now will we deal worse with *thee* than with *them*!"

And they pressed sore upon the man, even Bruce, and came near to break the door.

(The Citizens ram their shoulders against Bruce's imaginary door. Bruce puts up his hands to keep them out.)

But the Fairies put forth their hand, and pulled

Bruce into the house.

(They do so, then kick the door closed, keeping the Citizens out.)

And the Fairies smote the Citizens with blindness.

FAIRIES Smote! Smote!

NARRATOR So that they wearied themselves to find the door.

(The Citizens turn in circles twice and wander off.)

And the Fairies said unto Bruce, "We will destroy Bakersfield because the cry of these fools is waxen great before the face of the Lord!"

"Nay, destroy it not entirely," Bruce begged. But the Fairies answered not.

(The Fairies stand, arms folded, very determined.)

And Bruce went out, and spoke unto his father and mother and his friends, even unto his ex-lover, and said, "Up, get ye up, get ye out of this place, for the Lord will destroy Bakersfield!"

But he seemed as one that mocked unto his ex-lover.

(The Ex-lover appears carrying a flower. He taps Bruce on the nose with it and goes off unconvinced of any danger.)

EX-LOVER No!

And when the morning arose, then the Fairies hastened Bruce, and one of them said, "Escape for thy life! Escape to the mountain!"

And Bruce said unto them, "But I cannot

escape to a mountain,
lest some boredom take
me and I die."

(Bruce shows boredom.)

"Behold now, a city is
near to flee unto. Oh, let
me escape thither!"

And one Fairy said unto
him, "I have accepted
this request also,
because of thy
hospitality last
evening."

(The Fairies touch Bruce's body, up and down.)

"But haste thee at
once!"

(Bruce hurries up some of the platforms.)

Therefore was Bruce
settled in the city called
San Francisco!

(Bruce spreads out his arms, down on one knee, with a big flourish.)

And then the Lord
rained from a volcano
upon Bakersfield — and
upon Fresno — why
not? — brimstone and
fire from out of heaven!

(The Citizens re-appear, hiding their heads from the falling brimstone, then fall to their knees. Lightning flashes.)

And He overthrew those
Citizens, and all the
valley, and all the
inhabitants of those
cities, and that which
grew upon the ground.
Because the Lord did
not stint easily his
wrath!

(The Narrator shakes his finger.)

Grapes did wither on
their vines.

(One Citizen forms a vine and withers.)

And figs likewise from
lack of rainfall.

(A second Citizen shrivels up, from a different angle.)

The earth opened up
and *swallowed* the
remnants thereof.

(The Fairies make a slurping sound as the Citizens roll offstage.)

And thus did fog and
drought and ruin
descend upon the land.

(The Fairies make a fog-horn noise.)

But Bruce's ex-lover
looked back from
behind him at
Bakersfield and Fresno,
and he became a pillar
of dung.

(The Ex-lover re-appears with his flower, which he drops as he freezes.)

EX-LOVER Oh, shit!

NARRATOR And Bruce looked

toward all the land of
the valley, and, lo, the
smoke went up like the
smoke of a furnace.
And not a stone was left
upon a stone in the
cities of the valley, even
unto Colonel Sanders'
Kentucky Fried
Chicken and unto Dari
Delite! For the Lord
was exceeding wroth
with the Citizens'
unkindness to Bruce
and the two Fairies.

(Bruce waves. The Fairies bow.)

And likewise because
the Citizens were such
unmitigated simpletons
as to think that sin
affects the weather!

ALL (as one) Hah!

(The Narrator raises his arm and snaps his fingers as if controlling the light.)

BLACKOUT

THE WAYS MEN SHALL TOUCH

CHARACTERS:
NARRATOR
FIRST MIME
SECOND MIME

(The NARRATOR stands at the side of the stage with a big book. The MIMES act out the following sequences, making them flow in and out of one another.)

NARRATOR Gentlemen, I give you the laws! Here are the ways that men shall touch!

(Points to the two MIMES, who leap in sideways and take up positions opposite each other.)

Thou shalt compete for sustenance!

(FIRST MIME starts to pick an apple from the ground. SECOND MIME, a caveman, comes up behind him and hits him with a club. FIRST MIME is stunned but recovers and hits SECOND with a club. They hit each other and knock each other out. They lie stretched out.)

NARRATOR Thou shalt touch with manly mettle!

(FIRST MIME and SECOND MIME face each other with swords, very elegantly bow to each other, then start slashing like maniacs. Finally SECOND MIME runs FIRST MIME through and proudly places his foot on the fallen, striking a picturesque pose with the sword.)

NARRATOR Gentlemen, thou shalt touch to settle other questions of honor!

(FIRST MIME holds out a box of old-fashioned pistols to SECOND MIME, who takes one. FIRST MIME then takes the remaining pistol, and they walk five paces from each other.)

NARRATOR Gentlemen, are you ready?

(Both nod to him.)

NARRATOR Ready! (They assume a sideways stance.) Aim! (They level their pistols at each other.) Fire

(They shoot. SECOND MIME is hit. He bows very properly to FIRST MIME, then falls over dead. FIRST MIME clicks his heels and bows very properly to the corpse.)

NARRATOR Gentlemen, thou shalt touch if thy work be in circuses!

(FIRST and SECOND MIME tumble about the stage like acrobats. One of them lies on his back and lifts the other on his hands, or a reasonable facsimile of same. After several stunts, they take typical circus bows.)

NARRATOR Thou shalt touch if thou art engaged in manly athletics!

(FIRST and SECOND MIME begin to hand wrestle, first one about to win, then the other. FIRST MIME loses and falls to the ground.)

NARRATOR Of course it is written that if a man shall perform badly, he shall lose face!

(FIRST MIME pretends to remove his own face and hands it to SECOND, who scoffs at it.)

NARRATOR But men shall recover their face if they be real men!

(FIRST MIME dons boxing gloves and challenges SECOND to do the same. He does. They box. FIRST knocks out SECOND.)

NARRATOR (counting him out) Eight, nine, ten. The winner and new champion of the world!

(FIRST MIME smiles, holds his hands above his head like a champion, then, out of sportsman-ship, starts to revive SECOND MIME. FIRST lifts SECOND up and places his arm under SECOND's arm to support him. The other hand is between his legs, at the crotch.)

NARRATOR (shaking his finger) Uh ugh! Thou shalt not touch in unseemly ways!

(FIRST MIME looks guilty and drops SECOND like a sack of rocks.)

NARRATOR Unless one of thee shall be drunk!

(FIRST MIME grins, nods, points down at SECOND to indicate how drunk SECOND is. Then he lifts him and he staggers off with SECOND MIME.)

NARRATOR Got to watch 'em every minute. Never know where it might lead. (Pause, then look offstage.) Is that all the sports you guys know?

(FIRST MIME and SECOND MIME come running onstage as if playing basketball. They take several imaginary shots at a hoop. As FIRST goes up for a basket, SECOND stands up in front of him, brushing his front against FIRST MIME's.)

NARRATOR Foul!

(SECOND MIME protests.)

NARRATOR I say foul! Thou

touched his front with thy front!

(SECOND MIME dare not protest further and skulks off the court.)

NARRATOR Don't you guys even know how to play football?

(FIRST and SECOND get down as if to charge each other over the line of scrimmage. They push their shoulders together, until SECOND upends FIRST and scores with the football.)

NARRATOR Touchdown!

(SECOND jumps around like an idiot, out of joy, then slams the football in the end zone.)

NARRATOR (to FIRST) Thou may congratulate thy teammate!

(FIRST MIME smiles. As a teammate now, he goes over, slaps SECOND MIME on the butt.)

NARRATOR Enough!

(FIRST very rapidly removes his hand from SECOND's butt, looks chagrined.)

NARRATOR We'll overlook it *this* time.

(FIRST and SECOND almost faint with relief at being forgiven.)

NARRATOR And it is written that men may touch in times of crisis!

(FIRST MIME sits down, begins to weep, obviously grief-stricken. SECOND MIME comes on, mouths something. FIRST shakes his head no. SECOND then comes over and sits beside FIRST. After much uncertainty, SECOND places his arm around FIRST's back, to comfort him.)

NARRATOR (looking at his watch) Three seconds. That's almost beyond the allotted time! Thy crisis time is up. On to the next crisis!

(SECOND MIME falls over and lets FIRST assume a life-saving posture astraddle SECOND. He applies artificial respiration, while SECOND coughs out much water. After a few seconds, FIRST turns SECOND over, as if to breathe air into his mouth.)

NARRATOR No, thou shalt not apply mouth-to-mouth resuscitation! We know what that leads to!

(FIRST MIME looks guilty, stops applying artificial respiration, looks at SECOND MIME below him, examines the eyes, feels the pulse, decides that SECOND has died, gets up and walks off, leaving SECOND dead.)

NARRATOR Only seemly kinds of oral contact are permitted!

(SECOND is now a dentist. FIRST is sitting in a dentist's chair, with his mouth pried open by SECOND, who drills away. FIRST jumps around in some pain.)

NARRATOR Be a *man*!

(SECOND MIME yanks a tooth out of

FIRST, throws it down.)

NARRATOR And likewise it is written that a man may touch the mouth of another man if the second man be ill and in danger of death!

(FIRST MIME is now the doctor examining the SECOND as his patient, with a tongue depressor. Then he taps on SECOND's chest, listens to his heart. He mouths a word and SECOND coughs. FIRST taps on SECOND's back, asks him to cough again. This procedure is repeated several times. Finally FIRST, as the doctor, turns SECOND around, places both hands on SECOND's upper arms and shakes his head as though it's a terminal disease. He walks out, turning for a final hopeless shake of the head. SECOND realizes he's going to die and can merely tape his own chest helplessly.)

NARRATOR And men may touch each other lest they go naked before all eyes!

(FIRST becomes a clothing salesman, measuring SECOND for a pair of pants. FIRST's hand approaches SECOND's crotch with the tape-measure . . .)

NARRATOR Watch it!

(SECOND becomes a shoe salesman, fitting a shoe on FIRST's foot. There is some trouble getting it to slip on, and SECOND has to hold onto FIRST's knee. When he notices what he's done, he profusely apologizes — mimed.)

NARRATOR An abomination! (The shoe salesman cringes, starts to sneak out.) Art thou going to endure such an abomination from such as he?

(Indignant, FIRST rises and begins to pursue SECOND with a switchblade knife. They circle each other, both with switchblades now. Eventually FIRST stabs SECOND to death.)

NARRATOR That's more like it!

(FIRST grins at the praise, then kicks the body between the legs, to show an extra ounce of "courage.")

NARRATOR Thou shalt be honored for thy bravery before all eyes!

(FIRST jumps up, as a French general, and ceremoniously places a medal on SECOND's chest, then leans forward and touches his cheek to SECOND's cheek several times.)

NARRATOR All right, don't get all fruity about it! Jesus, couldn't you just pin the medal on him, without all that swish stuff?

(FIRST and SECOND jump apart guiltily. Then they look at each other, then begin to glare at the NARRATOR.)

NARRATOR (noticing them glaring at him but trying to ignore them, turning to the audience.

(FIRST and SECOND cross their arms defiantly.)

Dear friends, we have revealed the laws

wherein one man may touch the body of another man. Go ye and do ye in like manner.

(NARRATOR starts to leave, but he is stopped by FIRST and SECOND, who militantly begin to hold hands. The NARRATOR backs away in horror.)

NARRATOR Oh, my god! Oh, my god!

(FIRST and SECOND MIME hold hands even more defiantly.)

NARRATOR What will it lead to! What will it all lead to! Oh, my god! (He falls to one knee.)

(FIRST and SECOND embrace and kiss deeply, beautifully. NARRATOR see it, has a heart attack, falls down, dies.)

(The two kissing men hear the NARRATOR's body fall. They interrupt their kiss to look briefly at the corpse. They go back to their kissing.)

BLACKOUT

DESERT ISLE

CHARACTERS:
MAN, in a ragged T-shirt
TRANSVESTITE, in a life preserver, with two scarves tucked in as breasts; high-pitched voice

(As the skit opens, MAN is sitting alone, looking depressed. For a few moments he shifts position, looks disgruntled, dissatisfied, and restless. Then he gradually notices something in the distance. He stands up, shading his eyes to see better. Gradually he moves closer to the edge of the stage.)

MAN It's a boat! (He's doubtful but moves closer, still not sure.) Maybe it's a mirage! (Groans, covers his head with both hands, falls on the ground.) Why doesn't somebody save me! Save me! Damn it to hell, somebody save me! (He notices that something is getting closer.) It *is* a boat! My god, it *is* a boat! (Gets excited.) Oh my god, I'm rescued! I'm rescued at last. Real food! Civilization! Women! Oh my god, women, women, women at last! (Falls to his knees and beats on the ground in anticipation, then rises and begins to realize that it's too small to be a boat.) It's not a boat after all. It's just a . . . just a . . . what is it? Oh my god, it's just a woman in a life preserver! It's just a woman all by herself and she's coming here in a life preserver! (Covers his face with his hands.) Oh, no, it's just a woman all by herself . . . just a woman. (Begins to realize what a woman can do for him and starts rubbing his hands together out of lust.) It's a woman in that life preserver and she's coming this way. A woman! Oh my god, a woman's coming this way! Oh, thank you, God! Thank you! Thank you! (Kneels down for a quick prayer of thanks, then leaps up.) Come on, lady! Come on! (Starts waving her toward him, getting more and more excited.) Come on, lady! Come on, row those arms! Come on, come on! Tote that barge! Lift that bale! (Gets down on both knees, yelling encouragement, banging on the ground.) Come on, girl, you can do it! Come on, sweetie, get the lead out! Come on, gal, get yourself over her! Come on, come on, come and get it from me, hot momma baby!

TV (Enters from the audience, paddling in a life preserver.) Where in the world am I?

MAN (with a big smile) In paradise!

TV I am? I don't see any angels.

MAN Maybe not, but I know a devil you can meet. (Starts to stalk.)

TV I've been rowing for days!

(Takes out one scarf that makes up one breast.) My arms! My hair! (Fixes her hair.)

MAN I've been on this island for two years.

TV (arranging her wig, her gown, both imaginary) Oh, really? I was on this marvelous cruise out there, when this huge tidal wave came right along and threw us all overboard. But I was lucky and managed to get into this life preserver.

MAN You horny?

TV I beg your pardon? (Puts the scarf back as a breast, moves away.)

MAN I asked if you was horny. (He's having trouble keeping his hands off her.)

TV I don't know the meaning of this term . . . *horny.* (Shudders.)

MAN Ah, come on, don't play hard to get. I ain't had no sex for two whole years.

TV Pity.

MAN I thought you was a rescue party.

TV Obviously you *was* mistaken. (Goes on fixing hair.)

MAN How about a quickie?

TV Since it's been two years, I'm sure anything you might attempt would be a quickie.

MAN You're lovely. I love you. (Goes down on his knees.)

TV (smiling a bit) Oh, `you're just saying that!

MAN No, I'm not. I'm sincere. You're lovely. I love you. I wanna kiss you. (Hugs her legs.)

TV Oh, you naughty boy, how you talk! (Pats him on the head.)

MAN You're a real doll.

TV Now, now, I bet you say it to all the girls around here.

MAN No, I don't. I just say it to you. (Touches her crotch.)

TV Somebody probably told you the way to a girl's heart is through her skirts! (Pushes the life preserver down over her crotch quickly.)

MAN (groping himself) Come on, what d'you say, huh? You wanna do it?

TV My good man, such vulgarity! (Gesturing at MAN's hands.)

MAN (very fast) I think you's real pretty, and I love you, and I wanna kiss you and I wanna marry you! (On knees again.)

TV (teasingly) Aren't you sweet.

MAN Now will you do it?

TV (quickly) No.

MAN Please!

TV (quickly) No.

MAN Pretty please, with sugar on top.

TV (quickly) I'm on a sugar-free diet — no! (Turns back to him.)

MAN I'll give you a present. I'll give you two presents!

TV What sort of presents? (Turns around, interested.)

MAN How about a lobster and two coconuts?

TV Silly, silly boy, is that all you've got?

MAN (insinuatingly) I've got something better'n that, believe me. (Touches his crotch.)

TV Bragging?

MAN Wanna see it?

TV I've seen one before.

MAN Not like this one.

TV (to audience) Out of all the desert islands around here I had to pick this one!

MAN Come on, let's do it. Okay? I won't hurt you.(Grabs her from behind.)

TV *Hai! Hai!* (Assumes various karate poses, then kicks him away from her.) But we haven't been properly introduced.

MAN Jesus, you're strong!

TV (kittenish) Who me? (Fixes her hair.)

MAN I never met such a strong woman before.

TV Karate. (Affects a karate pose

and flicks a scarf at the same time.)

MAN Look, we're gonna be stuck here together for months, for years, maybe forever. We gotta work something out.

TV Says you. (Trying scarf around her head.)

MAN You can't fix your hair all the time, can you? You gonna need sex sometime, ain't you?

TV (airily) I prefer to drift with the mood of the evening. (Crosses stage while fluttering a scarf.)

MAN Do you want me to take you by force?

TV (dropping voice in pitch) Not likely, kiddo.

MAN Please, pretty please, with no sugar on top. I think you're lovely. I love you and I wanna kiss you and I wanna marry you and I want you to be the mother of my children. (Crawls across to TV on his knees, whimpering.)

TV — I can't be the mother of your children.

MAN — You can't? Are you sterile?

MAN — (sing-song) *Noooo!*

MAN — Are you on the pill?

TV — *Noooo.*

MAN — What's wrong with you?

TV — (same sing-song, but with a lower pitch) *I'm a man!*

MAN — (after recoiling at first, then deliberating, worrying, arguing with himself, agonizing over his decision) I can live with it.

TV — I don't think so.

MAN — Why not? I'm willing to overlook certain things. I'm not a queer, but I can make adjustments, considering the circumstances.

TV Well, I won't!

MAN Don't you wanna suck my dick?

TV Don't you care to kiss my ass?

(Turns away, sticks out rear end.)

MAN (after pause) I'd consider it . . .

TV Sorry, love, but it's not going to work out.

MAN But you're a transvestite!

TV Haven't you read your Kinsey? (Takes out both scarves and waves them in his face.) Honey, I'm *straight*!

(Exits, with a back kick.)

MAN (Groans.)

BLACKOUT

BOBBIE

CHARACTERS:
MOTHER
FATHER
BOBBIE (five years old, carrying a teddy bear; played by an adult)

(FATHER stands stage left, MOTHER on stage right. BOBBIE sometimes takes a few steps toward one parent or the other, building to a major dilemma.)

FATHER Dear Bobbie,
This is your Daddy. How are you? I'm fine, and I miss you a bunch. I wish you were here with me right this minute. I am taking steps at this very moment so that you can come and live with me. I hope you'll understand, even though you're only five, that Daddy loves you very much and that we're separated right now not because of me, but because of your mother. (Glares at

MOTHER., who sticks out tongue at FATHER.)

FATHER I'm afraid she has become very bad. You probably won't know what I'm talking about, but I'm going to tell you anyway — your mother has become a Lesbian-Separatist.

(BOBBIE, in the middle, raises his eyebrows.)

That's right. She has become a great big dyke! Of course she wasn't one of those when I married her, but now she hates men. Yes, I know that's hard to believe. I won't begin to tell you all the awful names she's called me —

MOTHER Fascist!

FATHER (to MOTHER) Pervert!

MOTHER Mr. Banality!

FATHER Ms. Les-banality!

(BOBBIE's head goes back and forth with each insult.)

MOTHER Asswipe!

FATHER Clit-licker! (to BOBBIE) Your mother is so filled with hate these days she won't even sing you a lullaby if it was written by a man. I couldn't begin to tell you the terrible things your mother is probably doing right this minute. But of course Daddy doesn't want to put bad thoughts — about cunnilingus and dental dams — in your sweet little head. 'Cause Daddy loves you very much indeed, and I want you to come and live with me just as soon as I can work things out.

Love,
Daddy

(BOBBIE toddles toward FATHER, is stopped by voice of MOTHER.)

MOTHER Dear Bobbie,

This is your Mommy. Don't go to your father, baby! He'll only hurt you, the way he hurt me. Yes, Bobbie, I left that man, and I'm glad I did, because your father knows nothing but contempt for women. He treated me like sh — poody. Yes, poody, Bobbie! No, I won't hand you a lot of sweet garbage like a lot of mothers. When I see poody, I call it shit! And, Bobbie baby, your father was nothing but one great, big piece of shit! (Glares at FATHER.)

FATHER Takes one to know one!

MOTHER Did he respect me? No, not once did he respect me! Did he sympathize when I told him I wanted to swim the English Channel? No, he did not sympathize. He told me I could swim in the bathtub. Worse! He told me a woman's place is in the sink! I'm sorry to have

to tell you this, but your
father is the worst sort of
male chauvinist pig. And I
grew sick and tired, tired
and sick, of his snorting.

(FATHER snorts like a pig.)

MOTHER And that's why I left him
and you. But I want you to
know I'm thinking of you
every minute, baby, and as
soon as we can manage it I
want you to come and live
with me and my new friend,
Barbette.

Love,
Mommy

(BOBBIE starts toward MOTHER but is
stopped by the voice of FATHER.)

FATHER Dear Bobbie,
This is your Daddy again.
I'm sorry I haven't come
for you yet. But the judge
still hasn't decided whether
you belong to your mother
or to me. I told that judge
that if your mother got
ahold of you, she'd turn

you into a weirdo like her.
I want you to know I'm
fighting for you, little tiger,
and I'm not giving up until
we're together the way we
used to be. Your old dad
won't let you fall into the
clutches of your mean old
monster of a mother!

(BOBBIE cringes at possible clutches.)

He won't let her turn you
into a hair-dresser!

(BOBBIE reacts in horror.)

Your father won't let her
turn you into some
simpering sissy twit!

(BOBBIE mimes being a twit.)

He won't let her get her
nasty Lesbian-Separatist
hands on you and make
you into a sicko like her.
I don't know to tell you
this, but your very own
mother sleeps with women

now, and she lets them
do ugly, disgusting, filthy
things between her legs —
things that only I, your
daddy, used to be able to
do. (Of course those
things weren't ugly and
disgusting and filthy when
I did them.) I won't say any
more because I don't want
you to have nightmares.

(BOBBIE shakes head no.)

Someday soon we'll be
together again, and then
we'll forget all about the
unnatural things your
mother's doing, and we'll
go to baseball games. Maybe you'll even play in the
Little League!

(BOBBIE swings a bat.)

And we can go fishing
together, and we can stick
worms on a hook and catch
great, big fish and kill them
and chop them up and eat
them!

(Simultaneously BOBBIE mimes hooking a worm, at first squeamishly, then more cruelly, then kills a flopping fish, and devours it raw.)

FATHER Love, Daddy.

(BOBBIE takes steps toward FATHER, is halted by MOTHER's voice.)

MOTHER Dear Bobbie,
How are you, baby? Mommy's very sorry that she hasn't been able to come for you yet. But she's working on it. No over-bearing, war-causing, porno-loving rapist asshole man is coming between you and me, you can be sure of that! So don't cry! I won't let your daddy have you. I won't let him turn you into a jerk who thinks the worst thing in the world he can call somebody is a —

FATHER (throwing insult) Cunt!

MOTHER Excuse my language, baby,

but you should know how
men are, so you'll know
how to deal with them
when you grow up. Avoid
the fuckers! I want you to
grow up happy. I want you
to wear your hair short,
and have fun and play with
yourself anytime you feel
like it.

(BOBBIE hops about, playing.)

Don't be ashamed of your
body. Because Mommy
wants you to be the best
adjusted person you can be,
as long as it's not a man,
and when we're re-united
we'll do all kinds of fun
things together. We'll go to
beauty contests and insult
the contestants! We'll
swim the English Channel
together, and your father
and nobody will tell us we
can't! We'll write long,
long pamphlets about
female oppression and
show everybody we can do
things as well as men —

better than men! And we'll
do it together, Bobbie, you
and me, me and you, me
and you, and you and me!
Love,
Mommy

(BOBBIE mimes heckling contestants, swimming the Channel, etc, as she mentions each thing, getting excited by the plans.)

FATHER (stopping BOBBIE cold)

Dear Bobbie,
Guess who this is! The
judge has decided to let you
come and live with me!
Isn't that wonderful? I'll be
there tomorrow to pick you
up.
Love,
Daddy

MOTHER Dear Bobbie,
This is your Mommy. I'm
coming for you tomorrow,
no matter what any bigot
of a judge or anybody
says. I love you, and I'm
coming to get you if it's

the last thing I do. Wait
for me!
Love,
Mommy

(BOBBIE runs back and forth rapidly between the two parents.)

FATHER Dear Bobbie,
This is Daddy again. I'll
be there in a little while.
Be ready!
Love,
Daddy

MOTHER Dear Bobbie,
Wait for me by the front
door. I'll be there in a few
minutes.
Love,
Mommy

FATHER That woman better not —

MOTHER — touch him!

(FATHER and MOTHER leave their positions, move toward BOBBIE at the center, see each other and stop short.)

FATHER What are *you* doing here?

MOTHER None of your business.

FATHER Oh?

MOTHER Out of my way!

FATHER Out of my way! I've come for Bobbie.

MOTHER So have I!

FATHER Well, you're not getting him! He's legally mine! (Grabs BOBBIE's arm.)

MOTHER I carried Bobbie in my Womb. That's more than you ever did for this child! (Grabs BOBBIE's other arm.)

All you ever did for him was squirt into me!

FATHER Bobbie's mine, and you're not getting him — ever!

(Pulls BOBBIE away. MOTHER pulls in the opposite direction.)

MOTHER Bobbie's mine!

FATHER (tugging) Mine!

MOTHER (tugging) Mine!

FATHER (very emotional) Unhand that child! He's my son, and I love him!

MOTHER Your son? Bobbie's my daughter, and I love her! (very emotional, tugging)

FATHER I thought Bobbie was a boy.

MOTHER Bobbie's a girl!

FATHER Bobbie's a boy, damn it!

MOTHER Bobbie's a girl, goddamn it!

FATHER A boy!

MOTHER A girl!

FATHER (louder) A boy!

MOTHER (louder) A girl!

FATHER Bobbie's a goddamn boy!

MOTHER Bobbie's a goddamn girl!

(MOTHER and FATHER both look at child.)

MOTHER /
FATHER Well?

(They shake his arms to make him/her speak.)

(BOBBIE squinches up face, undecided, shakes head, uncertain which he/she is.)

FATHER Well, I don't want it if it's a girl. You keep it.(Drops BOBBIE's arm.)

MOTHER Well, I don't want it if it's a boy. You keep it. (Drops arm.)

(Parents go in opposite directions, stop, look back at child, exit simultaneously.)

(BOBBIE hugs himself/herself, then hugs his teddy bear, then crumples up, touching forehead to the floor, a sad little pile, downstage center.)

SLOW FADE/ INTERMISSION

MR. RIGHT

CHARACTERS:
GANYMEDE, a Trojan shepherd boy about sixteen, wearing a toga, carrying a staff
ZEUS, a Greek god in the form of an eagle, just a beak for the nose, a laurel wreath; the actor can simulate flying by flapping his arms
TWO OTHERS

GANYMEDE (before the curtain, to the audience) "Mr. Right" — the story of a simple shepherd boy and a god!

(At rise GANYMEDE is dozing on a hillside, when suddenly ZEUS, waving his arms, making loud eagle noises, zooms in.

(GANYMEDE wakes up, frightened.)

GANYMEDE Fie! Fie! Be gone!

(ZEUS flutters toward him.)

GANYMEDE Oh, to have my father's bow with me! Eagle, be gone! (He drives the eagle partway off. The eagle crouches on chair as though it's a rock) *E*

ZEUS But I have come for thee, Ganymede.

GANYMEDE (amazed) But who art thou?

ZEUS I am Father Zeus. I have come for thee, in the shape of an eagle. (Makes a comic eagle noise.)

GANYMEDE For me? But why?

ZEUS I am Father of the Gods (GANYMEDE falls face down.), and I have seen thee on these Trojan hillsides and become enamored of thee, boy.

GANYMEDE Enamored of me?

ZEUS	Yes, beloved. I have watched thee from the domain of the Gods day following day as you strolled and slumbered on these hillsides, and today I have at last come for thee and wish to take thee back to Mt. Olympus. (ZEUS smiles.)
GANYMEDE	But, Sir . . . thou knowest me not.
ZEUS	I know I shall never rest until thou share my bed. Come, ride astride my back, and I will soar with thee to the Heavens — aloft, aloft, where thou, like us the Gods need never die!
GANYMEDE	(Takes a step forward, then stops.) My father! He will be angry if I leave here.
ZEUS	Leave him! Thou art the son of Tros and

Callirhoe no longer! Henceforth thou art mine alone. . . (an afterthought) And I thine.

GANYMEDE (Takes another step closer but halts.) Yet my father will have no one to tend his flocks.

ZEUS Well, beauteous boy, I shall give him recompense. I shall give him a golden vine that I much prize. (He removes the golden laurel wreath from his head, offers it grandly.)

GANYMEDE (Takes it, looks at it, bites it to test it, then says:) Ehh! (Not impressed.)

ZEUS Is this not recompense enough?

GANYMEDE Well, what can my father do with a golden vine? Why not just give him some gold coins?

ZEUS — MORTALS! Such mundane minds! (He crosses back to his "rock," then has an inspiration) AH! I shall gift your father with two immortal horses, swifter than any steeds on earth! (Offstage sound of galloping horses, made with coconuts perhaps.) How do you like that?

GANYMEDE — (Shakes his hand back and forth, not too impressed, but ZEUS doesn't notice.)

ZEUS — (descending from the "rock") Now come, sweet, comely lad, and climb aboard my eagle back, and we will flash to Mt. Olympus!

GANYMEDE — (still hesitant) Yet what will we *do* there once we arrive?

ZEUS (kneeling, over shoulder, prepared to fly) We will make love! Of course!

GANYMEDE But I am only a mortal. Won't my body corrupt in time, and fall away to nothingness? (coyly) And then what will become of me?

ZEUS Ah, delightful, calculating boy, I shall never forsake thee. . . . And *should* I do so, I vow I shall make thee into a star!

GANYMEDE Others have been *poised* such . . .

ZEUS (loudly) Shall I make thee into a whole constellation!?

GANYMEDE Well . . .

ZEUS It's thine, rapturous lad! I promise thee, as I am Lord of Everything!

GANYMEDE	(still not sure) Great Zeus, I petition thee that I may have a useful place among the divinities. (to audience) I don't want to be a star! (to ZEUS) But could I beg for the position of cupbearer to the Gods? (kneeling, one hand reaching ZEUS's crotch on the word "cupbearer.")
ZEUS	(looking down at the hand close to his crotch) Well, it will mean warring with Hera, my wife. But DONE!
GANYMEDE	My thanks, Royal Sir.(Bows.)
ZEUS	Now, well-made boy, whose beauty knots my heart, come, run, leap onto my eagle back! Come with me from lowly Mt. Ida to Mt. Olympus, and let me show you the delights

above that only the gods know!

(GANYMEDE looks around, a final decision. Then he comes running across the stage and leaps onto ZEUS' back. ZEUS flaps his wings, about to fly off.)

OFFICER (coming in) All right! Enough of this perverted filth!

(His partner grabs GANYMEDE and pushes him into a crouching position.)

ZEUS Who art thou?

OFFICER Trojan Vice Squad! You're under arrest for corrupting a minor, possible child molesting, and attempted sodomy! (Snaps handcuffs on ZEUS.) We're gonna cook your goose, you old *buzzard* you!

(OFFICERS raise ZEUS's arms, who makes a distressed eagle noise.

TABLEAU / BLACKOUT

SOMEWHERE OVER THE RAINBOW

CHARACTERS:
MAN
BAR PATRONS, with beer bottles
THE LOVER
THE ONE-NIGHT STAND

(Opens with the three BAR PATRONS arranged in exaggerated masculine poses around the stage. The MAN goes up to each one, striking various butch poses, such as chest thrust out, fingers looped in back pockets, crotch thrust forward.)

(Each PATRON turns away in an exaggerated way as he is approached, ending with a half-circle turn and a stomp away from the MAN. The third PATRON also blows smoke in the MAN's face.)

MAN (to audience) If only I could find a lover, I'd be happy!

(FIRST PATRON now comes down and circles MAN, then shakes his head in rejection. SECOND PATRON comes over and checks MAN's rear-end, taps him on the shoulder, then rejects him. THIRD PATRON then pulls out a tape-measure, finds MAN wanting. Exits.)

MAN If only I could find a lover, I'd never have to cruise again!

(One of the players, now the ONE-NIGHT STAND, leaps into MAN's arms, his body in a dying swan posture.)

MAN If only I could find a lover, instead of one-night stands!

(The ONE-NIGHT STAND gets insulted, hops down, gives the finger, and stomps off. MAN follows to exit, giving the finger too.)

(The LOVER, with a flower in his teeth, enters on the opposite side of the stage. He claps his hands.)

MAN (hearing the hands clap) Oh, I've found a lover at last!

(MAN and LOVER come toward each other in very slow motion, like a scene in a romantic movie, with some music underneath. They embrace.)

LOVER I love you!

MAN Say it again.

(They take turns throughout saying the lines downstage of each other.)

LOVER I love you!

MAN How much?

LOVER Lots and lots.

MAN Will you love me forever like it says in the songs?

LOVER Till two years beyond forever!

MAN (to audience) I knew it would be this way! (They leap off the platform, then begin to tango. Then they go backwards in the same pattern and bump hips, back where they started.)

LOVER I'm tired of dancing.

MAN You are?

LOVER Yes, let's do something else.

MAN Like what?

LOVER Can't *you* think of something?

MAN No.

LOVER You never think of anything!

MAN I think of things as much as you do!

LOVER You do not!

MAN I do too!

LOVER You're so stupid!

MAN You're not so bright yourself!

(Turn with backs to each other.)

LOVER I think I'll leave you.

MAN Go on, leave me. See if I care!

LOVER You never loved me!

MAN I did too love you.

LOVER No, you didn't. I could tell.

MAN I loved you! It was *you* that didn't love *me*!

LOVER What do you mean by that?

MAN You know.

LOVER I *don't* know.

MAN I loved *you* more than you loved *me*.

LOVER Like hell you did! I gave you the best three weeks of my life!

MAN All I asked of you was total devotion, and what did I get?

LOVER You got love. This is it — *this* is love!

MAN (to audience) I thought it was supposed to be different.

LOVER That's what's wrong with you — one of the things! You don't even know love when you have it. I've always wanted to tell you that!

MAN There are a few things I've always wanted to tell you too!

LOVER Like what?

MAN (leaning closer) You let the

hair grow in your ears!

LOVER I do not!

MAN Well, I'm not going to argue about it!

LOVER If you loved me, you'd argue with me!

MAN (to audience) This is worse than cruising ever was!

LOVER (pissed off) I'm leaving you.

MAN Good! I'm glad! Goodbye! Good riddance!

LOVER (turning back for exit line) I was the best thing that ever happened to you! (Exits.)

(The BAR PATRONS re-appear as the MAN looks toward where each exited earlier. All three turn away and stamp, rejecting MAN as one. MAN looks dejected, shoulders slumped.)

MAN (turning to audience) If only I could find a lover, I'd be happy!

BLACKOUT

THE FIANCÉ

CHARACTERS:
KING
QUEEN
PRINCESS GIDGET
FIANCÉ
NARRATOR

NARRATOR (using a large fairytale book) A long, long time ago in the distant Kingdom of Bizarria there lived a King and Queen.

(The KING and QUEEN, wearing crowns, enter through center screens, make trumpet sounds themselves with their mouths or with kazoos.)

NARRATOR And the King and the Queen were very royal and were greatly loved by all their subjects.

(The KING and the QUEEN sit on their thrones, which are angled, and throw kisses and waves to imaginary crowds.)

NARRATOR However, there was one very serious problem in the Kingdom of Bizarria — the Princess Gidget.

(GIDGET appears in a poodle skirt, does the Twist, waving to KING and QUEEN. She runs between the thrones.)

NARRATOR For the Princess, it must be told, had decided to select her *own* husband.

(GIDGET points to the screens. The FIANCÉ, who has been hiding behind the screen, extends a bare leg.)

KING What's that?

NARRATOR Said the King.

GIDGET My fiancé!

NARRATOR Said Gidget.

KING / QUEEN Oh, my god!

GIDGET He is the man I love!

(The FIANCÉ pops up at another screen, ducks back down. He's wearing a raincoat and appears to be a flasher.)

QUEEN But, Gidget —

NARRATOR Said the Queen.

KING You don't even know

this person!

NARRATOR Continued the King.

GIDGET Oh, I just love mystery!

NARRATOR Swooned Gidget.

KING But he isn't one of your official suitors.

QUEEN Where did you two meet?

GIDGET In the park.

(The FIANCÉ pops out from behind the center screen. We now see the raincoat clearly and that his pant legs are rolled up. He pops back behind the screens.)

QUEEN But we don't know anything about him!

NARRATOR The Queen argued.

GIDGET His name is Mr. Gordon.

NARRATOR Gidget replied.

KING Mr. Gordon? Doesn't he even have a first name?

GIDGET Yes . . . Flash.

(The FIANCÉ runs to another screen, peeks around, wiggles his pockets, runs out of sight.)

QUEEN This can never be!

NARRATOR Protested the Queen.

KING What are his family origins?

NARRATOR Protested the King.

GIDGET He's a peasant! Isn't that neat!

NARRATOR Cried the Princess Gidget. And at this answer her mother and father were at a loss for words.

(The KING and the QUEEN cover their mouths with their hands.)

For, you see, they *did* indeed wish their daughter to marry a peasant, to improve the waning stock of the royal line. But the question in their minds was whether Mr. Gordon was a *good* enough peasant.

QUEEN His appearance!

NARRATOR Grumbled the Queen.

KING Is he an artist?

NARRATOR Inquired the King.

GIDGET I didn't ask his occupation. All I asked was his love!

(GIDGET and the FIANCÉ wave to each other. Then he disappears behind the screens.)

NARRATOR The King and the Queen were still not satisfied. "What about his religion?" they asked.

GIDGET (hand on hip) Pish!

NARRATOR And what about their different educational levels?

GIDGET Double pish!

QUEEN But, Gidget, you have a

bachelor's degree!

KING And what has he got?

GIDGET His health! (She pulls out a yo-yo and starts to play with it.)

NARRATOR And the Princess Gidget told the truth, for she and her fiancé had had blood tests and both were negative! And still the King and the Queen of Bizarria argued with their daughter. They mentioned that the fiancé was *years* older than she.

GIDGET The years have only given him experience!

(Does Around the World with yo-yo.)

(The FIANCÉ pops up, slurps suggestively, disappears.)

NARRATOR Declared Gidget. They asked what she and Mr. Gordon would live on.

GIDGET Fiddly dee!

NARRATOR Remarked Gidget, who just wouldn't listen.

(GIDGET sticks her fingers in her ears.)

QUEEN What will our relatives say!?

NARRATOR Worried the Queen.

GIDGET Let them eat cake.

QUEEN What does that have to do with anything?

NARRATOR Retorted the Queen.

GIDGET I'm in love and that's all that matters!

NARRATOR Snapped the Princess.

KING But what can he possibly offer you?

GIDGET Companionship!

NARRATOR Simpered Gidget.

(The FIANCÉ opens center screens, then darts back.)

QUEEN I fear Gidget's going bananas!

NARRATOR Agonized the Queen.

KING And what about your children?

NARRATOR Begged the King.

GIDGET I hope they're just like their *papa.*

NARRATOR Gidget sighed.

QUEEN Daughter, you can't go through with this!

GIDGET Try and stop me!

NARRATOR Gidget contradicted.

KING What will the people of the kingdom say?

GIDGET Let them eat . . . pizza!

NARRATOR Gidget said wittily.

QUEEN Oh, my child, my child, you're making a terrible mistake!

NARRATOR The Queen said, wringing her hands.

(QUEEN forgets to wring her hands)

NARRATOR The Queen said, *wringing her hands*!

(Now the Queen wrings her hands.)

KING Oh, Gidget, what will become of you! Oh! Oh!

NARRATOR The King carried on. But at last there came an end to the *royal quarrel.*

(The NARRATOR garbles these two words several times.)

KING / QUEEN (correcting him sternly) THE ROYAL QUARREL!

NARRATOR When Gidget stated —

GIDGET No matter what you say I'm going to marry him!

QUEEN No! He doesn't even say anything!

KING Gidget, can't you see what he is!

GIDGET Mums, Dadums! Don't

you understand *any-thing* about romance?

(She turns wantonly to the FIANCÉ.)

He's great SEX! (Extends her arms to him) FLASH!

(The FIANCÉ runs downstage, turns his back to the audience, opens his raincoat toward GIDGET, the KING, and the QUEEN. The KING fans the QUEEN with his crown.)

FIANCÉ *Gidget!!*

(She runs down to him and he closes the raincoat around them.)

(The QUEEN faints across the KING's lap)

NARRATOR And they lived happily ever after!

QUEEN But he's a *sickie*!! (Her voice is falling off a cliff.)

BLACKOUT

BESTIALITY

CHARACTERS:
DUKE, a dog
SPOT, a dog
(Both wear collars)
Off-Stage Voice

(The action is played by both actors on all fours, sniffing, scratching, and "peeing" where appropriate.)

VOICE (off-stage) We've got the camera set up now! We'll be ready to shoot in a few minutes. Get your dogs ready.

(DUKE and SPOT enter from opposite sides, growl at each other, then hurry right over to smell each other's butts.)

DUKE (sniffing) Don't I know you from some place?

SPOT (sniffing) You seem familiar to me too.

DUKE You're making movies now, huh?

SPOT (coming downstage, facing

audience) Yeah, but I sure hope this movie's better'n the last one I made!

DUKE What was it?

SPOT You should pardon the expression, but it was a dog.

DUKE By any chance was it "Sylvia and the German Shepherd"?

SPOT (disgusted) No, I tried out for that, but they gave the part to a friend of the producer's. It's who you know.

DUKE Well, "Sylvia and the German Shepherd" was an artistic disaster. You're better off you didn't get the part.

SPOT I guess so. By the way, what's your name?

DUKE Duke. What's yours?

SPOT Spot.

BOTH How d'you do? (They sit up and shake paws.)

DUKE What movies you been in so far?

SPOT A few months ago I did "Dog Day Night" with Linda Love-lace. My master got me the part at the last minute. The Airedale who was supposed to do it came down with the clap.

DUKE Lucky for you! Have *you* ever gotten the clap from this work?

SPOT When I first started acting, I used to get it a lot. Then I learned to take a leak after every shot.

DUKE Ever do any water sports films?

SPOT Yeah, in this one picture I had to run out into a pond and retrieve a stick.

DUKE Is that all?

SPOT Oh, you meant did I ever . . . ? Oh yeah, once I had to piss on my leading lady. Managed to do it twenty-seven times.

DUKE Was it hard to do?

SPOT Oh, you learn to save it, you know, for the performance. (Lifts his leg and shows how.)

DUKE Ever made any S&M movies?

SPOT Yeah, I was in one with my master. Just a bit part. He whipped me a little too hard.

DUKE (nudging SPOT) So you *bit* him, huh?

(They laugh together.)

SPOT I would have if he hadn't started getting me straight scenes. Basically I'm a romantic lead.

DUKE I like stunt work myself. Had to do it on the wing of a 747 in one picture – "The Stewardess and the Springer Spaniel."

SPOT I saw that! It was a hot flick!

DUKE (affecting modesty) Why thank you.

SPOT	But I never would have recognized you.(Looks him over, crosses behind to examine the other side.) You're not a Springer Spaniel, are you?

DUKE	No, I'm a Bull Terrier, but I spend a lot of time on my make-up.

SPOT	I remember that scene with you and the stewardesses in the cockpit! (Remembering, he scratches one leg very fast.)

DUKE	I've had a number of offers since that came out. There's even talk I may be nominated for an Oscar.

SPOT	Really! How wonderful for you!

DUKE	But there's some cat that might win it. (dismissively) It does cat food commercials!

SPOT	Yes, those cats are getting in everywhere! (Scratches fleas.)

DUKE	(backing away because of the

fleas) What part are you trying out for today?

SPOT The second lead. So I'm a little nervous. (Goes to one side, urinates on scenery.)

DUKE (crossing at the same angle but on the other side of the stage) Do you have many lines?

(He spots SPOT's urine and SPOT spots his, and they hurry, in double cross, to urinate on the other's territory.)

SPOT Not many. But I do have several important barks when [some contemporary porn star's name] starts to climax.

DUKE I bet you steal the scene from her.

SPOT This could be my Big Film.

DUKE You sound ambitious.

SPOT I'm going to get out these cheap skin flicks and make it really big in Hollywood.

DUKE Your own dog house in Beverly Hills, huh?

SPOT I'm going to be the biggest thing since Lassie!

DUKE Be careful. You know what happened to Rin Tin Tin.

SPOT Yeah, lost his looks and couldn't get parts anymore.

DUKE I heard he wound up in the pound.

BOTH (in horror) No!

SPOT But I'm only two years old, and Rin Tin Tin didn't get his start until he was almost four.

DUKE It's rough-rough in Hollywood. Cat eat cat.

SPOT I've worked my way up, and there's no stopping me now!

DUKE You got an agent?

SPOT Yeah, and my agent's working on a deal starring me and

[Name a temporary sexy female movie star.]

DUKE (Says the star's name, impressed.)

SPOT And, furthermore, I may have my own television series!

DUKE Wow!

SPOT What about yourself? You got an agent?

DUKE Oh, I'm not ambitious. I'm just doing this film to make a little spare money.

SPOT You don't want to go to Hollywood and become a celebrity?

DUKE All I want is settle down, and raise a couple of litters.

SPOT Are you engaged?

DUKE Yeah, but I don't tell my fiancée I'm making porn films. She's a St. Bernard, and if she ever found out she'd beat the crap out of me.

SPOT A real bitch, huh? (They agree.) I'm afraid I don't have time for marriage myself. I want to concentrate on my career.

DUKE (nudging SPOT) And I imagine these movies keep you pretty 'busy' anyway, don't they!

SPOT Believe me, it's better than waiting for my old lady to come in heat twice a year.

DUKE Do you think they're about ready in there? (looking off)

SPOT Ah, they take forever! Would you mind helping me rehearse my part?

DUKE Of course not. What do I have to do?

SPOT Just stand there as if you're my leading lady. (Nods where.)

DUKE (Starts to play along, then looks back somewhat doubtfully, then decides to play along.) Is this okay? (Wiggles his butt.)

SPOT That's fine. (He mounts DUKE and pumps a little.) Arf! Arf!

DUKE (looking back at SPOT) You said those lines with such feeling! You're going to be a big star, I can tell.

SPOT Thank you, but my really big speech comes next. (Barks several times.)

DUKE You're going to be a howling success.

SPOT Sure hope so. (Pumps some more, howls loudly, then howls in pain.)

DUKE What's wrong, Spot?

SPOT I'm stuck, Duke! Can you get me out?

DUKE Sorry, haven't got any *spot* remover!

(SPOT howls at the awful pun. Other howls from off-stage join in.)

BLACKOUT

SEXEDUC ATION

CHARACTERS:
MOMMY, overly gushy, "progressive"
SONNY, about five, carrying a cuddly toy

(MOMMY and SONNY enter hand in hand. MOMMY arranges SONNY on a little stool as though she has something to tell him.)

MOMMY Sonny, before you take your nap, Mommy has something very important to tell you today. So I want you to sit very still and listen very hard. Okay?

SONNY Okay, Mommy.

MOMMY Mommy's going to tell you all about sex. Isn't that great?

SONNY (Jumps for joy at first.) . . . What's sex?

MOMMY Sex is a wonderful, wonderful part of life, a

wonderful, wonderful power in each and every one of us, and I want you to grow up to feel good about sex, and that's why I'm going to tell you all about it.

SONNY But what *is* it?

MOMMY Mommy's getting to it. Don't rush her, darling.

SONNY Is sex something *bad*?

MOMMY (kneeling beside him) Of course not! Sex is never bad. You mustn't think that for a minute. Sex is good and wholesome and clean, just like you. (She hugs him.)

SONNY What is it then? Is it like ice cream?

MOMMY A little bit, yes.

SONNY What flavor?

MOMMY Well, for some people it's like chocolate ripple. Umm! And for other people it's like . . . like pistachio peanut brittle. Umm! For me it's always been sort of . . . plain vanilla.

SONNY I don't like vanilla.

MOMMY Well, you're going to like sex, I'll bet you on that!

SONNY Okay, what is it?

MOMMY (getting up, standing in front of SONNY, taking a deep breath) See Mommy?

(She takes out an expandable pointer.)

SONNY I see you.

MOMMY (illustrating all her points by touching her body with the pointer) These are Mommy's breasts. (Rubs them slightly.) Sometimes people touch their breasts when they're having sex.

It's all very nice and very warm and wonderful.

SONNY Are those your boobies?

(MOMMY cringes.)

MOMMY These are my *breasts*, Sonny. There's no need to call them baby names any longer, is there?

SONNY Is it okay to call them knockers?

(MOMMY cringes again.)

MOMMY (trying not to be upset) No, Sonny, they're not knockers. They're *breasts*, and nice little boys should call them that.

SONNY Okay, I promise.

MOMMY And this is Mommy's navel.

SONNY I thought that was Mommy's belly button.

MOMMY Well, it used to be, but it's time that you grew up, and so you should call it the navel. Come on, say it!

SONNY The navel. (MOMMY echoes the word.)

MOMMY Very good! And this is Mommy's vagina! (Points with pointer.)

SONNY Vagina? What's that?

MOMMY Mommy would take off all her clothes and show you, but it's cold today. Mommy has a vagina and it's round inside.

SONNY What's it for?

MOMMY It's for . . . it's for the daddy's penis.

SONNY Daddy's penis?

MOMMY Like your pee-pee.

SONNY My pee-pee?

MOMMY Yes, daddies stick their penises into mommies.

SONNY (curling lip) Why?

MOMMY Because they want to, that's why. And mommies want them to.

SONNY I don't think I want to.

MOMMY When you get bigger, and your pee-pee gets bigger too, then you'll want to.

SONNY Does Grandma do this?

MOMMY Yes, Sonny, Grandma and Grandpa both do it! And so do Aunt Ruth and Uncle Bob — together! Isn't that wonderful!

SONNY I've never seem 'em. When do they do it?

MOMMY I'm coming to that, honey. But first let me show you all the parts.

SONNY (doubtful) Really?

MOMMY Let me go on, dear. See this? This is what the inside of Mommy's vagina looks like. It's got lips. And we call these *labia.*

SONNY *Labia*?

(MOMMY echoes and spells the word in the air with the pointer.)

MOMMY That's right! They're like *lips*. (Moves her lips toward him.)

SONNY (turning away, near tears) I don't want 'em to be like *lips*!

MOMMY (going to the other side of him) But they are, Sonny! They *are*! And guess what? Inside there's a part we call the clitoris.

SONNY (echoing) The clitoris.

(MOMMY echoes the word.)

MOMMY It's about this big, and it gets stimulated when the

daddy rubs his penis against it.

SONNY He rubs his penis against it?

MOMMY Of course sometimes he uses other things.

SONNY What other things?

MOMMY Well, his tongue for one. (Flicks tongue rapidly.)

SONNY Does he lick it?

MOMMY Yes, he does because it's nice, Sonny. It's very nice.

SONNY Can I go out and play now?

MOMMY But Mommy's teaching you about sex! And she hasn't finished yet.

SONNY (reluctantly) Okay.

MOMMY And deeper inside the mommy is the uterus, where the baby stays!

SONNY How did the baby get there?

MOMMY It came from the daddy's penis.

SONNY A whole baby? How did it get *there*?

MOMMY (a little flustered) Well . . . it came out of the daddy's penis in a liquid.

SONNY (screwing up his face) The baby was a liquid?

MOMMY That's right, darling.

SONNY You mean like pee-pee?

MOMMY No, darling. It's different from pee-pee. It starts out as a liquid that's a little bit sticky, and the sticky liquid shoots from the daddy's penis inside the mommy's vagina, past the labia, or lips (Makes lip noise), past the clitoris, which is about this big. (Show him.) And into some of the mommy's tubes!

SONNY It's *sticky*?

MOMMY Yes, it's sticky so that it will cling to some of the mommy's reproductive goodies, and a baby will result.

SONNY Is it always this way?

MOMMY Why yes, darling. Is it all becoming clearer to you now?

SONNY Does the sticky liquid come from those two things hanging down from Daddy?

MOMMY (kneeling) That's right, sweetheart! How clever of you to notice! Those two 'things' are called testicles. Isn't that a pretty word?

SONNY Testicles? (Wrinkles up his face.)

MOMMY They hang down from a daddy's body so the liquid inside won't get too hot.

SONNY Why do they got hair on them?

MOMMY Because . . . because (with extreme reverence) God wanted the testicles to be pretty!

SONNY So He put *hair* on 'em?

MOMMY That's right, darling

SONNY (unconvinced) Is that all? Can I please go out and play now?

MOMMY Honey, let me go on and explain everything, so you'll know how every bit of it works! (Pulls him back onto the stool.)

SONNY (sighs) Okay.

MOMMY It all begins when the daddy kisses the mommy and his penis fills up with blood.

SONNY (scared) With blood? (Moves stool away.)

MOMMY There's nothing to be afraid of! No blood comes out. It just makes it easier for the daddy to insert the sticky liquid into the mommy.

SONNY Why doesn't the daddy just put it in with a spoon?

MOMMY Well, that's a very good idea, Sonny, but if the daddy put the sticky liquid in a spoon, he might spill some. And we shouldn't ever waste things, should we?

SONNY I guess not.

MOMMY Mommy knows, darling. Trust her.

SONNY When the daddy puts his penis into the mommy's vagina does the baby come out then?

MOMMY Well, you see it takes longer than that! (a little laugh) First the daddy has to bounce up and down, and sometimes the mommy bounces too! (Demonstrates bouncing.)

SONNY Like a pony?

MOMMY Yes, sort of like a pony. And then the daddy bounces very hard, and the Mommy praises the daddy's performance!

SONNY Like a show?

MOMMY Yes, sweetheart, just like a show! And at that moment the daddy and the mommy *say* things to each other.

SONNY What do they say?

MOMMY They say, "I love you."

SONNY Oh. Is that all?

MOMMY Sometimes they say "other" Things. These can be very wholesome words, and nobody should be ashamed of these words when they're said *out of love.*

SONNY Is there any more?

(Reluctantly nods when she goes on.)

MOMMY Yes, darling, at last the daddy gives a final great big bounce (A bump is in order here.) And the mommy *sings* out in her joy!

SONNY Mommy sings?

MOMMY Sort of.

SONNY What happens to the sticky stuff?

MOMMY Well, when the mommy is singing, the sticky stuff, which we call sperm, (He echoes.) flies out of the daddy's penis into the mommy's vagina, and there it stays, and nine wonderful months later, it becomes a baby — just like you did!

SONNY Like I did?

MOMMY Yes, sweetie pie! Isn't this

all wonderful? Aren't you glad Mommy told you all about sex? (Hugs him from behind.)

SONNY Do *I* have to do all these things?

MOMMY (tapping his shoulders) Of course, Sonny! Take your nap now. Mommy has some baking to do! (Waves goodbye, exits.)

SONNY (crying) I don't want to! I don't want to!

(Slides to his knees, prays, heartbroken.)

Please, God!
Not Grandma!

BLACKOUT

BODY AND SOUL

CHARACTERS:
BODY, a male
SOUL, a male

(SOUL is sitting on a backless chair or stool facing the audience, with a blanket pulled up to his neck as if asleep, with a chair nearby.)

(BODY is on the floor between SOUL's legs, with his head angled so that his voice will project. BODY uses his arm (with the fist in a sock) to make SOUL's *extensive* penis.)

SOUL (waking up, no penis showing) Ah, another day! (Yawns.)

BODY (raising his arm between SOUL's legs to make BODY's penis rise) Ah, another day!

SOUL (pushing penis down) Oh, not again!

BODY Don't start putting me down already.

SOUL It's only six A.M.

BODY Don't give me any lectures, okay?

SOUL Can't you get lost for a few days! (Sits up.)

BODY I didn't bother you all day yesterday.

SOUL And what a relief that was.

BODY Just give me what I want, and I'll shut up.

SOUL No!

BODY We're going out, whether you want to or not.

SOUL I'm going to stay in and read.

BODY Listen, Mister, we're going out for a treat, and that's all there is to it.

SOUL Who do you think you are, giving me orders?

BODY If it weren't for me, you'd never go nowhere.

SOUL (getting cozy) Yeah, I'd stay here and just think and dream and —

BODY You'd be a vegetable in two weeks.

SOUL (sitting up) Because of you, I'm nothing but an animal!

BODY (waving SOUL's penis back and forth under the blanket) (in a sing-song) Sticks and stones may break my bones, but names'll never hurt me!

SOUL I used to be happy until you started bugging me!

BODY That's absolute horseshit! I've given you the happiest times in your whole puny life! Just give me what I *want*, and I'll go back to sleep.(Penis sticks up expectantly.)

SOUL (pushing it down) No! . . . It's dirty!

BODY You just slept for eight hours. Was that dirty?

SOUL That was different.

BODY The hell it was! It's okay to sleep for eight hours or to eat three meals a day, but when I ask for five little minutes you deny me!

SOUL It's immature.

BODY So it'll keep you youthful! Come on.

SOUL Why don't you go find somebody else to bother?

BODY 'Cause I'm stuck with you, that's why. (Waves penis.)

SOUL What if somebody came in now and saw you like this?

BODY Who cares! They're no different from you, simp!

SOUL They're not walking around with this big old thing sticking out all the time.

B0DY (coaxing) I give you a good time, don't I?

SOUL Well . . .

BODY (more coaxing) Do I or don't I give you a good time, hmm?

SOUL But you're always nagging me!

BODY Damn it, you keep me cramped inside your shorts most of the time!

SOUL If I give you an inch, you take a mile.

BODY I thought we were partners.

SOUL Not after that awful drip you had last month.

BODY A little head cold! For that I should be put in isolation?

SOUL I'm sorry, we're through. That's all there is to it!

BODY Okay, so I got us into a little trouble. So *beat* me. (Sticks up.)

SOUL No!

BODY Go ahead, beat me!

SOUL You'd just like that.

BODY Well, how about rubbing me on the chair then? (The penis points to the chair.)

SOUL I don't want to. (Folds arms defiantly.)

BODY Come on, just a little bit (sing-song) *Back and forth* on the chair, okay? (Waves penis.)

SOUL It'll make a stain.

BODY Naw, it'll put a nice polish on the wood!

SOUL No, I'm working on my self-control. (Crosses his legs.)

BODY If God didn't want me to spout off, why'd He put me here?

SOUL As temptation.

BODY He put me here because He knew what a lousy world He'd created and He wanted you to have at least a *few* good times!

SOUL But to please you I'll have to get up, get dressed, go out and find somebody who's looking for the same thing, and then we'll —

BODY (insinuatingly) Naw, you don't, pal. We can handle it . . . ourselves.

SOUL That'll grow hair on my palms!

BODY Then you won't need no gloves this winter.

SOUL I could go blind!

BODY I got a friend over in the school for the blind. He tells me the blind guys there see *better* if they do it!

SOUL It's no use. I'm swearing off — forever. I'm through with low-lifes like you.

BODY I'm sorry I'm not the high-society type. (Fakes tears.) Go ahead, abandon an old buddy.

Go ahead!

SOUL Don't be like that now.

BODY (More tears.) Go ahead, leave me after all I've done for you!

SOUL Oh, come on, don't be hurt.

BODY Go out with your high-falutin' friends!

SOUL Don't be mad.

BODY What do you expect me to do, jump for joy?

SOUL From now on I'm going to be spiritual, that's all.

BODY You're throwing me over for some artsy-craftsy creeps and I'm supposed to accept it?

SOUL Just don't be mad at me, okay? Please.

BODY Well, I *am* mad at you!

SOUL Come on, that makes me feel bad.

BODY Well, it don't make me feel so hot neither!

SOUL Say you're not mad at me, ok?

BODY (Reluctant, silent.)

SOUL Please! Huh? What do you say?

BODY Well . . . maybe . . . (slyly) Shake on it? (Penis sticks up.)

SOUL Sure! There! (Before he can think, he grabs the penis and shakes it.)

BODY Thanks. (SOUL continues to hold the penis.) (slyly) Feels *good*, don't it?

SOUL (his face betraying his true feelings) I'm not sure . . .

BODY Come on, just a little shake or two more.

(Reluctantly SOUL begins to stroke the penis a bit, then faster and faster.)

That's right! Way to *go*!

(SOUL begins to use both hands to stroke the penis, louder and louder, more ecstatic)

Way to go! Way to go! Way to Go! Way to go! Way to go! Way to *go*, you mother-fucking *motherfucker*!

(The penis jerks about frantically, then ends up spitting. The actor for BODY under the chair makes the sound and shoots detergent or colored plastic string that comes in an aerosol bottle. There are several phases of the ejaculation. Then the penis falls over limp. There is one final little spurt.)

BODY (sighing) Thanks, pal. I needed that. (Singing out operatically) See you *tomorrow*!

(SOUL, realizing he has been duped, wipes his slimy hand on the blanket, then gives a final little shake with both hands.)

BLACKOUT
END OF PLAY

YOUR TOWN

[Winner Cable Car Award, Outstanding Dramatic Show, San Francisco, 1978.]

["... is a witty commentary on the family done in a style loosely modeled on *Our Town.* The piece is briskly directed by Dan Turner and well-acted ... by the entire cast. The climactic downpour of babies is hilarious."
— Robert Hurwitt, *Berkeley Barb*]

CHARACTERS:
- STORYTELLER
- DAD
- MOM
- SIS
- JUNIOR

Style: The Storyteller narrates from a Little Golden Book. The actors are adults. The actors mime appropriate actions, make appropriate noises, and say the dialogue.)

TELLER Once upon a time there was a Man.

(The Man appears.)

And the Man was alone.

(Man cups hand over forehead looking for others.)

And of course it is not good for Man to be alone.

And so he met Woman.

(A Woman appears. They stare at each other. They wave.)

The Man and Woman liked being together. They had fun.

(Man and Woman play tag, chase each other around the stage, the Woman laughing.)

TELLER Man began to think he would like to spend all his time with Woman, and he brought her bon-bons. He brought her flowers.

(He does.)

Woman gave Man a kiss.

(She kisses him on the cheek.)

The Man brought the
Woman more bon-bons
and flowers.

(He heaps them on her.)

The Woman was impressed
and gave the Man
encouragement.

(She puts his hand on her breast.)

Finally the Man brought the
Woman an engagement ring,
six swans a-laying, and other
tokens of his affection.

(He runs about gathering things.)

The Woman gave the Man
her body.

(She leaps into his arms.)

Man and Woman were very
happy together. They had
lots of fun. But then they

decided to stop having fun
and get married.

(Man and Woman assume pious matrimonial poses, coming down the aisle, etc.)

At first they had an
apartment, which they
fixed up together.

(Pantomime of painting, hammering, etc.)

And the Man worked at his
job and the Woman worked
at her job.

(Man pantomimes digging ditches; the Woman types.)

Man and Woman did not
mind paying rent or working
long hours, because they had
each other in the evenings
and were often having fun.

(Woman leaps into Man's arms again.)

And guess what? Before you
could say Jiminy Cricket,

Man and Woman had an
announcement to make.
Surprise! Surprise!

(Woman is pregnant.)

Naturally the Man was
ecstatic!

(He looks disgusted at first, but finally is coaxed by the Storyteller and jumps for joy.)

For the Man was going to be
a father! He made the
Woman quit her job and stay
home.

(He drags her away from the typewriter, seats her.)

Because he didn't want
anything to happen to her or
the little baby that she now
carried in her tum-tum.

(He is solicitous, making sure that she is comfortable, etc.)

Finally the big day came.

(The Woman opens her mouth, screaming, clutching her stomach, falls over.)

The Man helped the Woman
to the hospital.

(Slowly she walks through a doorway with the Man assisting.)

The Woman went to see the
stork, and the Man waited.

(We see her lying sideways, having severe labor pains. The Man is sitting and pacing nervously.)

At last the little bundle came
into the world.

(Woman gives a big groan as if pushing out a big load.)

And the Man went in to see
his wife and little baby child.

(He enters hospital room. She is holding the baby near her. He looks at it.)

t was a baby!

(Man picks up the bundle and dances

around the room with it, tossing it into the air several times. Woman reaches up, afraid he'll drop it.)

Finally the day came when they took their little package home.

(They leave the hospital, enter their house.)

DAD It's time we bought a real house.

TELLER Said the Man.

DAD A place where Junior can play.

MOM But we don't have the money!

TELLER The Woman said.

DAD I'll work overtime!

TELLER Said the Man. And he did.

(Man pantomimes working furiously digging ditches.)

MOM Oh, how wonderful!

TELLER Said the Woman.

MOM Now we can put a down payment on a house! (She gathers up the money he's earned.) You've worked so hard, dear.

TELLER She said.

MOM I love you very much.

DAD I don't mind.

TELLER Said the Man.

DAD 'Cause now we are a Mom and a Dad.

(Fanfare. He puts his arm around her shoulder; she holds the baby. They look like a photograph.)

TELLER Soon after, Mom and Dad were blessed with another addition to their growing family. . . . It was a girl! (Mom now has two bundles in her arms.) Naturally Dad

was overjoyed — although
he had to take a second job
to pay the bills.

(Dad trudges off to work, then works too hard, digging ditches and packing boxes, scurrying about.)

And before you could say
hippity hop, Junior was
taking his first steps.

(Junior enters, taking baby steps, almost falling as Mom and Dad watch and encourage him.)

TELLER And then before you could
say Jack Robinson, Junior
was off to school.

(Junior waves bye-bye to Mom and Dad.)

Junior liked school. because
they had slides and teeter-
totters, and because Junior
liked to play with the other
children:

(He slides, etc., and then punches but the other children.)

You see, Junior was a real boy!

(He takes a fighter's stance, punches.)

And little Sis was a real girl!

(She looks demure.)

Little Sis also liked school because she learned to read and write and play hop-scotch and jump-rope and meet boys. (Mime of each quickly.)

Mom and Dad were very pleased with Junior and Sis, and Junior and Sis were very pleased with each other. (They hug.)

Except sometimes.

(The children assume boxers' stance.)

Sometimes Junior wanted something Sis might have.

(He beats her up, grabs a toy from her.)

But of course Mom and
Dad told Junior that was
not the way to behave.

(The parents give the toy back to Sis, who hits Junior with it.)

Naturally, despite their
occasional disagreements,
Sis loved her brother
very much indeed, and he
loved her.

(They stand almost face-to-face yakking at each other and then stick their tongues out at each other simultaneously.)

TELLER They were an average, but
wonderful, family. They
went everywhere together.
On picnics!

(The four pantomime eating, throwing napkins and scraps every which way.)

To the zoo, to see the wild
animals, who were so
pleased to wait in their
cages waiting to be seen.

(The four look in the cages.)

They loved to take long
walks together and enjoy
nature.

(They stroll hand in hand, throwing gum wrappers, beer cans; the kids jump up and down on the flowers and grass.)

Just a typical family!
And nothing could come
between them.

(They assume positions like soldiers in a row with fixed bayonets.)

They looked out for each
other, and they became very
closely knit.

(They get tangled in each other like a huge pretzel.)

At last came the day when
Junior was old enough to go
to high school. He became
captain of the baseball
team and spent a lot of time
catching a ball.

(Junior catches a baseball several times, throwing it to himself.)

Both Mom and Dad thought it was a good sign that Junior spent so much of his time catching a ball. They knew it would make him grow up to be healthy, moral, and well-educated!

(Mom and Dad applaud when Junior catches the ball again.)

And then Sis went to high school too. She was a cheerleader because she was pretty and had personality.

(Sis does a cheer with exaggerated gestures and too much "personality.")

Everybody liked Sis — because she always had a smile on her face.

(She smiles too much.)

Needless to say, Sis had many boyfriends. Everybody thought the whole family was keen.

But of course we mustn't tell a

lie — they did have their
spats. Mom some-times fought
with Dad.

(She yaks at him.)

And Dad sometimes fought
with Junior.

(Dad turns from the argument with
Mom to one with his son.)

And Junior sometimes fought
with Sis. (He turns to her,
carrying on the chain effect.)
And Sis sometimes fought
with Mom.(Sis turns to Mom,
hands on hips, mouth
wagging, to complete the
circle.)

But at least they kept their
spats in the home!

(They all scream at each other all once.)

The years marched on and
Junior and Sis grew and grew.
They even got bigger than
their Mom and Dad! So big
that —

(They shoot up like weeds.)

That's because they ate plenty of wholesome foods. Frosted cereals every morning. And plenty of butter and french fries every night. Finally Junior became a strapping young man.

(Junior strikes a manly pose.)

And it was time for him to go to college. But because Junior had spent so much time playing baseball, he didn't know how to read and write, and so instead he went into the army.

(Junior marches.)

They were very proud of Junior for wearing his uniform with such honor.

(Junior salutes them.)

He became a corporal in twenty-seven days. And then he got promoted to sergeant in a month and a half.

He was a natural leader. He
had found his niche in life:

(Marches around, saluting, giving
orders.)

Sis came to see Junior off on
the ship that was to take him
away to The War. They had
forgotten their disagreements
of the past and fell into each
other's arms.

(They embrace, but reluctantly. Mom
and Dad have to force them.)

Yes, Junior was going off to
fight The War. He didn't
know where it would be; he
didn't know who had caused
it, what it was about, or when
it might end. But it was his
duty to go. This was his very
first War and he was sure it
would be the very last War.

Besides if the economy was in
a bad way, and somebody had
to help create jobs.

During the War, Mom was

able to get a job of her own.
She made airplane parts in the
same factory where Dad now
worked. In fact, they stood
side by side and made airplane
parts together.

(They do so.)

Even Sis got a part-time job in
the airplane factory while she
finished high school.

What a patriotic family they
were!

(All three stand side by side making
airplane parts.)

Junior, meanwhile, was off
fighting the Enemy.

(He has a rifle, creeping through the
battle zone.)

Mom and Dad prayed for
Junior.

(They kneel and pray.)

For he was their only son and

they didn't know how else to
help him except to pray.

Some of the other boys were
dying.

(Junior dodges bullets, tries to catch the
bodies falling about him.)

I guess those other boys'
parents didn't pray hard
enough.

Yes, it was hard times for the
family. Because, while Junior
was off in the War, Sis
unfortunately got pregnant.

(She holds her belly.)

She was afraid that Mom and
Dad wouldn't understand
because she wasn't married,
and so she pretended nothing
was wrong and went on
making airplane parts to win
the War and improve the
Economy.

(Sis sucks in her stomach, ties a thick
cord around it.)

But finally Sis could pretend no longer, and she had her little baby, which she hid in her dresser drawer.

(She hides it, pushes the drawer shut.)

She was terribly afraid that Mom and Dad would find it and make her go to a school for Bad Girls, and so she never told them about the little tike.

However, one day Mom was tidying up Sis's room and noticed the baby in the dresser drawer.

(MOM opens it, expresses surprise.)

She lifted it up.

(She cradles it.)

And confronted Sis with the evidence.

MOM Is this your child? (Holds it out.)

SIS It must be a foundling;

TELLER Sis said.

MOM Who is the father?

TELLER Mom demanded.

SIS It was one of my boyfriends.

TELLER Sis confessed.

MOM You were supposed to have boyfriends but not sex!

TELLER Mom reprimanded.

SIS I'm sorry.

MOM Were you in love?

SIS So much so I couldn't see straight.

MOM Well, as long as you were in love!

TELLER Mom said, taking Sis into her forgiving arms.

(They embrace.)

SIS But he wouldn't marry me!

TELLER Sis explained.

MOM Never mind! You're a mother and I'm a grandmother now!

TELLER Mom rejoiced. Mean-while, Dad was having a heart attack at the airplane factory.

(Dad clutches his chest, collapses.)

It was the strain of all those years of hard work and all the worry about Junior and Sis. Mom and Sis dropped everything and rushed to Dad's side.

(He lies on the floor. They kneel beside him, then run back for the baby they've dropped.)

DAD I think I'm passing over.

TELLER Dad whispered.

MOM Don't die, Dad —

TELLER Mom begged.

DAD I'm afraid it's curtains for me.

MOM (Grabbing the baby bundle and holding it toward him.) But look at your grandson, Dad!

(Angel voices.)

DAD (Slowly sitting up.) My grandson?

MOM Isn't he beautiful?

DAD (With wavery voice, tears in his eyes, hand extended.) My grand . . . son! Let me hold him before I die.

(They give him the bundle.)

TELLER And before you knew it Dad began to feel his heart get stronger. He hugged that little tike. The warmth of that little breast against his was better than heart surgery. Yes, Dad was up and about in no time.

(Dad leaps up and prances about.)

And now Sis and Dad and Mom were even closer than they had been before.

(They make a tight hugging circle.)

All that was missing was Junior, who was so far, far away . . .

(They look off in the distance for him.)

All they could do was pray for him.

(They all kneel and pray.)

And finally one summer afternoon Junior came home —

(Junior comes toward them, limping.)

Yes, Junior came home from The War!

MOM Our prayers have been answered!

TELLER Mom shouted.

JUNIOR I'm crippled for life.

TELLER Junior said.

DAD Just look at your nephew
and you'll be cured!

TELLER Dad advised.

(Dad holds up the baby. Junior takes it, hobbles around with it, finally falls down but manages to toss the baby underhand to Sis before he drops it.)

SIS Aren't you better?

JUNIOR There's nothing left but the
shell-shock.

TELLER Alas, Junior was wrong. The
euphoria faded and he was
limping again before the day
was out.

(Junior limps around.)

Not long after that, Mom
noticed that Junior was
depressed.

MOM You need to get married.
That'll perk you up!

TELLER So Junior got married to a very nice girl down the block.

(Carries a dummy across the threshold.)

They rented a house not far from! Mom and Dad and were able to get a thirty-year mortgage at eleven percent interest because Junior was a veteran. Soon Junior opened his own gun shop. And sold lots and lots of weapons with which people could shoot birds, animals, and each other. He turned a nice profit and helped the economy once again, and in no time he purchased a second home in the country.

Sis, in the meantime, had turned into quite the young lady and married a man she'd met in the airplane factory.

She forgot about the baby's father and in practically no time became a respectable matron of the community who wrote to the post office to complain about the unsolicited pornography that was being left in her mail box.

(Shakes her finger like a matron.)

TELLER Mom and Dad were growing gracefully older, with a few grey hairs here and then a few white ones there.

(They put on grey wigs, then white ones.)

They sat on their porch (in rockers) and talked about the good old days.

DAD We had some times, didn't we?

TELLER Dad said.

MOM We sure did.

TELLER Mom agreed.

DAD Sure is good to relax.

MOM Sure is.

(She pats Dad's hand. He collapses.)

MOM Dad? (She shakes him. No response.) Dad?

TELLER Unfortunately Dad did not answer. For, you see, he had gone to his reward.

(Dad rises from rocker and drifts off.)

A lifetime of work, a loving family, a little relaxation, what more could a man want? Yes, Dad died that day, but Dad died happy.

DAD (pulled off by force.) I don't want to go yet:

TELLER And so now Mom was left all alone. She wanted to see Sis and Junior, but most of the time they were busy with their friends and families. Of course they did call Mom up when they needed a baby-sitter.

(Junior and Sis come in and dump some baby bundles on Mom then exit.)

And so Mom grew older and
sat alone and took up tatting
and watching TV and trying to
make ends meet.

(She sits and tats and rocks.)

And every Christmas Junior
and Sis came without fail and
everybody exchanged presents
and they had a big turkey and
they all loved each other so
much they were about to burst.

(Quick hugs, quick exchange of
presents, belches, rapid exits.)

But finally one Christmas
Mom wasn't there anymore.

(We see an empty rocker, rocking.)

Yes, Morn had gone away.
She had wanted to be with
Dad, but that wasn't the way
the good Lord meant it to be.
You see, Junior and Sis had
had to put Mom in a Home.

MOM No!

(We see Mom in a wheelchair in a straight-jacket.)

TELLER You see, Mom had gone a little funny in her head in her old age.

(Mom twitches, tries to get free. Junior and Sis shake their heads sadly.)

MOM Goddamn you fucking kids! Let me out of here!

JUNIOR Now. Mom, just get hold of yourself.

(She strains in the straight jacket.)

MOM I have got ahold of myself! Ungrateful sons of bitches!

SIS Look at your granddaughter, Mom!

(Holds up her hand to indicate a growing child.)

MOM What the fuck do I care! She doesn't give a shit about me!

TELLER Mom replied.

SIS Mom, if you don't simmer down, we're not going to bring you any presents next Christmas.

MOM I'm bored silly! Get me out of: this fucking place!

SIS You're better off with people your own age, Mom.

MOM I hope your kids put you away in a home someday!

TELLER Mom shouted. Unfortunately Mom shouted a little too much and gave herself a stroke.

(Collapses, falls out of the wheelchair.)

Of course Junior and Sis gave their mother the nicest funeral money can buy, and they still visit her grave every single Mother's Day.

(They appear solemnly and drop two wreaths on the grave.)

But life goes on, and Sis and Junior's kids are growing up.

GIRL (Played by actress who played Mom.) Mom, Junior hit me!

BOY (Played by actor who played Dad.) She hit me first!

SIS Be quiet, both of you! Junior, behave yourself. You're the troublemaker!

BOY Shut up! You're an old poop!

SIS Don't you talk like that to me. I'm your mother!

BOY You're an old poop!

SIS I am not an old poop!

BOY Old poop! Old poop!

SIS You shut your mouth!

CHILD Don't have to! (Acts snotty.)

SIS Why can't you be good like your sister!

BOY She's an old poop too!

GIRL I am not!

(They yak and stick out their tongues in the same way the children did earlier.)

TELLER By golly, it sure makes you feel good all over? People getting married, people, having kids, (Starts throwing stuffed frogs. Their kids having kids, and those kids having more kids, (More stuffed frogs from everyone.) And those kids having kids, and everybody loving each other, 'cause there's one thing in this world you can always count on, and that's the family.

(There should eventually be a huge pile of stuffed frogs on the stage.)

Well, I guess I best be mosey-ing along. It's getting late and it's about time for bed. . . . Good night now!

(He waves.)

BLACKOUT

BENEATH THE SURFACE
SAN FRANCISCO, 1979

BENEATH THE SURFACE
— a satirical comedy

[A shorter version of this play was first performed in San Francisco in 1979.]

"I really enjoyed it."
— Robert Chesley,
Bay Guardian

NOTE: These character "types" existed in the last quarter of the twentieth century. Naturally they don't exist now.

CHARACTERS: (12)
young NATIVE AMERICAN
lower-class BLACK MAN
middle-class BLACK WOMAN,
young LATINO,
middle-aged, conservative WHITE MAN,
liberal WHITE WOMAN
old ASIAN
young, effeminate GAY MAN
young LESBIAN
HANDICAPPED WOMAN,
FOREIGNER
LOUDSPEAKER VOICE

STYLE: The actors need not be literally of the categories mentioned above. They can wear representative partial masks or makeup.)

SETTING: The play opens with eleven passengers entering a subway train one by one, almost a fashion show, then taking seats or standing. It should be a stylized set with an exit door frame downstage. All the characters are exaggerated versions of their types, some reading newspapers or magazines. One is dozing, another tatting, some staring at nothing, one hanging onto a strap, etc. The FOREIGNER is eating something suspicious out of his handkerchief, surreptitiously. He is dressed eccentrically, perhaps with some sort of odd head-cloth. He carries an oversized sausage.

(Throughout the action, the characters echo certain words or say lines as a chorus. They should also ad lib as necessary during interactions.)

(MUSIC as the lights dim and the train goes into a tunnel, with the characters miming the movement. After a few moments, the train starts to slow down, the passengers lean in one direction, then they come to a jerking halt.

Uncertain, they stay in their seats, etc. looking at one another with a few weak smiles, gestures, very polite.)

VOICE	(over loudspeaker throughout) Excuse me, ladies and gentlemen, this is the Transport Authority. I'm afraid we've had a momentary delay. But we'll have you through the tunnel shortly.

(Immediate sound of mechanical difficulty with the P.A. system. Some passengers laugh a little. The WHITE MAN gets up and looks out a window or tries to, but he can't see much.)

WHITE MAN	I think we may be trapped. (He laughs, not believing it.)
BLACK WOMAN	They're never going to get the kinks out of this contraption!

(She laughs too and waves her hand at the interior.)

NATIVE AMERICAN (going to a window) Sure is black out there.

WHITE MAN We're stuck in the middle of the tunnel.

WHITE WOMAN You mean we're still under the water?

WHITE MAN Water, water everywhere, but not a drop to drink!

VOICE Ladies and gentlemen, sorry for this inconvenience. We've had a little power failure, but we'll be underway in no time. There's nothing to worry about, believe me.

HANDICAPPED WOMAN (on metal crutches) I could get there faster if I walked! (Laughs.)

GAY MAN I should've brought my roller skates!

LATINO How far it is, out of here?

GAY MAN Wouldn't know. I'm a stranger here myself.

LATINO I bet over a mile.

BLACK WOMAN We may have to swim out.

WHITE MAN I got stuck like this last week. No sweat!

LESBIAN The authorities are certainly taking their time!

ASIAN What we think's wrong?

WHITE MAN (cutting off the LESBIAN) Just some mechanical problem. We'll be chugging along any minute now.

LESBIAN (to WHITE MAN with spite for being interrupted) Perhaps you ought to get out and see what's wrong

	— on the track, I mean.
WHITE MAN	What?
WHITE WOMAN	Does it seem stuffy in here to you?
GAY MAN	Does to me a little bit.
WHITE MAN	Not to me!
LESBIAN	Maybe you don't notice stuffy when you see it.
WHITE MAN	Maybe we should all sit down and be quiet.
NATIVE AMERICAN	(to LESBIAN) You think the air supply's cut off?
WHITE MAN	(cutting off the LESBIAN again, sniffing) Seems all right to me.
GAY MAN	Maybe we should all carry canaries or parakeets. (The others don't get his point.)

	We should carry them — to check the air!
LATINO	(almost under his breath) You carry a parakeet, if you want one. (Rolls his eyes.)
GAY MAN	(going to a window, holding his throat, a little too theatrical) We're trapped! We're trapped forever! Why me? Why me?
HANDICAPPED WOMAN	Should we make a run for it?
GAY MAN	(archly) Think you got it in you, honey?
HANDICAPPED WOMAN	I'm hell on wheels. (Holds up her crutches. They laugh together.)
ASIAN	I hope we start soon. Need medication — home. Heart. (Taps his chest.)

BLACK WOMAN	It's in the Lord's lap now.
ASIAN	Confucius' lap.
LESBIAN	Maybe we should do something.
GAY MAN	Like what? Stop breathing?
LESBIAN	You can stop if you want.
GAY MAN	I — never mind. I'm splendid in a crisis. (Stifles a scream.)
VOICE	Ladies and gentlemen, we're still have some small difficulties with the power system. Please be patient. We'll get back to you momentarily. Don't panic, please.
GAY MAN	(to VOICE) Screw you, Mister! Get us poor mortals out of here!

BLACK
WOMAN We won't be here long. I feel it in my bones.

HANDICAPPED
WOMAN I wish I had bones like that.

BLACK
WOMAN The Lord will provide!

GAY MAN It looks like the Lord got us into this. He'd better provide.

BLACK
WOMAN When our time comes, it comes. When it doesn't, it doesn't. The Lord of Subways is on our side.

GAY MAN If I knew you better, I'd say that was a lot of baloney.

LATINO (looking at the FOREIGNER) What if we run out of food?

NATIVE
AMERICAN And drink.

(The FOREIGNER hunches over his food, still nibbling, eyes jumpy.)

LATINO (to the FOREIGNER) Don't worry! I don't want that ugly stuff.

BLACK MAN I'm getting tired of waitin' here.

WHITE MAN Let's open a window.

GAY MAN (ironically) "When God closes a door, he opens a window." Get it? *The Sound of Music*!.

LESBIAN (to WHITE MAN) They're all locked. I thought you'd know that.

WHITE MAN You sure? (trying a window) You're right.

LESBIAN Surprised?

BLACK MAN Maybe we should smash it.

WHITE WOMAN The Transport people will be mad if it's just a

t

temporary delay.

BLACK MAN Want us to smother in here?

WHITE WOMAN I don't want anybody to smother anywhere at all.

BLACK MAN Well, I think we should smash it.

(He goes to a window, takes a hidden pipe out of his jacket.)

ASIAN We can pretend it's ghetto.

(The BLACK MAN looks back with a scowl.)

WHITE WOMAN If you ask me, it's just needless destruction of public property!

BLACK MAN When things is bad, you gotta do something about 'em.

(He starts prying a window open.)

GAY MAN Let's do this thoroughly. Anybody got any spray paint?

(Pretends to put graffiti on the walls.)

ASIAN Somebody come along pretty soon.

LESBIAN We can't just sit here passively twiddling our thumbs waiting for somebody else to do something!

HANDICAPPED WOMAN What do you suggest? I can't leave too easily. I don't think the tunnel is accessible to folks like me.

LESBIAN Oh, let the men decide! They will anyway.

WHITE MAN I haven't said a word!

HANDICAPPED WOMAN Now let's all be cool and collective, and we'll get through this mess.

WHITE WOMAN	Yes, a little politeness goes a mighty long way to make each day a little brighter.
GAY MAN	(ironically) Courtesy is contagious.
VOICE	I'm sorry, ladies and gentlemen. We still haven't been able to repair the generator that runs the subway trains. I'm afraid you'll have to wait a while longer. Hang in there!
GAY MAN	Oh, barf! It's easy for him to say.
ASIAN	Have deck of cards! (Takes out the cards, shows them) Any like to play?

(Most of the others decline.)

HANDICAPPED WOMAN	I'll take you up on that offer. I'm pretty good at cards. It's something one can do sitting

	down! (She hobbles over to the ASIAN.)
ASIAN	(to LESBIAN) Sure?
LESBIAN	No thanks.
GAY MAN	(swooping by) No? They're playing Old Maid!
LESBIAN	Why don't you play then?
GAY MAN	Funny! Is that the famous lesbian wit?
BLACK MAN	I hope we're not gonna be stuck down here all day. Freakin' Jesus!
GAY MAN	I know! We can put on a show! All singing, all dancing! I can do my Faye Wray impression! (Screams as if King Kong is coming.) We'll raise oodles of money for those kids in the orphanage!
NATIVE AMERICAN	What orphanage?

GAY MAN	Obviously we have a cultural gap here. I get to play the Judy Garland part.
LATINO	We don't got no dresses along.
GAY MAN	Oh, a touché from Tijuana! (Sings.) "South of the border, down Mexico way. That's where I felt in love when the stars above came out to play!"
LATINO	(standing up) *Puta!*
GAY MAN	*Puta* am I? You're as observant as you seem. Only *putas* charge and I'm free! (defying him with more singing and dancing) M-M-M-*M-M-M Mamacarro! M-M-M-M-M-M-Mamacarro!*
LATINO	Don't sing that! (Takes swing, misses.)
WHITE MAN	(separating them) Okay now! We're in enough trouble already!

NATIVE
AMERICAN We'll be into cannibalism in another hour.

GAY MAN I want the white meat!

(Starts to dance on the seats.)

BLACK MAN You got something against dark meat?

NATIVE
AMERICAN Or red meat?

GAY MAN I'll eat the meat I choose. Even cannibals can be choosy.

LATINO *Maricone!*

GAY MAN Does that mean fairy? Don't you know any insults in English? Cocksucker —
aha, beat you to it! (dancing on the seats some more, singing) "I took it all, against the wall, but did it MY WAY!"(Takes a bow.)

WHITE WOMAN	Sit down and behave yourself.
GAY MAN	Yes, Mother. (He sits with his legs together, folding his hands like a schoolboy.)
WHITE WOMAN	There's no sense in getting everyone all riled up. Our adrenaline level is already above normal.
GAY MAN	I was trying to be entertaining.
WHITE WOMAN	Perhaps you try too hard.
GAY MAN	Perhaps you don't try hard enough.
WHITE MAN	Don't be snotty with her.
GAY MAN	Is she your wife? Only you have the right to be snotty with her?

WHITE MAN I don't know who she is. That's not the point.

GAY MAN I wasn't being snotty to anybody. I apologize for being interesting!

BLACK WOMAN Hey now! We're getting on each other's nerves. Why don't we all sit still and you watch — this train'll start moving again. How much you want to bet?

(All sit quietly for a few moments; the train doesn't move.)

GAY MAN (after the silence, to BLACK WOMAN) Okay, you lose . . . Hey, I'm thirsty!

NATIVE AMERICAN No, you're not.

GAY MAN What do you mean I'm not?!

LESBIAN You're just trying to get all the attention.

GAY MAN	Pardon me for living. You want my part of the air? (He scoops several handfuls and throws them at her.)
LESBIAN	No thanks. Never know where it's been.
BLACK WOMAN	Maybe we should all sing something!
GAY MAN	Yeah, a spiritual! (giving a sexual meaning to the song) "I'm a-comin', I'm a-comin', for my head is bendin' low!" (Moans after each phrase.)
BLACK WOMAN	Hey now! Let's sing — together. It'll keep us out of mischief.

(She gets up and makes the others sit down in a group, then begins to direct them. They are reluctant, but a few start to follow her lead.)

BLACK WOMAN	Let's see. "My momma

done tole me when I was in knee pants, my momma done tole me, hon —"

LESBIAN (jumping up) I won't sit here and hear that a woman's a two-face, a worrisome thing who'll leave you to sing the blues!

GAY MAN "In the night." Hey, you're not bad. Do you know "The Man I Love?" (Sings some of it.)

BLACK WOMAN (cutting him off) Come on, let's sing another one then!

(Mutters; some try to think of a song.)

WHITE WOMAN Group singing lifts the spirits!

HANDICAPPED WOMAN I know one! (Sings) "When you walk

through a storm keep your chin up high —"

OTHERS (joining in) "And don't be afraid of the dark. At the end of the storm is a golden sky and the sweet, silver call of a lark."

(The OTHERS begin to weaken on the lyrics.)

HANDICAPPED WOMAN (going on, too loudly, too enthusiastically) "Walk on! Walk on! With hope in your heart and you'll never walk alone — " (Her voice cracks on a high note.)

GAY MAN (meaning the campy situation) I love it! I *love* it!

WHITE WOMAN This is so nice. I mean really and truly. (She is too bright, too cheerful.) I think we should all be grateful the subway broke down like this.

There is so little communication in the subways of today!

ASIAN So nice. So nice.

(OTHERS nod agreement.)

WHITE WOMAN We all spend so much time going here and going there we just never get a chance to practice our conversation. Think how it would be if people actually conversed down here instead of . . .

ASIAN What she say?

WHITE WOMAN It's about time people said hello in this world. (She shakes a few hands) Hello! Hello! Hello there! Why don't we all introduce ourselves and get to know more about each of us? (Some mutters of protest) I'll start! I'm Mrs. Margery Gilbert and I'm going to visit my sister. We go shopping together. The little street artists near where she lives have such attractive and tasteful trinkets and we just love them so much. (Turns to the BLACK MAN) And who is this black gentleman?

BLACK MAN (standing as if in a classroom) I'm —

WHITE WOMAN Say hello first!

BLACK MAN (mocking her) I'm Willie E. Davidson and I'm — I'm just ridin' round. (He sits quickly.)

WHITE WOMAN Well, isn't that nice. (not letting it die, to BLACK WOMAN) And why don't you tell us something about yourself?

BLACK WOMAN (incensed at the

BLACK MAN) Some of us can talk. Some of us are role models. I'm Grace Abdullah Babu-llah, and I'm a Black Muslim. (Laughs.) No, I'm Grace Bloom-ington, and I'm on my way to work. I'm Assistant Personnel Specialist for Alcohol, Tobacco, and Firearms for the United States Government. And soon to be office manager!

BLACK MAN (ambiguously) Congratulations, mama!

(The BLACK WOMAN points to the next likely speaker, the ASIAN, and goes over to him.)

BLACK WOMAN And you, sir?

ASIAN (standing) I'm Chester Hing, and own own restaurant in city back there. Am thinking of to buy one more restaurant that I'm going to look. And I like all my new friends here to come to Hing's Palace and say, "Howdy, Hing!" We got special pork fried rice, friendly service, cheap prices. Dim Sum all day.

GAY MAN — Cockroaches?

ASIAN — Cheap prices, friendly service. And we got special pork fried rice too. Eat soon. Come fast. Thank you, my subway friends. (Sits.)

WHITE WOMAN — (to HANDICAPPED WOMAN) And what do you do, dear? Let me help you.

HANDICAPPED WOMAN — (not wanting help) My name is Estelle Avery and I'm handicapped — and proud to be so. I've been on crutches since I began to walk at the early age of eight months. And for a living I'm a broadcaster for a Pacifica radio station. I'm also a Leninist-Marxist-Trotskyite! (to the next person) And what do you do, may I ask?

LATINO — I'm Alfredo Pedilla and I'm from Mexico, and I've been in America for fifty-five years. (He holds up two fingers.) And I pump gas, yes? And I love America, yes? (Forces the HANDICAPPED WOMAN back by walking aggressively toward her. Then he salutes.) (to LESBIAN) And what about you, honey? What do you did?

LESBIAN — I'm Kris Schumacher and I run my own photographic laboratory. And — ah — and I don't think it's necessary to reveal anything else about myself. I'm a perfectly normal, well-adjusted citizen.

GAY MAN (just barely audible) Closet case.

LESBIAN Screaming queen. (to next person) And you?

NATIVE AMERICAN Ted Parker. Used to be Ted Redwing. I was born and raised on an Indian reservation. Now I'm waiting for the Bureau of Indian Affairs to find me —

GAY MAN An affair?

NATIVE AMERICAN A job.

WHITE MAN (eagerly) My name is Evans Horton. I'm the president of my own well-known company, Horton Tool and Die. "At Horton's we'll die for you — or at least tool!" You've seen my ads? (Hands out business cards.) I have a lovely wife, Marlene, and two handsome boys, Brad and Burt.

	And I'm going to miss my luncheon appointment with a very important client. (He smiles.) (to GAY MAN) And who, dare we ask, are you?
GAY MAN	(sulking a bit) Oh, I wouldn't want to make a nuisance of myself.
WHITE WOMAN	Oh, come now! Everybody has to introduce him- or herself. It's a rule!
LATINO	Come on, Herself! Make a nuisance.
GAY MAN	(bridling) My name is Sabu the Elephant Boy, and I used to be in pictures!
WHITE WOMAN	Really?
GAY MAN	No, seriously — God knows we need more seriousness in this world. I'm Marty

Maynard and I'm a full-time faggot! (Strikes a pose, then sits.)

WHITE WOMAN (embarrassed) Have we forgotten anybody?

(All eyes turn toward the FOREIGNER, who is still eating. He sinks down in his seat.)

Oh, of course, the foreign gentleman. What's your name, sir, if you don't mind telling us?

FOR'NER (squirms because they are all looking at him; he shakes his head to indicate that he doesn't speak or understand very well.)

HANDICAPPED WOMAN Why don't you tell us where you're from? I'll bet it's someplace exotic!

(The FOREIGNER gestures that he doesn't understand.)

WHITE
WOMAN — By the way, what is that you're eating? It looks very interesting.

(The FOREIGNER tries to hide whatever it is in his handkerchief and sticks it inside his clothes.)

BLACK MAN — (not pleased) You're not illegal, I hope. Taking jobs —

WHITE
WOMAN — (hurrying on) Well! We've finally met one another. You see! A little ray of sunshine can make even the darkest day radiate all over us.

GAY MAN — (pointing to the roof) And we owe it all to fate!

VOICE — Ladies and gentlemen, we've —

(The VOICE is cut off abruptly by static. The OTHERS are unsettled by this; they mutter.)

GAY MAN (sing-songy) I'm getting scared, and I don't mind saying so!

WHITE WOMAN Everything is going to be fine. What do you say we all hold hands together?

LATINO Hold hands!

(There are some protests, but they begin to hold hands, except for FOREIGNER.)

WHITE WOMAN (encouraging) Come on! Come along now!

(The LATINO doesn't want to hold the GAY MAN's hand and switches places. At last they are all in a circle holding hands, with some coughs, some embarrassment.)

LATINO What do we do now?

NATIVE AMERICAN I went to a séance once. It was sort of like this. I heard from my ancestors.

GAY MAN What did you hear?

NATIVE AMERICAN It was sort of hard to figure out. We had a bad connection.

LESBIAN I hate this!

WHITE WOMAN Wait now, wait! We've gone this far. Let's play a little game I know!

GAY MAN (slapping hands against the hands of the person next to him) Patty-cake, patty-cake, baker's man!

WHITE WOMAN No, not that one, although that's a very nice game too. I'll whisper something about somebody in the circle and everybody passes it on to the next person, and — guess what! — it goes all the way around and then back to this end.

BLACK MAN What for?

GAY MAN Don't ask!

WHITE WOMAN You'll see.

OTHERS All right. Okay. Go ahead. Why not., etc.

(WHITE WOMAN whispers to the one next to her. Quickly the message goes around the circle, ending with the person on the far side of the WHITE WOMAN. The audience hears it each time.)

(The ASIAN changes it to "Handicapped people are fairy mice.")

NATIVE AMERICAN (saying what he heard) Handicapped people are hairy lice.

HANDICAPPED WOMAN (incensed) Well, thank you very much!

WHITE WOMAN Oh, that's how this game works! Everything gets all scrambled up. What I really said was: Handicapped people are very nice.

HANDICAPPED WOMAN Well, let me try one then! (She whispers and the message goes around the circle to the person next to her, the ASIAN. The audience does not hear this one each time.)

ASIAN Socialism is cancer.

(The OTHERS snicker.)

HANDICAPPED WOMAN (angry) Socialism is the answer!

WHITE WOMAN See! Isn't this clean, wholesome fun?

GAY MAN I'm tired of it.

BLACK MAN Wait! I've got one. (He whispers. It goes around. The audience hears this one. The ASIAN changes it to "crocks.")

LATINO	(aloud) Black guys got the biggest crocks.
BLACK WOMAN	(to BLACK MAN) The biggest what? (Smirks.)
BLACK MAN	Timepieces! (He points to his watch.)
BLACK WOMAN	Oh, you!
GAY MAN	It isn't *always* true, you know.
BLACK MAN	How do you know?
GAY MAN	They once used me as a guinea pig in an experiment!
WHITE WOMAN	(trying to head off any fighting) Let's try one more round! What do you say?
LESBIAN	Oh, please!

(Some start to go back to their seats.)

GAY MAN — Ah, and it was just about to turn into an orgy too!

NATIVE AMERICAN — Gay man always speak with great dignity.

GAY MAN — Indian suck butt with forked tongue. Oo, it sounds like heaven!

ASIAN — I show card tricks!

WHITE WOMAN — That sounds like fun!

(ASIAN stands up and fans the deck.)

ASIAN — You want gamble?

WHITE WOMAN — No, no, no gambling. Let's be on our best behavior.

ASIAN — Okay, somebody pick card.

(There is some fuss over who'll do it. Finally they decide that the HANDI-CAPPED WOMAN should be the one. She picks a card.)

ASIAN	(with flourish) Got one?
HANDICAPPED WOMAN	Got it.
ASIAN	(building suspense) Now put back in deck. (She does. He shuffles the cards, then pulls out a card and names it dramatically.) Your card was — [Actor fills in wrong card.]
HANDICAPPED WOMAN	Why, no. It was — [Actor fills in right answer, shows the card.] (She is embarrassed for him.)
GAY MAN	(a real put-down to ASIAN) Oh, sit down, for god's sake!
ASIAN	(embarrassed) Guess didn't do right. But know another really good one — (Starts to arrange cards.)
VOICE	Ladies and gentlemen,

this is the Transport Authority again. I'm afraid we can't get you out.

(The shock of the announcement causes the ASIAN to let fly all the cards he has spread out for his trick.)

We suggest that you make yourselves as comfortable as possible, and please try not to use any more air than you absolutely have to. We've developed some problems with the air circulator in the tunnel. Just make yourselves comfortable, please!

(They are getting frightened now.)

NATIVE AMERICAN Maybe this is really the end of us all.

(All are sober now; they all help pick up the cards, overly helpful.)

GAY MAN (to LATINO) Sorry I made fun of you before.

LATINO — It's okay. I shouldn't have put you down so much.

LESBIAN — (to GAY MAN) I'm sorry too.

GAY MAN — I guess I acted sort of silly.

LESBIAN — I shouldn't have been so grouchy.

GAY MAN — Oh, we all have our off-days.

WHITE WOMAN — I want to apologize for scolding you.

GAY MAN — I understand how you must have felt.

(There is a round-robin of apologies and forgiveness, except for FOREIGNER, who is conspicuously off to the side.)

NATIVE AMERICAN — Everybody's passed the peace-pipe now.

WHITE WOMAN — It's real nice, isn't it?

GAY MAN (after a yawn) But on the dull side. Hey, I know! Let's make up cheers for each other!

WHITE MAN Cheers?

GAY MAN Like basketball cheers. Only not for teams. For all of us here. It should be fun, and it'll pass the time.

WHITE WOMAN And cheers should make us 'cheerful,' right?

GAY MAN I'll start. "2-4-6-8! I feel safe 'cause my friends are straight!"

(The GAY MAN does some cheerleader moves to accompany his words. The OTHERS applaud when he's through.)

LATINO Another one! Please!

GAY MAN Okay. "1-2, please don't panic. There's no need when you're friend's Hispanic!"

(More applause.)

GAY MAN (to NATIVE AMERICAN) Now you try.

NATIVE AMERICAN (a little shy but trying) "Who sees you through when you're sort of trapped? (needing help) Ah, ah —

GAY MAN (helping out) "Nobody else but the — " (Points to HANDICAPPED WOMAN)

HANDICAPPED WOMAN (finishing the compliment) " — the handicapped!"

GAY MAN " — with black folks on board we won't get zapped, because they — they —" (points to WHITE MAN and WHITE WOMAN)

WHITE MAN " — know how to adapt and — and —" (passing it on to:)

WHITE WOMAN — " — they are very apt!"

GAY MAN — (keeping it going) "And 2-4-6-8! Our Asian friends are really great!

ASIAN — (picking it up) " — 9-10! Who is better than —" (passing it on to:)

NATIVE AMERICAN — (picking it up) " — a Native American"!

GAY MAN — (spotting the FOREIGNER) "All the way down the car, hey! All the way down the car! Zis boom bah! Zis boom bah! Let's give a hand for the man who's come so far! Let's hear it for — (to FOREIGNER) What's your name?

(The FOREIGNER won't answer, shakes his head, tries to hide.)

GAY MAN — Don't let it die! What's your name? (The FOREIGNER shakes his head harder.) Come

	on! (to OTHERS) Give me an F!
OTHERS	(except the FOREIGNER) F!
GAY MAN	Give me an O!
OTHERS	O!
GAY MAN	Give me an R!
OTHERS	R!
GAY MAN	(seeing that it's frightening the man and that the cheer is petering out) Give me an I . . .
OTHERS	(losing momentum) I . . .
GAY MAN	(giving up) Oh, well . . . fuck it.
ASIAN	How much air left now?

(Sniffs the air.)

(All the rest sniff the air to see.)

WHITE MAN	Seems hard to breathe, doesn't it?

HANDICAPPED WOMAN	Do you suppose we'll just keel over all of a sudden, gasping and choking, our fingers digging into our throats like —
BLACK WOMAN	Now let's not lose our heads! I bet we have a whole lot of air left.
LATINO	Maybe we only got enough for a few of us.

(ALL look around at each other with growing resentment. They breathe loudly in unison.)

BLACK MAN	(to FOREIGNER) Do you got to breathe so hard? (FOREIGNER cowers.)
LESBIAN	You're breathing sort of hard yourself.
BLACK MAN	I am not. (Moves away, pounds his chest.)
LESBIAN	Don't move around so much. You're using up the air!

BLACK
WOMAN If we just sit still, there'll be plenty for everybody.

HANDICAPPED
WOMAN (to the BLACK WOMAN) You're so heavy you take up twice as much air as anybody else.

BLACK
WOMAN My lungs are the same size as yours!

HANDICAPPED
WOMAN Prove it!

BLACK
WOMAN I don't have to prove it. It's a God-given right to breathe!

HANDICAPPED
WOMAN When the Revolution comes, if people don't watch themselves, they'll be allowed to have only one lung!

BLACK MAN (jumping up) Now watch your mouth you — you lame duck!

HANDICAPPED
WOMAN (raising her crutch) Watch who you're calling names, Sambo!

GAY MAN Sambo? I haven't heard that in years!

HANDICAPPED
WOMAN I'm sorry. It just sort of slipped out.

WHITE MAN Please! Let's all simmer down. There's enough air. We simply have to conserve it, that's all.

(ALL sit, but they nervously watch each other to see who's breathing too hard.)

WHITE MAN (Takes a couple of quick breaths.) I'm sorry. I did it because I'm nervous.

(Several others take extra breaths behind their hands, pretending not to be stealing them. Suddenly the FOREIGNER jumps up and kneels down close to the air vent and tries to wave more fresh air into his face.)

WHITE MAN (standing) Come back

here, you creep!

(All stand, shout at the FOREIGNER.)

BLACK MAN (going to grab the FOREIGNER) Get away from that vent!

(When he touches him, FOREIGNER uses his large sausage to knock the BLACK MAN down. Then the FOREIGNER waves everyone else back with the sausage. He kneels again, breathing the air, keeping watch on the rest.)

BLACK MAN (stunned) Oh, my head! My head! (He staggers back to a seat.)

LESBIAN Don't wave that sausage at us! It's a symbol of phallic domination!

ASIAN We let you people into country and you steal our air!

LATINO (to BLACK MAN) Now you're breathing twice as hard, man!

BLACK MAN I can't help it, man.

BLACK
WOMAN You don't have to breathe that heavily! Stop right this minute!

BLACK MAN Get off my back, woman!

LATINO (under his breath) Dirty colored person!

BLACK MAN (under his breath) Greasy, illegal alien spic!

LATINO I spit on your mother's eyebrows. All three of them! (Pulls a knife.)

(Gasps from the OTHERS.)

BLACK MAN Get away from me, you Mexican crud! It's people like you takin' our jobs! I can't get no job on account of you! And besides, all you grease balls got dandruff!

LATINO (pointing to the ground in front of him) Come over here and tell me

	I've got dandruff in my hairs! Come on, I dare you!
BLACK MAN	(pointing to the ground in front of him) You come over here! Come on, let's see you come over here!
LATINO	I do crummy work! Lousy work, that's all I can get. Pumping gas in the fields!
BLACK MAN	You fuck up your own country, and then you come here to fuck up ours, you enchilada-eating wetback!
LATINO	It's not so great here, let me tell you that!
BLACK MAN	It's still better than where you came from. Go back where you belong!
LATINO	You go back to Africa! Everybody here came from someplace else! I'm no different, just a

little later. (Sings) "God bless America, land that I love!"

WHITE MAN Some of us were actually born here.

NATIVE AMERICAN My people were here first! And what do I have? I've had to sit back and watch. First the white man and now the niggers and the spics!

WHITE MAN How do you think anybody every got any land? By taking it, that's how! Even you holier-than-thou "Native Americans" took it away from each other. You took it away from the animals!

HANDICAPPED WOMAN The English took it away from somebody else, and so did the Germans and so did the French.

GAY MAN — And the Red Chinese took Tibet, and the Soviets took Afghan-istan. Or tried to!

HANDICAPPED WOMAN — That's different!

WHITE MAN — You Indians don't seem to mind taking advan-tage of white civiliza-tion!

NATIVE AMERICAN — Yeah, your air pollution! Progress is your most important product!

WHITE MAN — If you were so great and noble, Chief Running Mouth, how come you couldn't handle the firewater? You couldn't be satisfied with a nice Dubonet or two, or even three, before dinner. Oh no, you had to guzzle it by the gallon!

NATIVE AMERICAN — Because you knocked

down our teepees, that's why!

WHITE MAN Don't hand me that buffalo dung. You knocked down the white man's teepees first!

NATIVE AMERICAN You weren't satisfied with sharing! You had to have it all! Every bit of this country!

WHITE MAN We made this a great country. George Washington! Abraham Lincoln! Gerald Ford!

NATIVE AMERICAN By making our horses drink your detergents, that's how you made it great!

WHITE MAN We make the best detergents in the world, and your horses loved them!

NATIVE AMERICAN You destroyed our civilization!

WHITE MAN	We gave you toilet paper!
GAY MAN	And don't forget "Depends."
WHITE WOMAN	Whoa now! This talk is getting out of hand!
WHITE MAN	I'm a minority in my own country!
WHITE WOMAN	That's true. I try to be fair, but now I'm supposed to give you people quotas and Affirmative Reaction or whatever it's called. I'm a woman and I deserve some quotas myself!
WHITE MAN	Quotas, my ass! You women have had things your way for the past umpteen years and you're still whining! I guess you won't be satisfied until you're in charge of everything!
GAY MAN	Whoa! Whoa now!

Why don't we all cool this discussion.

HANDICAPPED WOMAN — Oh, why don't you sit down, you liberal! Who asked you?

WHITE WOMAN — I think he's right. We're using up the air this way!

BLACK WOMAN — It might be good for you to lose some air for a change. Might give you some idea what it's like to do without. Like certain people have had to do without all their lives!

WHITE WOMAN — Don't turn on me now! I'm just trying to make peace. After all, we are a melting pot. So melt

BLACK WOMAN — All dressed up so nice and refined! Going shopping, huh? You have more money than I'll ever see in my whole life and all you have to do is go shopping! Pooh!

WHITE WOMAN — Just a second now. All you and your kind have to do is sit around and get fat, I suppose.

BLACK WOMAN — I'm not fat. I'm calorie-challenged.

WHITE WOMAN — You're so fat you can hardly move! I suppose I'm to blame for that! I'm to blame because you're a great big saturated-fat blimp who blames everybody else for her problems! I've had it with you blacks!

BLACK WOMAN — Not too fat to clean your house! Haven't been too fat to take care of your babies!

WHITE MAN — That's because you've

had so much experience with babies! Illegal babies!

BLACK WOMAN — And we're going to have a whole lot more, Mr. Honky!

ASIAN — Many children good!

BLACK WOMAN — (to ASIAN) Yeah, you're trying to swamp *us*, aren't you?

WHITE WOMAN — (to BLACK WOMAN and ASIAN) The world can't support the ones you do have and you're going to have even more. Typical! Typical of you people!

BLACK MAN — Pay us enough and we'll support the ones we have! We're just crawling along because you've got everything!

WHITE MAN — Then why don't you

better yourselves! Bring yourself up to our level.

HANDICAPPED WOMAN — Some of them have bettered themselves.

BLACK WOMAN — My brother's a lawyer! I have a responsible job with Alcohol, Tobacco, and Firearms!

GAY MAN — To say nothing of *using* Alcohol, Tobacco, and Firearms!

BLACK WOMAN — You've had all the advantages, Whities! And now it's time we had some. We're not going to tap-dance for you anymore!

WHITE WOMAN — But let's face it. Some of you don't do diddly!

BLACK MAN — Bullshit! I do diddly! I do diddly!

BLACK WOMAN — Slaving away on your plantations and sweating in your factories, and you have the nerve to say —

WHITE MAN — But you liked being slaves! At least you had jobs then!

WHITE WOMAN — You're the ones with the privileges now. Nobody's giving me free cheese for doing nothing but sitting on my big behind!

WHITE MAN — And the percentage of criminals in your category is —

BLACK WOMAN — I'm not a criminal. I'm a hard worker.

WHITE MAN — For every one of you, how many of your kids acts like rude, witless animals, and I'm not supposed to notice when they Mau Mau

me. Oh no, if I even
complain because I'm
mugged, I'm supposed
to be *prejudiced*!

WHITE
WOMAN — And your literacy rates!
(Tsks.)

BLACK MAN /
BLACK WOMAN — Racism!

WHITE
WOMAN — Oh, fuck, shut up about
'racism'! It isn't racism
to point out your faults
as they are!

WHITE MAN — We've bent over
backwards for you
and you still can't get
your act together!

BLACK
WOMAN — I can do any job any
white man can do!
But they won't give me
a chance. You don't see
me with my own tool
and die company!

WHITE MAN — I built that company

from scratch! If you want one, then you do the same.

ASAIN Like us!

(The OTHERS whisper "Fight! Fight!" trying to start a fist fight.)

BLACK MAN You treated us like cattle and sweated us and beat us and lynched us and took away our educations! You took away our self-respect. You think I asked to be called Willie?

WHITE MAN I'm taking my life in my hands right this minute because I'm telling you what I really think!

BLACK MAN It's the color of my skin you hate! That don't make no sense. No sense at all!

WHITE WOMAN I don't give a fuck what the color of your

skin is, but when I see a spade, I don't call it a shovel! Come on, when was the last time either of you read a book? Go ahead, name a book!

BLACK WOMAN — *Uncle Tom's Cabin*!

WHITE MAN — A recent book!

BLACK WOMAN — We're too busy cleaning your house to have time to read!

WHITE WOMAN — Too busy playing basketball! Aha!

BLACK WOMAN — You give us rotten schools and expect us to get a decent education?

WHITE WOMAN — You made them rotten. You don't wait around expecting someone to *give* education to you! You have to take pains and make an effort. We Jews have been

	oppressed too, but we did something about it ourselves.
ASAIAN	Like us!
BLACK WOMAN	Yeah, the Jews made money off us blacks!
GAY MAN	And we gays have gotten it from all of you bastards, and what have we done in return — oh, just given you most of your art and —
OTHERS	(together) Oh, shut up!
BLACK WOMAN	It's you Whites, and now the Asians, who have done it to us. There isn't one of you I'd give one bowel movement for!
ASIAN	Good. Don't want your bowel movement. We put in internment camp –World War II! Internment camp!

BLACK WOMAN — Oh, get over yourselves! I've stayed in Motel 6's that were worse than your so-called internment camps!

WHITE WOMAN — (to BLACK WOMAN) You're as much a racist as anybody else!

BLACK MAN — What did I ever get out of this country except to work on an assembly line all day, breaking my back to make ashtrays for rich folks to put their butts in! We got screwed, that's what we got. Screwed!

HANDICAPPED WOMAN — And screwed is all we outsiders are ever going to get! It's only when glorious Marxist-Leninist Trotskyism takes over that those who have been throttled by the system are going to get a chance for the future!

GAY MAN — You can take your Fidel Castro and your Red China and your Russia and shove 'em up your Trotsky!

HANDICAPPED WOMAN — They're helping starving people all over this globe.

GAY MAN — They're just exploiters like anybody else. They want their colonies; they want power, just like the Romans. Just like the Americans!

HANDICAPPED WOMAN — You're full of middle-class crap! You double-income, no-kids wimp!

GAY MAN — What have the Communists ever done for gay people except persecute them? The glorious Marxists are just another group who want predictable, tame little robots who do exactly what they're told, when they're told.

HANDICAPPED WOMAN There'll be no room for degenerates like you when the universe goes (reverently) *Commie.*

GAY MAN You call me degenerate — and you have the bad taste to be deformed? You hobbling, wobbling freak, and you — you try to scorch the hair off my chinny chin chin! (Shows his butt to her.)

HANDICAPPED WOMAN You bet your sweet penetrated posterior I come down on you! I may be deformed, but I'm not sick inside like you!

GAY MAN Not sick? You're practically a hospital all by yourself!

HANDICAPPED WOMAN — You make me sick! Prancing around like you've got a hot dill pickle up your behind.

GAY MAN — I'm sorry I don't waltz the way you do! Smell her! Listen to the cripple! Do you hear me? Not handicapped! Not 'physically challenged!' Cripple! Who'd ever want to spread-eagle you on the sheets? The crutches would get in the way. You know something? I want to gag when I see you. Gag! (Gags exaggeratedly.) And they give you a parking sticker for it!

HANDICAPPED WOMAN — Your opinions don't interest me in the slightest. You should have been an abortion.

GAY MAN — Like you?

HANDICAPPED WOMAN — You queers can't even reproduce!

GAY MAN — And what do you reproduce, huh? Maybe little flippers for arms? And we're supposed to stand around and get all goo-goo-eyed because one of you manages to play "Chopsticks" on the baby grand with your flippers!

HANDICAPPED WOMAN — I don't have flippers! How dare you pick on somebody like me! You disease carrier! (Attacks him with her crutch.) You've given it to all of us!

GAY MAN — I don't have a disease, goddamn it. But you should all be grateful to the gays who do. Not only do they not add to the population explosion, they positively reduce the surplus by dying for you!

VOICE (over loudspeaker) Oh, shut up, all of you! I'm tired of listening to you.

GAY MAN (incensed) I beg your pardon!

VOICE I think I'll leave you all down there.

HANDICAPPED WOMAN Hey, wait a minute. We're not at our best right now!

VOICE Here's an announcement. We almost have the air supply fixed. So calm down.

NATIVE AMERICAN Almost fixed?

VOICE But I feel obliged to inform you that we've developed a problem in the side of one of the subway cars. A small problem.

LATINO What problem?

VOICE — Water is slowing seeping into the subway cars.

GAY MAN — Seeping in!

VOICE — We may try to evacuate you. Please stand by.

HANDICAPPED WOMAN — Evacuate us?

LESBIAN — They'll be taking women and children first of course?

HANDICAPPED WOMAN — Right!

ASIAN — Hold on! Very sick and tired of giving place to women and children first.

(The MALE CHARACTERS agree. Yeah! Way to go! That's saying it. Etc.)

LESBIAN — You men think of yourselves first, last, and always!

WHITE MAN — You want me to suffocate or drown

	instead of you, and then you want my job afterwards! No way, lady! And I've got all the privileges?!
ASIAN	Want to scream I'm so sick of sacrificing, sacrificing!
GAY MAN	Right on!
ASIAN	Just as much as I sick of her (meaning the HANDICAPPED WOMAN) I sick of you faggots! Always your rights this and your rights that! You give me a headache!
GAY MAN	And I'm going to keep on yelling for my rights until I get 'em.
ASIAN	Free to do what? Play with each other's ding-dong!
BLACK MAN	You faggots and you Asians don't mind buying up property and pushing my people out

of their homes so that you can be free!

GAY MAN — Oh, I'm so sorry. You must so proud of your slums!

BLACK MAN — We have families to support. We can't spend our money on Vaseline!

ASIAN — You homos destroy family. People like me carry on human race!

GAY MAN — Honorable Oriental not kind to men who suck pee-pee. (Bows mockingly.)

ASIAN — You have no respect for elders, no respect!

GAY MAN — Maybe you don't deserve any respect. Breeder!

NATIVE AMERICAN — (cutting in) Listen, I'm not defending no squaw-man like him, but it's time somebody told you old gooks off. It's the old guys like you that's keeping us young guys down.

ASIAN — Lazy round-eye!

NATIVE AMERICAN — It's you old, worn-out geezers that hang on to the jobs and the money and us young guys can't get nothing.

ASIAN — You want me sit around on bench and dry up?

NATIVE AMERICAN — You won't give me an inch so I can get a little bit for myself!

ASIAN — You expect me give up everything — my restaurant, savings? Give it to some no-good bum like you who's never worked days and months and years like me!

NATIVE AMERICAN — Goddamn it, you never

move aside so I can get in. You don't even know when to get out of the way!

ASIAN — Nothing wrong with me just because I old! Can out-think and out-work you any day! See? (He does one quick push-up, very wobbly.) Out-fuck you too!

NATIVE AMERICAN — How can I work when you people got everything sewed up! You lend each other money and do favors for each others and buy up all the property. And besides your fortune cookies don't even tell the truth!

ASIAN — They do too! It's you Indians who don't know how to adapt like we do. You want take everything I have just 'cause you young! Nothing! You get nothing from me!

LATINO I tried to start a company making Indian fortune cookies — they would tell the truth — but you've got a monopoly on the market!

ASIAN (coming at the NATIVE AMERICAN with fists flying) Okay, come on then! Come on, you big brave brave! You can't even hang on to your own goddamn country!

(ASIAN swings at NATIVE AMERICAN, who holds him away with one hand, the old man still swinging, not connecting.)

NATIVE AMERICAN Watch it, you shriveled-up old Chinaman!

ASIAN I show you, Geronimo! I show you!

NATIVE AMERICAN I ought to cut you up into chow mein, you old, yellow coolie!

VOICE	Ladies and gentlemen, how are you doing down there? Is the air holding out? Do you see any water?

(They look for cracks, for water seeping in.)

GAY MAN	(looking for water, to VOICE) I don't think it's as far as this car yet.
VOICE	Did they say something down there?
GAY MAN	Yes!
VOICE	(aside) I can't hear them. I broke a switch the last time I spoke to 'em. I wonder if they can hear *me*.
ALL	YES!
VOICE	Hey, down there! Why don't you knock on the side of the train if you're still alive!?

(Some move to the side of the subway car.)

WHITE
WOMAN We don't have anything to make noise with!

BLACK
WOMAN Why don't you pound your white head against the wall. It's hard enough.

WHITE
WOMAN Why don't you pound your big, black behind. They ought to be able to hear that all the way to Mars!

BLACK MAN I could knock my dick against it?

GAY MAN That should be fun.

LESBIAN Don't you dare!

GAY MAN Frontal nudity offends her, even if it'll save her life.

LESBIAN Your extensive knowledge of musical comedy is exceeded only by your expertise in pornography.

(The FOREIGNER runs over and starts banging his sausage on the floor, then taps his chest and temples with his fists, praying in some odd ritual. It should be extreme.)

WHITE MAN What is he doing?

(The FOREIGNER continues the odd praying, which should be of no recognizable religion.)

LATINO The Pope warned us about people like that.

GAY MAN So what?!

WHITE WOMAN We do not allow praying on public vehicles!

BLACK MAN He's worshipping the Devil, that's what! I read about it in the *National Inquirer!*

WHITE WOMAN He's going to bring the wrath of God down on us. Thou shalt not have strange gods before me!

HANDICAPPED
WOMAN — The opiate of the people! That's the kind of drug that should be banned.

WHITE
WOMAN — Religion made this country great, but not that one!

GAY MAN — For the Pope's sake, let's not argue religion.

VOICE — Folks? Anybody there? I think they must be dead down there.

ALL — NO!

LATINO — We're not dead! Let's bang on the wall together!

(They find whatever they can: shoes, crutches, to bang on the wall, the seats.)

VOICE — (in between the banging) Hey, I think I heard something. (They all bang very hard at this.) Yes, I think I hear something, very faintly.

Ladies and gentlemen, if you're still there listening, try not to panic. The electricians are working on the power. We're trying to get you before the air gives out. Or the water fills up the tunnel. But there is one new problem I suppose I should tell you about.

ALL New problem!

VOICE It's possible you could be electrocuted when the power comes back on. The water and the wires have somehow gotten crossed and a — and a —

GAY MAN (very whiny, tiny voice) Stop it!

NATIVE AMERICAN (quietly) Oh my God, we're all gonna drown like rats in a toilet bowl.

VOICE We're sure everything's going to be fine. In the

	meantime, we wish to play you a musical interlude.

(MUZAK comes in at once — "Some Enchanted Evening." They stagger to their seats. The MUZAK is out of tune.)

WHITE MAN	I thought things like this only happened in movies.
LESBIAN	Typical of the way men think. It's not real until it happens to them personally.
WHITE MAN	Don't jump down my throat.
LESBIAN	You going to stop me?
WHITE MAN	I don't hit women.
LESBIAN	Since when?
WHITE MAN	Don't start!
LESBIAN	You don't hit women. Just rape them!
WHITE MAN	Christ, I've never raped

anybody in my whole life!

LESBIAN (looking at her watch) There's still plenty of time left!

WHITE MAN You're not being fair.

LESBIAN Fair? Have you and your kind ever been fair to oppressed women? Have you ever 'allowed' downtrodden, underpaid women to be themselves. Huh? You always forced them to wait on you, to surrender themselves totally to your carnal pleasures and you male wants! Always!

WHITE MAN What stale garbage! You can do anything any man can do, plus all the old benefits and privileges of being a woman. And you're still belly-aching.

LESBIAN	Can I get the jobs at the top that are reserved for men? I ought to be a brain surgeon or a Giants catcher, or both, but *am* I?
WHITE MAN	Maybe it's because of you personally! Maybe it's you that's not so hot! Not women. Just you!
LESBIAN	I've had to work for men who weren't worthy to kiss my elbow! Oh, but how they tried!
LATINO	Nowadays some weak, stupid broad can take away a man's job because she happened to be born without a . . . member.
LESBIAN	Yes, that's the real meaning of your clubs — for "members" only! But I'm ecstatic that I don't have a member! You despise women! Deep down in your

	mind you think we're lower than lizards.
LATINO	I love women! I'd own two of them if I could!
LESBIAN	You think a woman's a simpering piece of meat for you to slobber over in your harem!
WHITE MAN	Don't oversimplify us, you humorless sow!
LESBIAN	It would be impossible to oversimplify you. I'm a sow to you. Well, I won't call you a pig. You'd only consider it a compliment.
WHITE MAN	You hate me more than I hate you!
LESBIAN	You aren't good enough to hate. (Echoes of "hate.") I pity you.
LATINO	You're not even a real woman! How dare you speak for all women and what they want.

LESBIAN — If it weren't for lesbians there wouldn't have been a women's movement! You can't stand it that I don't want your prick anywhere near me. You can't get around me by gripping my head in the crook of your arm and forcing me wherever you want. You can't stand the thought that some of us don't need you, don't need you for a minute for anything!

WHITE MAN — You need a man for all the heavy work, building and lifting. Deny that if you dare!

HANDICAPPED WOMAN — And you need a woman for all the puke work.

WHITE MAN — Puke work? You think it's easy to be a man? All privileges and no heartaches? Who do you think fights and dies in the wars — men, that's who! Not women!

Men! (Echoes of "men" from the men.)

HANDICAPPED WOMAN — And who starts the wars, heh? Men, that's who! Not women! (Echoes of "women" from the women.)

WHITE MAN — That's so simplistic it doesn't deserve an answer.

LESBIAN — It doesn't deserve an answer because you can't think of one, jerk!

WHITE MAN — I can think of all the woman who've forced their boys to go off and fight wars for them!

LESBIAN — (her arm around the WHITE WOMAN) You don't see this woman raping and killing!

WHITE WOMAN — Oh no, I don't rape!

LESBIAN — It's only men who do that!

(Gestures at the LATINO, who gives a big, goofy grin in reply.)

WHITE MAN	I read all the time about wives dousing their poor husbands with Mazola oil and setting them on fire. And I'm supposed to be happy that you're just as nasty as we are — as some men are!
LESBIAN	You men deserve everything you get. And that's why I brought this along! (Reaches into her clothing as if going for a weapon.)
LATINO	Oh my God, she's got a gun!
LESBIAN	No, something even more deadly than a gun!
GAY MAN	What is it? What is it?
LESBIAN	(pulling them out with a flourish) Eleven petitions for women's rights!

(Some boos, some hisses, groans, various unsympathetic reactions. The LESBIAN goes around with a pen trying to get signatures.)

LESBIAN How about you?

WHITE WOMAN Oh, my husband doesn't let me sign anything without his permission.

LESBIAN (to BLACK MAN) How about you?

BLACK MAN I can't write!

LESBIAN (to HANDICAPPED WOMAN) How about you at least?

HANDICAPPED WOMAN Not right now, okay? My leg sort of hurts.

LESBIAN And you, Latino baby? Here! Write L-a-t —

LATINO Why don't you shut your mouth, lady?

LESBIAN Why don't you make me?

LATINO (threatening to slap her) You big-mouthed wore, somebody ought to slap you down where you belong!

LESBIAN (taking off her jacket) You just try it, Mr. Macho. I've got a black belt! I'll twist your head off and bowl my way to Mexico City!

LATINO (cautious but still coming toward her) You think I'm scared of a woman? A woman?

LESBIAN Come over here, big boy! Come see what momma's got for you!

(She grabs the LATINO in a head-lock. He screams.)

BLACK WOMAN (hitting the LATINO with her purse, although he can't move) You leave her alone!

LATINO (breaking loose, moving way) You want me to

	leave her alone? Who says so?
BLACK WOMAN	(coming closer) I say so!
LATINO	And who are you, black momma?
BLACK WOMAN	Don't mess with me, Pancho. I'll cut your two-inch dick off and throw it all the way back to the Equator!
LATINO	You think I'm gonna let a couple women order me around?
HANDICAPPED WOMAN	(making a third confronting him) How about three women?
WHITE WOMAN	Make that four.
LATINO	(intimidated) I'm not afraid of you. (He backs away, beating on his

chest.) You're all lesbians with small tits!

(The women form a line with the BLACK WOMAN in front, thrusting her large breasts into his face.)

BLACK WOMAN — Look at the big, brave Latino!

LATINO — (still intimidated) You're asking for it!

(Each woman comes to the front of the line to deliver her insult.)

BLACK WOMAN — What you going to do — run us over in your spic-mobile — the kind with the little fringed balls hanging in the back window!

LESBIAN — And the loudspeaker on the outside with the Mexican Hit Parade. Sure makes me want to jump inside your car, big boy!

WHITE

WOMAN (helping encircle him) Zooming down the street in your low-rider car like some adolescent asshole who think he's a big man because he drives fast!

HANDICAPPED WOMAN With statues of the Virgin Mary stuck every damn place you can think of!

LATINO Don't you make fun of me! I'll kill you all!

LESBIAN How? Get in you car and honk us to death? See how you are! All you know how to do is screw something or kill it!

LATINO Someday I'm gonna get you, lady, and hold you down and screw you with my statue of the Virgin Mary! How you gonna like that?

LESBIAN We're not taking it anymore! We're not

taking it!

LATINO — You're not changing me! You're not cutting my balls off. You want me to be like that? (Points to the GAY MAN.)

GAY MAN — You should die to be as good as I am. I'm talented, barf hole!

LESBIAN — At least he's not hung up on his goddamn macho balls all the time!

LATINO — Because he ain't got none!

GAY MAN — (testing his testicles) Excuse me, I believe I detect something here. Yes, by god, I think there actually just may be something hanging from my body!

LATINO — (grabbing his own testicles and parading about) My balls are bigger! See that? I've

	got big balls! But a real man can't get nowhere. Not with the queers and the women ganging up on him.
GAY MAN	Goddamn, you have such predictable notions of manhood.
LATINO	I done did all right so far, Miss Nancy Face! (Shows his testicles again.)
LESBIAN	Well, it's time to trade in your testicles, kiddo. You're going to change your sexist ways if it's the last thing we do!
BLACK WOMAN	Now just a minute there. It's one thing to stop the men from stomping all over us, but I'm not one of those feminists. I want my man to take care of me and every now and then give me some good, hard lovin'!

LESBIAN — You call that rutting on your body love?

BLACK WOMAN — Sister, you do it your way, and I'll do it mine.

LESBIAN — But don't you see how men have used your poor, beautiful body — and for what? They're insensitive and clumsy brutes — (The men growl as one.) — who don't know the first thing about how a woman's clitoris responds!

GAY MAN — Draw us a diagram, why don't you!

BLACK WOMAN — All I know is some of my men sure know how to give me that tingle, and I don't get that from a woman.

LESBIAN — How do you know until you try? As long as you depend on men and their spouting, sticky

	poles, they'll overlook the true needs of your sexual openings!
BLACK WOMAN	Listen, if you don't need men, fine. You stay away from them. You let me have 'em, hear, once in a while!
LESBIAN	I'm just trying to save you from —
BLACK WOMAN	I know what it's like to be put down and beat up. I don't want that anymore, that's for sure. But I don't want to get drafted either! I don't want that kind of equality!
LESBIAN	For heaven's sake, you won't be drafted!
BLACK WOMAN	That's the way I heard it.

LESBIAN	It doesn't mean women will have to fight in the army like men.
GAY MAN	Oh? It doesn't?
LESBIAN	Not in combat situations.
GAY MAN	You'll leave getting killed for the men, hmmm? Long live equality!
LESBIAN	Step aside. The patriarchy has had its day.
GAY MAN	We men — you should pardon the expression — are not going to hand you all the cushy parts and take all the stinky, awful parts for ourselves. Come on now!
LESBIAN	When women take control, there won't be any awful parts. No more wars. Or dishpan hands!
GAY MAN	(after a long laugh) What a laugh! Dear

	Dora Dykewoman, you don't really believe for a moment, do you, that people are going to change?
LESBIAN	People have been taught how to behave. They can change.
GAY MAN	Yes, look at us here today — drawn together in our mutual plight. Utterly transformed!
LESBIAN	Nothing's ever going to change if women don't change it with their poor, bleeding hands!
LATINO	Well, I'm not changing for you, you lesbian mother!
GAY MAN	I can almost wish you success if you can change him. A thick burrito up his be-hind might do wonders for his disposition. Only don't go tromping over all of us in your high-

	heel boots when some of us aren't guilty.
LESBIAN	There isn't a man alive who isn't guilty of something!
GAY MAN	Oh yeah, look at the blood on my hands — from your poor, bleeding pussies!
LESBIAN	Pussies are not funny!
GAY MAN	Give me a list of what's not funny! You don't want equality. You want to tell me what I can say and what I can't.
LESBIAN	It's only right that you should pay for what you've had and we haven't!
GAY MAN	I have a crummy job in a deli. I haven't got any special advantages. I'm fed up to here hearing how you poor women have suffered! Don't you think I've suffered

	because I'm a queer? (Echoes of "queer.")
LESBIAN	I really could care less.
GAY MAN	You lesbians have had it easy compared to us. They don't arrest you. They couldn't run the military without you. And they don't even know it! And they don't beat you up nearly as much as they beat us up!
LESBIAN	And we don't cruise the johns in police stations either! We don't prance around, calling attention to our effeminate mannerisms. And we form long-term couples!
GAY MAN	I don't have to act like some straight, square, wholesome moron — for nobody.
LESBIAN	You're probably a drag queen lip-synching to Diana Ross records. Degrading women!

GAY MAN	The goddamn gall of you dykes in your Levi's and your men's outfits and men's haircuts telling me about drag!
LESBIAN	(softer momentarily) You're the first male I've talked to in twelve years, and that's only because I'm stuck in this awful place.
GAY MAN	(softer momentarily) Yeah, I liked it better when you were talking to yourself too.
LESBIAN	Oh, no you don't. As women with our heads held high, we'll decide when and where we go. Not you!
GAY MAN	Sweetie, you're so grouchy you must need a new tampon — maxi!
LESBIAN	If I never hear another prissy joke, another nelly put-down, another

verbal rape, it'll be too damn soon.

(The LESBIAN slugs the GAY MAN, knocking him down.)

GAY MAN — Jesus, what are you doing!

LESBIAN — Expressing myself!

(OTHERS applaud.)

GAY MAN — When a man's as rude, as one-sided, and as violent as you are, he gets locked up someplace! You get applause.

LESBIAN — You think I don't know I'm not the only person who's ever had a hard time in the history of the world? I know that. But it's my time at last and I'm not giving up until I get what I want! You understand that?

GAY MAN — But we 'perverts' have got to stick together against them.

(The GAY MAN and the LESBIAN both look back at the other passengers, then shudder.)

If we're ever going to get anything.

LESBIAN That's the only reason we'll ever stick together. There's nothing in this world I want from you!

GAY MAN And there's even less I want from you. So let's just make use of each other while we have to.

LESBIAN Yes, that's how you like it — the woman always has to compromise!

VOICE Ladies and gentlemen, I have an announcement.

(ALL listen intently.)

The power is back on. I repeat, the power is back on. We're not positive, but it looks like all your yakking down there has raised

the temperature and
triggered the generator.

(The passengers cheer.)

But there is a problem.

(The passengers groan.)

It seems we may be able
move the train through
the tunnel, but because
of the water and the
weight the cars might
slip back, killing you all
instantly.

(Louder groans.)

So what we suggest is
that you pick among
yourselves and send out
one person to test the
passageway. Once that
one person is through
the tunnel, we'll know
it's safe and we'll bring
you the train through. If
that person doesn't
make it, then we'll try
something else. So pick
someone from among
yourselves to see who'll

be the guinea — ah, the chosen representative.

GAY MAN Don't everybody speak up at once.

WHITE MAN Well, it could be like committing suicide.

GAY MAN It's a chance to be a hero.

LATINO Or a goat.

GAY MAN Why don't we all talk about it. Say why you want to go or why you don't. One final game?

WHITE MAN I don't want to go because I have an important business to look after.

(OTHERS object.)

The world needs the tool and die work I provide!

(VOICES object.)

GAY MAN Is that the best you can

say about yourself?

WHITE MAN I'm a valuable member of society, and you can't afford to lose me.

BLACK WOMAN Pooh! Who needs tool and die?

GAY MAN (to BLACK WOMAN) You want to go?

BLACK WOMAN I can't go. I've got a family to look after!

(OTHERS with families object.)

Well, I've got little babies that need me!

(VOICES say "Ahh" ironically.)

They need me to grow up to be upstanding citizens!

WHITE WOMAN Send her! She won't be missed.

BLACK WOMAN	How about you? Why don't you go?
WHITE WOMAN	I've got — I've got —
BLACK WOMAN	I know — shopping to do!
WHITE WOMAN	My husband! My children!
BLACK WOMAN	They don't need you. When was the last time you even had sex with your man? And your kids — they're on their own now. They won't miss you.
WHITE WOMAN	They will miss me. . . . Won't they? (She is distressed to see how little she'll be missed.)
GAY MAN	(to BLACK MAN) What about you?

BLACK MAN Me?

GAY MAN Yeah, you. Why shouldn't you go?

BLACK MAN I don't like tunnels!

(OTHERS object.)

Okay, okay, I don't want to go because I've got to look for a job.

GAY MAN Boo! That's not reason enough.

BLACK MAN Well then . . . let me see. I never had to do this before. I don't have to go because it took so long for me to get here, to be born and grow up and learn things. I'm just gettin' started! I can't go now! And I just joined a sports team!

(OTHERS pooh-pooh his reasons.)

LESBIAN	You can't go because you have to stuff a ball through a hoop?
BLACK MAN	You go, bitch!
LESBIAN	Me? (looking around, caught out) I can't go.
BLACK MAN	Why the hell not?
LESBIAN	Because — because I'm changing the world.
GAY MAN	How much have you changed it, really?
LESBIAN	I've changed it some. I've changed it a lot! But there's so much more to be done. It's not right for . . . for —
GAY MAN	For women to take chances?
LESBIAN	Why don't you go?
GAY MAN	Me? Who'll be master of ceremonies? . . . Who'll keep you amused?

(OTHERS object.)

	I can't go! I won't go! I'm the most important person in this car!

(Louder objections.)

	I'm going to turn this all into a musical comedy! I have to survive to do that!
LATINO	It won't sell. So you might as well go. You're just a clown!
GAY MAN	You go!
LATINO	No, I have a lot of gas left to pump yet!
HANDICAPPED WOMAN	I'll go!
GAY MAN	You will?

(OTHERS encourage her.)

HANDICAPPED WOMAN	Yes, I'll go, dragging myself every inch of the way. This afflicted,

humiliated body will save the rest of you!

(OTHERS say "Hurray!")

Though I have some pretty serious doubts about who's worth it! But I'll go! (She starts toward the door.)

NATIVE AMERICAN — She can't go! She'll get her crutches caught in the third rail and kill us all!

(The OTHERS realize this and ad lib: "That's right!" "Sit down!" "Get back, crip!" Etc.)

HANDICAPPED WOMAN — (to NATIVE AMERICAN) Then you have to go!

NATIVE AMERICAN — Go? I can't go!

HANDICAPPED WOMAN — Why not?

NATIVE AMERICAN — Because — because I'm one of God's creatures. I have a soul.

BLACK WOMAN — We all have souls!

NATIVE AMERICAN — But mine's pure. The Great Spirit doesn't want me to go. I'm too young to die!

GAY MAN — (to ASIAN) Well, pops, it looks like it's you!

ASIAN — (looking over his shoulder as if for somebody else) Me? No, sir! No baby!

NATIVE AMERICAN — You're old. Your time's up. You've had your day. You won't be missed.

ASIAN — (hurt) Won't be missed? (Looks to the others.) You won't miss me? Not even little bit?

(The OTHERS don't answer, look away.)

I see. I do not speak English well. But I am a piece of work. I am a human being. I am not only today. (Meaning the bad events of this day.) I am also inventor of wheel! Tamer of fire! Maker of microscope! Electricity! Morse code! Radio! Vaccines! Trips to moon! And I get better! I promise! I be good! I be good! I'm too young to die!

(The ASIAN sits.)

GAY MAN Well, who does that leave?

(All heads turn toward the FOREIGNER. The FOREIGNER realizes they are looking at him, shakes his head no. He gets up and backs away, shaking his head vigorously.)

GAY MAN We voted. And you won.

(OTHERS grab the FOREIGNER and push him toward the door, with various ad libs: “No one could do it better.” “This is terrific of you.” “You don’t know how much this means to us.” “How can we ever thank you?” Etc. (They arrange him in front of the door, just about to propel him down the tunnel.)

VOICE — Ladies and gentlemen, we don’t see anybody coming out, so we’ve decided to try moving the train. Please stay in your seats until the vehicle has come to a complete stop at the terminal building.

(The passengers mime the train starting up, going faster and faster, knocking them every which way; the lights blink on and off. MUSIC under to suggest movement through the tunnel. It should be loud and frightening, with all the people on the train jarred and knocked about.) (Lights up on all sprawled.)

GAY MAN — (plaintively) Are we there yet?

VOICE Ladies and gentlemen, I'm afraid the train has stalled again.

(Huge groans from the passengers.)

But you're not very far from the terminal. Just a few yards. But please stay in your seats until we give you the all-clear. Thank you.

(The FOREIGNER immediately rushes to the exit, waiting to be the first out.)

OTHERS Hey, sit down! Hey, come on, buddy! Get back in your seat! You didn't want to go before! Etc.

(The FOREIGNER stays where he is.)

WHITE MAN Get that foreigner! Let's get him!

(OTHERS yell and jump up and grab the FOREIGNER and throw him to the floor. They surround him so that he is blocked from the audience.)

VOICES — Dirty foreigner! Taking our air! Knocking me down! Eating that nasty stuff! Saying those terrible prayers! In unison: Smelly! Filthy! Creep! Crumb-bum! Animal! Monster! Etc.

(They say "Etc." too.)

WHITE WOMAN — (whispering as she did earlier in the whispering game) Foreigner!

(The word "Foreigner" goes around the circle.)

ALL — (with a final big kick) FOREIGNER!

GAY MAN — Well, at last we've found something we can agree about!

VOICE — Ladies and gentlemen, please, we're ready

now. Make you way out slowly, one by one. The rescue squad is just fifty yards from where you are. The fresh air is waiting for you all!

(They gather their belongings, then step one by one over the FOREIGNER's body, all off in the same direction through the frame doorway.)

VOICE Okay, they're coming out now! I can see them! Oh, the media are here. Just arriving now, with their cameras. (change of tone) What an ordeal for these people! What a – um – terrific bunch! Would anybody like some coffee? How about sandwiches? Hey, somebody make some sandwiches for these brave people! How about some donuts? Hey, somebody go out

for donuts for these
wonderful, marvelous
heroes!

(When all the passengers have gone, the FOREIGNER wakes up, starts to rise slowly. He gathers his belongings, especially his big sausage. He should take his time with his exit. Just as he limps through the exit door he bangs his sausage very hard on both sides of the doorframe, making it sway or ring or both.)

FOREIGNER (Growls loudly — the first time he's spoken — and limps off.)

BLACKOUT
END of PLAY

BEER AND RHUBARB PIE

[The one-act version was first produced by Theatre Rhinoceros, S.F., 1980]

"An important success." (Best of 1980)
— Robert Chesley, *San Francisco Bay Guardian*

"A sure sign of the growth of gay theatre."
— Mark Topkin, *Bay Area Reporter*

"Sensitive and often witty, *Beer and Rhubarb Pie* contains scenes charged with buried
hostilities and the heat of sexual tension."
— Dean Goodman, KEST-AM

". . . eloquent in its simplicity and contributes to a richer understanding of gay life."
— *San Francisco Sentinel*

"It was one of best readings that GPC [Gay Performances Company, NYC] ever did.
— GPC Producers, 1990

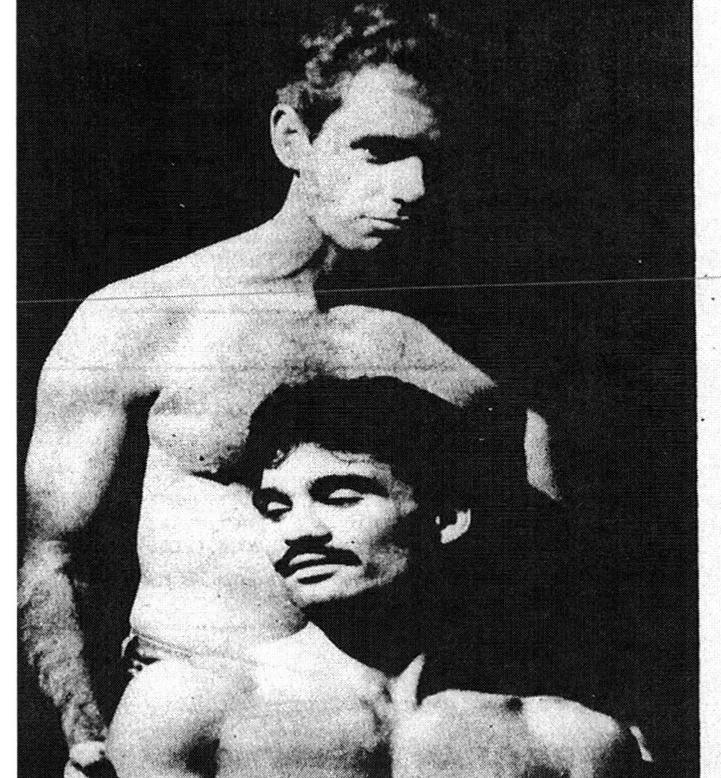

Theatre Rhinoceros Scores Again

BEER AND RHUBARB PIE.
By Daniel Curzon.

THE LINE FORMS TO THE REAR.
By Cal Yeomans.
At the Theatre Rhinoceros.

Les Attitude

Two very good and very simple gay one-act plays are appearing at the Theatre Rhinoceros, located in the Goodman Building on Geary Street. These two little dramas make minimal use of production and staging, but each is eloquent in its simplicity and contributes to a richer understanding of gay life.

In *The Line Forms to the Rear,* actor Blaine Souza presents a touching and a well-modulated performance as an ex-drag queen quietly living with his mother in a mobile home in Florida. In an extended soliloquy, this single character narrates his aspirations to show business, a resultant nervous breakdown and his current, complacent life crocheting, shopping at the K Mart where it's air-conditioned, and performing "mercy sex" with any and all takers at the local glory hole. The script, by Cal Yeomans, is distinctly minimalist, but is solid and full of small observations. This story of a downtrodden gay man is a cautionary tale: don't let this happen to you.

Beer and Rhubarb Pie, the second play of the program, by the *Sentinel*'s own Daniel Curzon, is somewhat more elaborately staged. This is the story of a gay man and the macho Cuban carpenter who's doing repair work in the kitchen. The carpenter is supposedly straight. "I don't bend over," he says defensively. "I suppose you leave that to your wife, too," the gay man replies.

Richard Staven is adept as the gay man who can't help but pick up on the sexual curiosity of his uptight friend. Thomas Mark steals the show as the hot carpenter, turning in a very funny portrayal. Although the brief exchanges of "sex talk" at the finale are just short of being embarrassing, the play's point is made effectively and economically—it doesn't hurt to loosen up.

Beer and Rhubarb Pie and *The Line Forms to the Rear* continue in weekend matinee performances through November 30.

Richard Staven and Thomas Mark in Daniel Curzon's *Beer and Rhubarb Pie.*

BEER AND RHUBARB PIE

CHARACTERS:

LEN, a gay man in his thirties, attractive, dressed in Levi's and tee-shirt

FERNANDO, a masculine, muscular Cuban in his forties, with a Spanish accent, dressed in workman's t-shirt and soiled work pants.

ROSA, Fernando's wife, in her thirties or forties, full-bodied, pretty, Spanish accent, talkative.

BOB, Len's roommate and ex-lover, in his thirties, a little overweight, not effeminate, just playful.

SETTING: 1) The kitchen of Fernando and Rosa's San Francisco apartment.

2) The kitchen and an alcove of Len and Bob's flat, with an attached alcove containing a daybed.

3) Rosa's office. The kitchen of Len and Bob's flat.

TIME: Not long ago.

ACT I
Scene One

(Fernando is sitting at the table drinking a glass of milk. Rosa is offstage.)

ROSA (Offstage) So do you think we should do it or no?

FERNANDO (No answer, takes a sip of milk.)

ROSA (Offstage) I read this article in *Reader's Digest* which said it's no good idea to have

	another kid if you're just doing it to help save the marriage.
FERNANDO	(No reply, takes another sip of milk.)
ROSA	(Offstage) What do you think, Fernando?
FERNANDO	(No answer)
ROSA	(Offstage) Fernando, are you still there?
FERNANDO	Yeah.
ROSA	(Offstage) Can you hear me? What do you think? Should we have another kid or no?
FERNANDO	Let me think about it.
ROSA	(Offstage) Well, tell me what you think about it now.
FERNANDO	I don't know what I think about it now.

ROSA	(Offstage) You must to have some ideas.
FERNANDO	(No answer, takes a sip of milk.)
ROSA	(Offstage) Fernando?
FERNANDO	(No answer, he sniffs the milk to see if it's sour, isn't sure)
ROSA	(Offstage) Are you still there? Huh?
FERNANDO	(No answer)
ROSA	I read that not talkin' is a form of violence!
FERNANDO	(No answer.)
ROSA	(Offstage) Fernando? (Entering, half dressed, still putting on clothes) Oh, you are there! You dead or something?
FERNANDO	No.

ROSA	Why do I gotta always drag everything out from you? Why don't you talk to me?
FERNANDO	I talk to you.
ROSA	No, you grunt. I talk to you, but you won't talk to me. What is it? I read this article about men who won't talk to their wives. They're not healthy. Do you know that?
FERNANDO	(Doesn't answer.)
ROSA	That article was so true I couldn't believe it. In *Cosmo* magazine. It was you they was talking about. The husband who won't open up. Keeps everything locked up inside. You never know what he's thinking.
FERNANDO	(Changing the subject)

You workin' today, Rosa?

ROSA — Of course I'm workin' today. What do you think I'm getting ready for? (She puts on more clothes) Mrs. Mattingly said if I was late again she'd dock me. Boy, I hate her guts. So what do you think — should we have another kid or what?

FERNANDO — (Doesn't answer, sips milk.)

ROSA — *Querido*, don't leave your glass in the sink like you did last time. Gets all sour and smells bad, okay? And why don't you put that skylight in here like you said you would? We'd get more ventilation and stuff wouldn't smell so terrible. You got work today?

FERNANDO Got a job over in the Castro later. Some guy's broken steps.

ROSA Is it that guy I work with? His *friend*?

FERNANDO I guess.

ROSA We could afford another kid, now that Alfredo and Ignacio are almost grown up. They could even take care of it. We can afford it. Maybe we could have a little girl this time. I'd like that. Wouldn't you? (Smiles) . . . Rosanna.

FERNANDO (Shrugs)

ROSA What kind a answer is that?

FERNANDO (Shrugs again) Is there any beer in the house?

ROSA You want beer now?

FERNANDO Yeah.

ROSA	You want beer in the morning?
FERNANDO	Yeah.
ROSA	You want beer?
FERNANDO	That's what I said.
ROSA	There ain't any.
FERNANDO	In the house?
ROSA	Yeah.
FERNANDO	Give me some money.
ROSA	For beer?
FERNANDO	Give me some.
ROSA	No.
FERNANDO	I want some beer.
ROSA	No.
FERNANDO	Okay, I don't want any beer.

ROSA I thought you wanted it.

FERNANDO Doesn't matter.

ROSA (Getting her purse) Here's some money.

FERNANDO I don't want it. Forget it.

ROSA I don't get you. I never know what you're thinkin'. You've got to learn to communicate, Fernando. I communicate. Do you see me communicating right now? You oughta try it. It'd be good for you. Be good for our marriage. What do you say to that?

FERNANDO You're gonna be late for work.

ROSA This is more important. I read this article that said people should always make time for

	interpersonal relationships.
FERNANDO	For what?
ROSA	That's what we got — an interpersonal relationship.
FERNANDO	(Skeptical) Oh?
ROSA	You feelin' upset about somethin'? The fact that you're not workin' that much? I read where men don't like it if their wives make more than them or got nicer jobs. Are you mad at me because I got promoted and you got laid off?
FERNANDO	(Gives her a "what do you take me for" look)
ROSA	You sure? You resent me 'cause I've changed during the time we been together? I'm not the quiet, little Rosa you

	married. Does that make you angry?
FERNANDO	(Doesn't answer)
ROSA	You can tell me. Maybe you're holding it in, all this anger. It's no good for you and it's no good for our relationship that you got all this negative inside of you. You've got to let it out, Fernando. Like a big cloud over your head, like in the cartoons, okay?
FERNANDO	I'd better get ready for that job. (Gets up.)
ROSA	Are you gonna leave your glass there?
FERNANDO	You said no to leave it in the sink.
ROSA	I didn't say leave it there neither.
FERNANDO	(Too patient) Where do

	you want me to leave it, Rosa?
ROSA	You could wash it.
FERNANDO	It's all right where it is.
ROSA	No, it isn't.
FERNANDO	Why isn't it?
ROSA	It's dirty, that's why.
FERNANDO	So what?
ROSA	It attracts cockroaches! You want cockroaches?
FERNANDO	Cockroaches need milk sometimes. The little baby ones. They get tired of garbage.
ROSA	(Quietly angry) Leave it. I don't care. I don't want to be a nag. You're making me a nag.
FERNANDO	You got free will, Rosa.

ROSA I got to get ready.
(Exits)

(Fernando watches her leave, stares at the glass, picks it up, starts to put the glass in the sink)

ROSA (Her voice stopping him) Is that glass still on the table?

FERNANDO (Changes his mind because of her and puts the glass back on the table, gets his tool box)

ROSA (Coming back, more dressed, putting on an earring) Are you hungry?

FERNANDO No.

ROSA You sure? You didn't eat.

FERNANDO I'm fine.

(Rosa takes the glass from the table and puts it in the sink, moves away)

FERNANDO I thought you said no to leave it there.

ROSA I don't got time to wash it now. You wash it later?

FERNANDO No.

ROSA Then leave it. I give up!

FERNANDO (Under his breath) I wish you would.

ROSA What?

FERNANDO Nothing.

ROSA You're not communicating again. If you got somethin' to say, speak up. I speak up.

FERNANDO (Looking in his tool box) Have you seen my awl?

ROSA Your what?

FERNANDO My awl. A-w-l. It's

pointed and it's —

ROSA — I haven't seen it. Have you seen my other earring?

FERNANDO — No.

ROSA — Well, I can't go with just one. Screw it! (Removes the one earring and throws it on the floor)

FERNANDO — (Turns his head very slowly and looks at the earring.)

ROSA — I'm leaving . . . Do I look pretty?

FERNANDO — (No reply)

ROSA — I left that article on communication in the bathroom. You should read it. Really.

FERNANDO — (No reply, doesn't look at her.)

ROSA — See you later, honey? . . . You look nice.

FERNANDO — Sure.

ROSA — Maybe we could eat out tonight or somethin'. Take the kids. My treat. What do you say? McDonald's isn't so bad. . . . We could have fishwiches. They're . . .

FERNANDO — . . . Sure.

ROSA — I didn't mean to be hard on you just now. You know I love you. I'm trying. I am trying.

FERNANDO — (Not looking at her) Yes.

ROSA — So . . . well, I'd better be going or I'll get docked.

FERNANDO — Yes.

ROSA — (Trying for humor) Do

you love me, *guapo*?

FERNANDO (Not looking at her)
Yes.

(Rosa waits a moment, unsatisfied, but she must go.)

ROSA It's hard. I mean, it's. . .

(She gives up, shrugs and leaves)

FERNANDO (Knowing she's out of earshot) You know what, Rosa? I don't think we oughta have another kid. What do you think?

(He takes the glass, looks at it, then throws it into the trash, stares at it as the lights fade.)

Scene Two

(Dinner time, the same day. Rosa enters with a bag. Fernando is at the table with his head down, asleep)

ROSA (Sees that he's asleep,

	tiptoes around, putting some groceries away)
FERNANDO	(Hearing her, waking, rubbing his eyes) Oh, hi.
ROSA	Sorry. Didn't mean to wake you.
FERNANDO	That's okay.
ROSA	Was that job hard today?
FERNANDO	I didn't go.
ROSA	Didn't go. Why not?
FERNANDO	The guy called me and said today wasn't a good day for him.
ROSA	I didn't see Bob at work. I guess that's why. So you sat around here all day?
FERNANDO	Yeah.

ROSA Sleeping?

FERNANDO Yeah, some of the time.

ROSA Mrs. Mattingly docked me half an hour pay.

FERNANDO That's a shame.

ROSA (After thinking about his remark) Is that supposed to be funny?

FERNANDO What?

ROSA What you just said.

FERNANDO What did I say?

ROSA Never mind.

FERNANDO You don't like what I say? I'm trying to communicate. Isn't that what you want?

ROSA Is that what it is? I had a hard day today.

FERNANDO I'm sorry.

ROSA	I don't get to lay around sleeping all day. And now I got to cook somethin' for you and the kids.
FERNANDO	No, you don't.
ROSA	Sure I do.
FERNANDO	No, you don't. I ate already. The kids can fix their own.
ROSA	They'll eat something cold.
FERNANDO	You don't need to cook anything, Rosa. You worked hard today.
ROSA	I did work hard.
FERNANDO	I know you did. I believe you. Cold isn't so bad.
ROSA	I just feel guilty when I . . .

FERNANDO	Stop feeling guilty. There's no need to feel so guilty.
ROSA	I'm trying to be a modern woman, all right? I'm not going back to the old days!
FERNANDO	You're succeeding, Rosa. You're succeeding!
ROSA	You don't like it.
FERNANDO	Rosa, believe me, it doesn't bother me. It bothers you!
ROSA	(Says nothing, sits down.)
FERNANDO	(After a moment) That guy said to come the day after tomorrow, about the steps.
ROSA	Did he really?
FERNANDO	His name is Len.

ROSA Good.

FERNANDO And he'll pay me in cash, under the table. Okay? And we'll live happily ever after.

ROSA Don't get upset.

FERNANDO I'm not upset!

ROSA You are too upset.

FERNANDO I'm not upset.

ROSA Why won't you admit it when you're upset? What is wrong with you? I think you should see a doctor — a vet.

FERNANDO (Laughs.)

ROSA That's better. You're too tense.

FERNANDO I'm not tense. Look. (Shows her an exaggerated relaxed posture) See?

ROSA	That's not how you relax.
FERNANDO	You got all the answers on how to relax?
ROSA	I didn't say that.
FERNANDO	Let's not fight, okay.
ROSA	Are we fighting? I thought we were talking. I thought we were beginning to talk, like real people. Are you bored, is that the trouble? Are you bored with our marriage?
FERNANDO	No.
ROSA	If you're bored, say so.
FERNANDO	I'm not bored.
ROSA	I think you are. Why won't you say so?
FERNANDO	I'm not bored!

ROSA	Well, I am! There, I've said it. I'm bored, Fernando. I'm bored. Why are you making me act like this? I never used to be so grouchy all the time. I no trying to be like this. Just can't help it. I don't like myself right now.
FERNANDO	(Starts to say something, holds back.)
ROSA	What was you gonna say?
FERNANDO	Nothing.
ROSA	I could see it. Why did you stop?
FERNANDO	You don't want to hear.
ROSA	I do! That's what I've been sayin'. What is it?
FERNANDO	Rosa . . .
ROSA	I'm listenin'.

FERNANDO	Do you think we got a good marriage?
ROSA	Sure. Basically. Don't you?
FERNANDO	Sure. Of course.
ROSA	That's not the question.
FERNANDO	It isn't?
ROSA	We'll talk it out, and then everything will be all right again. What is it?
FERNANDO	I don't know. I feel uneasy. I feel . . .
ROSA	A mid-life crisis, that's what it is.
FERNANDO	(After a look at her for her glibness) I'm not middle-aged yet.
ROSA	Sure you are. We married young and our kids are almost men, and so you're having

	your mid-life crisis early, but that's what it is.
FERNANDO	(Dryly) You should work as a therapist, Rosa.
ROSA	I've thought of that. But I suppose it's too late to change jobs now. I always thought I'd like to do that. Funny you should notice.
FERNANDO	(Dryly) Telling people what's wrong with them. I can see you sittin' behind a desk, Rosa, sharpenin' your pencil, fillin' in the forms.
ROSA	(Pleased) Can you?
FERNANDO	(Mocking her but so that she doesn't notice) Wearin' your earrings and markin' down those mid-life crisises.

ROSA	I'd be good. . . .You makin' fun of me?
FERNANDO	Would you notice if I was?
ROSA	What's that supposed to mean?
FERNANDO	Nothin'.
ROSA	I try not to make fun of you. . . . This time I'm not taking that for no answer. Say what's on your mind, for God's sake!
FERNANDO	You want me to say what's on my mind? I might tell you.
ROSA	Good! It's about time.
FERNANDO	You sure you want to hear?
ROSA	I want to hear! We've gotta clear the air here.
FERNANDO	Okay, for starters,

never mind the beer. Take that glass of milk this morning.

ROSA — What about it?

FERNANDO — You just had to have your way about that, didn't you?

ROSA — You had to have your way!

FERNANDO — It couldn't just sit in the sink for a while. It had to be washed, right then. No! I didn't feel like washing it, and so I don't got to wash it. I been feeling depressed and I don't feel like washin' no goddamn glass at that time.

ROSA — Keeping busy is good for you when you're feeling depressed.

FERNANDO — You read it somewhere. Don't tell me, I can

guess. But it's not just the glass. It's more'n that. You want to have another baby? I'm not workin' and there's a population explosion and you want to have another baby. But even if that wasn't true, you know why you want to have a baby? Because you don't know how to fill up your life otherwise. You complain about workin' so hard and workin' so much, but the truth is time hangs heavy and you don't got enough to make your life make any sense. You want a baby 'cause it's some kind of toy that'll keep you so busy you won't have time to think about how stupid and worthless your whole life is.

ROSA That's not —

FERNANDO Let me say what I have to say. You want me to communicate. I'm communicatin', Rosa. You know what really bugs me about you, honey. It's not 'cause you talk up more than you used to — all your women's stuff and your articles. You always talked up, actually. That is not it. It's what you say, Rosa, that's what bugs me. All this goddamn crap about not holdin' things back from each other. "What are you thinkin', Fernando?" "Tell me, Fernando." "I'm thinkin' this at this very moment, Fernando. Isn't that deep of me, Fernando?" "I'm expressing my anger, Fernando." "There's a little feeling over here in the back of my brain,

a little smudge I ain't
shared with you.
See it, Fernando?"
(Holds out his finger as
though it's got dirt on
it) "Show me your
smudge, Fernando.
Let's talk it out. Let's
analyze it. Hey, there's
a thought you had
you didn't tell me
about. That's bad,
Fernando. You can't
have secrets from me.
A husband and wife
shouldn't have no
secrets from each other,
Fernando."

ROSA — They shouldn't!

FERNANDO — They should! There are lots of things — lots of them — that people shouldn't tell each other or they can't go on.

ROSA — You get them out and then you deal with them. You work out the problems and you have a — a breakthrough.

FERNANDO — You have shit on your finger and then all you can do with it is sniff it!

ROSA Don't be vulgar.

FERNANDO Just speakin' my mind, Rosa. Maybe my mind is vulgar.

ROSA (Getting up) The kids'll be home from practice soon. I'd better get —

FERNANDO I'm not finished yet. Don't you want me to finish?

(Rosa sits back down)

FERNANDO You know what else? Our marriage. Our whole marriage. It sucks.

ROSA I'm trying to save it. We've grown apart, but I —

FERNANDO But why, Rosa? Why save it? Because we have such a strong, rich sex life? Huh? Because we have so many things in common? What things? Because you're afraid your mother will think you're a bad woman if you get a divorce? Because the Church won't let you get one? Because you have two kids who ain't out of high school yet and couldn't survive on their own for five minutes? Because you're afraid to go to McDonald's for fishwiches by yourself, afraid to sit in the booth alone? Because, never mind all your articles and your new self, deep down inside — *er es torpe*! It would tear you apart to be without a man, any man, even me. That's what holds this marriage together, woman. Bane — Bane — what's the word I want? Ba —

ROSA Banality.

FERNANDO Right! That's it. That's me! That's you!

ROSA . . . Why are you trying to shit on me?

FERNANDO I'm not trying to shit on you, honey, *guerida*. I thought you wanted to know what I'm thinking. Our problem isn't that we've grown apart. We've grown together! We've said everything forty-seven thousand times. Our problem isn't that we haven't had time for a little vacation getaway — just the two of us, like in the ads and the articles. Our problem is

not we don't commu-
nicate. Our problem is
we've reached the day
when — if you tell
about how awful Mrs.
Mattingly is one more
time, I'm gonna puke.
And if I tell you one
more time about all the
good jobs I'm gonna
have, you oughta puke.
The only trouble with
us, Rosa, is that we
been together for too
long. Not too distant,
too close. And we don't
like what we see up
close. People like us
wind up starin' at each
other across the table —
nothin' to say, and to
make us feel alive we
start pickin' at each
other, pickin' and
pickin' at each other
until we pick each other
to death. Commun-
ication is what's killed
us, Rosa. Most guys
won't admit it, but you

wanted me to speak my mind? Well, this is it! I think we got no chance in hell 'cause I don't want to spend no more days with you for the rest of my life, and as soon as I can manage it with the money, I'm gonna leave you. There's nothin' left, but we cling to each other 'cause we're too god-damn chicken to call it off. But loneliness is better than what we got. There's just one thing wrong with our marriage, honey. It's exhausted. Exhausted. Exhausted! And, please God, let's have the guts to say so!

ROSA (After a pause) Is that really how you feel?

FERNANDO No, I'm pretendin', Rosa. I'm pretendin.'

ROSA	I didn't think things were that bad.
FERNANDO	(Lying) . . .They aren't.
ROSA	They're not?
FERNANDO	I was just blowing off steam. Don't mind me.
ROSA	Don't mind you? Where do we go from here? To pray to St. Jude? For hopeless causes?
FERNANDO	(Doesn't say anything.)
ROSA	Are we finished?
FERNANDO	What do you think?
ROSA	I'm not sure. You said some very mean things.
FERNANDO	You know, it's funny, I feel better.
ROSA	Really? I feel awful.
FERNANDO	I guess I oughta thank you.

ROSA You're not welcome.

FERNANDO Thanks anyway.

ROSA Where do you get off with all them —

FERNANDO You didn't say if I spoke up it had to be nice.

ROSA But I didn't —

FERNANDO Don't ask for what you don't want, honey.

ROSA (To be funny) Yeah, but just 'cause I asked you to wash a glass . . .

FERNANDO If you can't stand the heat, Rosa, get out of the kitchen.

ROSA So where does this leave us? . . . Is our marriage over?

FERNANDO (Doesn't answer.)

ROSA Well?

FERNANDO (Doesn't answer.)

ROSA Fernando?!

FERNANDO (Doesn't answer.)

(Lights fade)

ACT II
Scene One

SETTING: (Dinner time the same day, Len and Bob's apartment. The set change should be quick, probably with the second kitchen on the reverse side of Act I's set. No intermission here)

(Humming or singing a current tune, Bob is putting the finishing touches on the meal he has prepared, placing the silverware, napkins, pouring the wine, etc. He sets down the plates of food, looking proudly at his handiwork. Bob sits down to eat, waits for Len offstage. Puts his napkin on his lap. Waits.)

BOB Where the fuck are you?

LEN (Offstage) On the phone!

BOB Slop's ready!

LEN (Offstage) Go ahead. Start without me.

BOB (Disgusted) I will not start without you. This is a first-class international gourmet meal — beef wellington, carrots delmonico, and potatoes florentine, with rhubarb pie for dessert. Get your ass in here and eat it.

LEN (Offstage) I don't eat with my ass.

BOB I work my fingers to the bone and what do I get — elegant conversation from my roommate: "I don't eat with my ass." (Sniffs his wine, swallows, then gargles with it. Gets up and goes closer to Len's side of the stage, gargles.)

LEN (Offstage) What's that?

BOB (His mouth full) Chef Robert is tasting the wine.

LEN (Offstage) What?

BOB (Swallows the wine) Chef Robert is tasting the wine.

LEN (Offstage on telephone) I'll talk to you later, Sally. I've got to go . . . Yeah . . . Bye. (Hangs up)

BOB Why do you always start a phone call just about the time I finish one of my wonderful meals? Is it a comment of some kind?

LEN (Entering) Yes.

BOB (Annoyed) What do you mean yes?

LEN Yes as in yes.

BOB My meals are — the Pope has declared my meals so exquisite they're on the Index of Forbidden Foods.

LEN They're too fattening.

BOB Life is short.

LEN (Pointing to Bob) But fat is long.

BOB I am not fat.

LEN Let's not get into it. You look very nice tonight.

BOB I am not fat.

LEN You were thinner when we were lovers.

BOB Was I? Didn't keep us lovers, did it? Skinny as a speed freak and it wasn't enough to keep you happy.

LEN Are we going to rehash that again?

BOB I am not fat.

LEN All right, you are not fat.

BOB Eat!

LEN I'm not very hungry.

BOB You just want to be skinny, so you starve yourself. I can hear your stomach rumbling from over here.

LEN You're projecting.

BOB Wrong psychological term.

LEN Eat if you must.

BOB I do not eat any more than I ever did, and you know that. I'm older now. It stays with me now, that's all.

LEN Eat less.

BOB I will not eat less! It's not fair. And I will maintain that until the day I die.

LEN (No reply.)

BOB I am perfectly normal-looking. It's society that's fucked up.

LEN Why won't you accept the fact that you are overweight and do something about it?

BOB In any other period of history, in any sane culture, I would be considered a dish.

LEN I still think you're a dish. Very tempting and tasty.

BOB You do?

LEN Sure.

BOB Hah!

LEN I don't know what you think, but I didn't stop . . .because of your weight. Sometimes I even wonder if we couldn't — (Stops, embarrassed, gets up to get something) Excuse me.

BOB Did I forget something?

LEN I'll get it. (Gets it, sits back down.)

BOB You shouldn't have been so reluctant to . . . when we were still lovers.

LEN You shouldn't have been so sensitive.

BOB Len, I could live with getting rejected in the bars by strangers, but — funny old me! — I didn't like being rejected by my 'lover.'

LEN It was only a few times —

BOB Not being one to force anyone to pay his Biblical debt, I refrained from rape — but let's not dwell on ancient history. Let's dwell on now —

LEN If we —

BOB — I live in a very severe little kingdom called Anorexia. Terrible place, boys and girls. You should see their movie stars! By comparison, they make concentration camp inmates look like fatsos. In Anorexia who do they want to fuck most? Why, shriveled-up, emaciated bird-people, that's who. We're a nation of aviary necrophiliacs!

LEN Bob —

BOB Thou shall not eat sugar. Thou shalt not pinch an inch. Thou shalt look like a stick and be called vile if thou veerest from the Law of Skinny, a law made by a life-denying, arbitrary, unrealistic, unfair — did I say that already? — bone-humping sicko society, and I'm not going to take it any longer.

LEN (No answer.)

BOB Have I made my point?

LEN Yes. Let's eat.

BOB (Pushing food away) I don't want it.

LEN Bob.

BOB Who cuts your hair — Sweeney Todd?

LEN Bob!

BOB I'm not eating ever again.

LEN (Takes a bite.) It's quite . . . quite . . . ah . . . (Purses mouth, tasting.)

BOB Did you ever see a cat lick another cat's ass and then purse its mouth like this (Purses mouth) as if to say, "What is that I'm tasting?" That's how you look right now.

LEN Why are you being so nasty tonight?

BOB Because I'm fat.

LEN You're not fat.

BOB I'm fat. Society is wrong, but I give up. I'm a fat pig.

LEN You are not a fat pig.

BOB Now you're going to tell me to join a gym.

LEN No, I'm not. I like you the way you are. But it wouldn't hurt you if you worked on your muscle tone a —

BOB Aha! See!

LEN I won't say another word.

BOB You'll just make sly comments about how full my plate is. Watch my mouth chewing and grinding every "self-indulgent" bite, but of course not saying a word.

LEN (Putting his fork down) Okay, what's wrong, Bob?

BOB Go ahead, eat. I'll just chomp on this breadstick. (Grabs a breadstick and bites off a piece angrily.)

LEN You've been on edge lately.

BOB (Faking melodrama) And you don't even know why!

LEN Why?

BOB I'm not going to say.

LEN Why?

BOB It's our anniversary and you forgot.

LEN Our anniversary?

BOB Yes, a year ago today we stopped being lovers and became that much more important thing to each other — roommates.

LEN God, you're right. It has been a year.

BOB And you didn't even bring flowers — or candy.

LEN I'm a heartless boor.

BOB You are. That's why I can't eat.

LEN (Cautiously) Maybe we made a mistake.

BOB About what?

LEN A year ago.

BOB Breaking up? Hardly. We've never gotten along so well.

LEN (Looking down, not wanting to be too explicit) I just wonder sometimes, that's all.

BOB I wonder sometimes too.

LEN You do?

BOB (Cleaning away the plates) But we made our separate beds. Now we must lie in them.

LEN (Holding on to his plate) I'm not finished yet.

BOB Yes, you are! (Grabs Len's plate, takes it away.) We're on a diet.

LEN What about that pie?

BOB No pie! (Gets the rhubarb pie, displays it, then puts it away.) Who wants to eat rhubarf anyway!

LEN Rhubarf? You're so bad. So excessive.

BOB And you love me for it, Martha! It's your turn to do the dishes. (Leaves them right where they are.)

LEN You're a slob.

BOB No, I care not for the things of this world. (He goes into the alcove and throws himself on the daybed, face down.)

LEN (Cleaning up) What's wrong?

BOB Nothing.

LEN Sure?

BOB I'm frustrated.

LEN At work?

BOB Yeah, there too. I put a credit where a debit should've been. Mostly just plain old sexually frustrated.

LEN I thought you were seeing that German guy behind us. The once-a-week backrub mit orgasm.

BOB Doesn't do it.

LEN (Cleaning up). . .I'm frustrated myself.

BOB Yeah? I thought you were out tricking with all the other skinnies.

LEN I go out, I cruise, I don't talk to anybody, I come home alone.

BOB Sounds hot.

LEN (Coming closer to the daybed) Remember the first time we had sex on this daybed?

BOB (Sitting up, not wanting to have sex with Len) Not really.

LEN We did.(Patting the daybed) Right here.

BOB I didn't know you were sentimental about beds.

LEN Just pointing out a fact.

BOB Odd, I remember this daybed as the place where you first removed my hand from your thigh when I touched it. Or was it the fifth or sixth time you removed it?

LEN I was going through a bad time then.

BOB For six months?

LEN I still loved you.

BOB He still loved me! If there's no sex, you're not lovers.

LEN How mechanical.

BOB Not mechanical. Why put up with all the crap you have to if there's no love-making to go with it? When you gotta spew, you gotta spew.

LEN Sorry I was so unforthcoming.

BOB You hurt my sense of myself, Len, and you don't seem to realize it. Really.

LEN I didn't — I didn't — (Starts to deny this, changes his mind.) I'm sorry.

BOB You want to have sex sometime? . . . Now?

LEN Do you?

BOB I asked you first.

LEN It's crossed my mind, yes.

BOB You mean really start up again, as . . .?

LEN (Shrugs lightly as though that's a real possibility.) Maybe.

BOB (Gets up from the daybed.) Well, I don't want to.

LEN You don't want to? (Covering up) Well, I don't want to either.

BOB Good. Now that I'm starving myself I'm too weak to have sex anyway.(Falls on the daybed, starving.)

LEN You're a bastard, do you know that?

BOB (Lightly) No, I don't.

LEN Why did you lead me on just now?

BOB I didn't lead you on.

LEN Yes, you did.

BOB A skinny thing like you wanting to make it with a tub like me? Impossible!

LEN You did it to get back at me.

BOB That's me. Vindictive Bob. Waits for a whole year for his former lover to stick out his throbbing man tool — just so he can whack it off in one fell swoop. Or is it one swell foop? I seem to recall you had one swell foop.

LEN I'm sorry I brought it up.

BOB (With an innuendo) You're frustrated, you brought it up. I understand. I'm a man. When you gotta spew, you gotta spew.

LEN We had some good years, didn't we?

BOB Did we? Remind me.

LEN That time we went to New York and saw a puppet show outdoors on the sidewalk.

BOB Oh, yes, those little bug-eyed puppets. . . . I don't remember them.

LEN And the time your father called me and asked if I was seducing his son.

BOB And I got on the line and told him he was a Cro-Magnon Piltdown Neanderthal and to stop harassing us!

LEN Right! . . . Don't you remember any good times?

BOB Let me see, George. Or am I George? The time we took our son to the orphanage and left his there. That was fun.

LEN Son?

BOB The little bugger. You know.

LEN Little bugger?

BOB The one we never mention in public.

LEN I don't know what you're talking about.

BOB Our son! Our son! All gay couples have imaginary sons. Driven crazy with their inability to reproduce — it's well known. But we got rid of our little bugger and our marriage has been perfect ever since. We don't drink much, but we eat to excess. We make jokes. We are perfection itself.

LEN We're not that bad.

BOB (Singing) "Is that all there is?"

. . .Want some pie? (Going to it, taking it out of hiding.)

LEN I am still hungry.

BOB Yeah! Talk dirty to me! Describe each pornographic bite. What are you doing now? Lifting the sugar-saturated filling to your lips? Snuffling through the rhubarb bits with your tongue?

LEN I'm going to have some. (Gets the pie.) But just a sliver. (Cuts a tiny piece.)

BOB It's terrible when you get a sliver in your throat. Have you ever had that? You get it from going down on Pinocchio.

LEN Sure you won't have some? It's hot and sticky? (Holds out the sliver sexily.)

BOB No, no, no, you can't tempt me.

LEN Sure?

BOB And you shouldn't have any either. Give me that. (Tries to take the sliver of pie away from Len.)

LEN No way.

BOB I'm just doing it for your own good. (Tries to get the pie.)

LEN (Running away with the pie) Keep your hands off! *Nein, nein, nein*!

BOB Come on, Len. Hand it over.

LEN Stay away! (Runs around the table.) Stay away!

BOB (Suddenly stopping) What's wrong with this picture? Aren't you supposed to be chasing me?

LEN Okay, if you like. (They switch roles and Len now chases Bob.) Come here, you!

BOB (Running around the table) Oh, no! Oh, please no! Not pie!

LEN Yes, pie! (He grabs Bob from behind and starts to force the piece into Bob's mouth too Hard.) Take that, you anorexic! Eat! Eat!

BOB (Pulling away, angry) I said I didn't want it! (He knocks the piece to the floor.)

LEN (The playfulness over, looking at the pie on the floor) Sorry. When you gotta spew, you gotta spew.

BOB . . . My place or yours?

LEN Where is this going, Bob?

BOB Can't tell yet.

LEN Come over here.

BOB (Turns away, not answering.)

LEN Come over here.

BOB (Quietly) I don't want to.

LEN (Hesitates, then comes over to Bob, hugs him from behind.) How's that?

BOB (Stiff, resistant) Is somebody there?

LEN (Kisses the back of Bob's neck.) Guess who?

BOB Wouldn't know. (Moves away.) I didn't feel a thing.

LEN (Feeling rejected) Tonight must not be the night.

BOB And no night's going to be.

LEN I really hurt you, didn't I?

BOB I'm all scars.

LEN How can I make it up to you?

BOB Don't think you can.

LEN That's what I get for trying to break a taboo.

BOB (No reply.)

LEN The lovers-to-roommates-to-lovers-again taboo. Tougher than incest.

BOB Aren't men the masters of their fate?

LEN One time this guy and I met. Remember Paul?

BOB No.

LEN Anyway, I knew he and were both very attracted to each other, but we didn't act on it. We became friends, and of course you know you can't have sex with your friends. What would people think. But then one time, this guy and I went rafting together, about four years after we'd first met. We'd spent a real happy day together, and that night I reached out from my sleeping bag to his . . . and touched his stomach . . . and waited.

BOB And?

LEN He picked up my hand very gently . . . and moved it away. And then he went to sleep, and eventually I went to sleep, and we never said a word about it, and after that he never spoke to me again . . . (About Bob's recent rejection of him) I guess I never learn, do I?

BOB You made that up.

LEN No, I didn't.

BOB I'm going to bed.

LEN So early?

BOB Got a big day tomorrow.

LEN I suppose you need your rest then.

BOB Yeah, I'm pretty bushed. Goodnight.

LEN Good night. I'll watch some TV or something. Maybe I'll go out.

BOB I didn't mean to . . . to get back at you. I wasn't —

LEN Sure, I understand. Goodnight.

BOB Good night. . . (He leaves, feeling bad about what he's done.)

(Len looks after Bob for a moment, then goes to the sliver of pie on the floor, looks at it, sadly takes a taste with one finger, smiles, takes a second taste more slowly, remains with his finger in his mouth but not sucking it.)

(Lights fade)

Scene Two

(Three A.M. that morning. Len is sitting in the near-dark at the kitchen table. Bob enters in his robe.)

BOB You still up?

LEN Yeah.

BOB (In order to have something to say) Did you call that repair-man yet for the steps? Fer-nando, I think his name is.

Rosa-from-work's husband?
He needs the job.

LEN He's coming. (Not sure of the time) Today? Tomorrow?

BOB How much is he going to charge?

LEN I don't know yet. Shouldn't be too much.

BOB Are you mad at me?

LEN Mad?

BOB Because of . . .

LEN Don't worry about it.

BOB I don't want us to stop being roommates.

LEN Oh, I know. The mortgage is so good.

BOB Not what I meant.

LEN People shouldn't be ashamed of economic realities. It's the basis of most couplings. Folks like it. Keeps 'em together. The state likes it. Everybody nice and orderly. You know where all those dicks are going.

BOB I meant I don't want us never to speak again.

LEN We're speaking — even as we speak.

BOB You coming in?

LEN In a little while.

BOB I put a mint on your pillow, on your bed. But you didn't come in, so I . . .

LEN (A bit cool) That was thoughtful of you. Like a fancy motel. Thank you.

BOB (Trying to keep the conversation going) You know, I always wondered when I was a horny teenager if they meant what I thought they meant on those family shows: "Are you coming to bed, dear?" Did that mean they were going to have sex? Or did it just mean, "Get in here. You're keeping me awake?"

LEN The latter, probably.

BOB . . . Are you coming to bed?

LEN It's almost time to get up.

BOB No, it's just a little after three.

LEN Your pie was good.

BOB I'm glad you liked it.

LEN I cleaned up the piece we spilled.

BOB That was nice of you.

LEN I'm a very nice person.

BOB You are.

LEN . . . Where do you think we'll be ten years from now, Bob?

BOB Who knows.

LEN Dead?

BOB Thriving.

LEN My fleet of trucks will be up from three to — wow! — count 'em — six or seven. I'll have a paunch and take a vacation to the Bahamas in the winter, maybe one to a cold climate in the summer. I'll think I'm pretty hot shit. What do people use that expression anyway? Who ever wanted to be hot shit?

BOB (Softly) You shouldn't feel sorry for yourself, honey-babe.

LEN That's another thin I've never understood. Why shouldn't I feel sorry for myself? I do it so much better than anybody else.

BOB You have a good life. You have friends.

LEN "Is that all there is?"

BOB You're self-employed. You're educated. You're not sick. You have a VCR.

LEN Not enough. I'm tired of them all.

BOB And your roommate.

LEN I'm . . . tired of him too.

BOB I don't blame you.

LEN He's a prick teaser.

BOB And a grudge holder.

LEN And a mean bastard.

BOB And a sore loser.

LEN And a . . . lousy cook.

BOB Hey! I draw the line there. I am not a lousy cook. And I was just beginning to feel sorry for you too.

LEN Everything seems so empty, that's all.

BOB	But it is empty! What do you expect?

LEN	Well, not *everything's* empty!

BOB	Of course it is. Where have you been? This is it. This is life . . . Don't scream.

LEN	Is joking the answer?

BOB	For some of us. You don't laugh, you don't live.

LEN	God, that's grim.

BOB	Only if you expect the world . . . from the world.

LEN	I guess I do. I feel like my life is falling apart. And I don't know what to do about it.

BOB	Jog! Eat, drink, and be merry! Pray to Buddha! Boycott grapes! All of these? None of these?

LEN	What keeps you going if you really think life is so . . . ?

BOB Sad? Unsatisfying? Meaning-
less? Why, not thinking of
course. Happiness is not
thinking. Happiness is not
comparing yourself to others.
I take that back. Happiness is
comparing yourself to that baby
in the next ward, the one who
was born addicted to heroin,
the one with brain damage and
the open spine.

LEN Stop it.

BOB I'm serious.

LEN That's not going to work for me.

BOB I don't know what to say then.

LEN Maybe . . . maybe it'd be better
to take something. Just . . . do it.

BOB Come on now.

LEN I mean it.

BOB I know you do. That's why I'm
worried.

LEN Just . . . cease.

BOB And leave your poor roommate?

LEN . . . Come with me.

BOB I hope we never feel this bad at the same time.

LEN No more problems with love or sex or dirty dishes.

BOB Or debits or credits or fat.

LEN I'll get a gun and shoot you and then myself.

BOB What if you change your mind in the middle? I'd better whack you with the skillet and then eat myself to death.

LEN You're making fun of me.

BOB No, I'm not. I'm trying to —

LEN Don't humor me.

BOB (Silence.) You want a hug?

LEN I'm not trying to blackmail you into having sex with me. I get lonely. You get lonely.

BOB I know that. Let me hug you. (Goes to Len.)

LEN I'm good-looking and I can't find a lover. What do ugly people do, for god's sake?

BOB Rub against tables. (Hugging Len) How's that?

LEN But is it sincere?

BOB (Hugs him harder.) Is that better?

LEN (Grudgingly) Hm.

BOB There, there, all babies cry in the dark.

LEN Why don't you want to have sex with me?

BOB It's too late —

LEN In the game?

BOB Something like that.

LEN Do you want me to beg?

BOB No.

LEN Do you want me to sneak into your bed in the middle of the night?

BOB No.

LEN What do you want?

BOB I don't know.

LEN You said you were frustrated.

BOB I know.

LEN God, I must be pretty bad if even that won't do it.

BOB I'm sorry.

LEN You'll rub my back or my adenoids or cook for me and god knows how many other things, but where it really matters, you won't rub. Doesn't make any sense.

BOB Go figure.

LEN How many people in the universe can't get anybody to put their hands on that spot that really aches?

BOB Forty-eight million three hundred and twelve.

LEN You're serious, aren't you? We're never going to be lovers again, are we?

BOB (No answer.)

LEN Are we?

BOB . . . No . . .

LEN (After a pause) Take your hands off me!

BOB What?

LEN (Pushes his hands away, gets up.) I don't want you to touch me.

BOB All right.

LEN In fact, you've got a nerve coming over here and putting your hands all over me.

BOB Len . . .

LEN Who do you think you are, you fat slob!?

BOB (No reply.)

LEN I'm so hard up, I have to settle for you? Not on your life, chubs!

BOB I'm going back to bed.

LEN Go back to bed. Play with yourself under the covers. See if I care. You think I don't hear you in your bed in there? You think I can't smell that coconut oil mixed with your sperm? You think I can't tell when you come? Why wouldn't I? You sound like a beached whale about to die!

BOB (Quietly) Shut up.

LEN Where's your famous sense of humor now, fatso? You and your great philosophy of life. You haven't got one tenth of what I've got going for me — in looks, in my job, in my friends. So don't tell me how to live, you porcine second-rate Ann Landers!

BOB Shut up, Len!

LEN Reject me! You son of a bitch! You've got a nerve rejecting me! You don't even know how to suck cock right. You're the crummiest, lousiest cocksucker I've ever known.

BOB You managed to suffer through it.

LEN You think you're such a lover. Well, you're not. What we had wasn't love. It was getting off together. That's what it was. When you gotta spew, you gotta spew! If I hadn't needed to come so bad, I wouldn't have spent two seconds with you!

BOB That says a lot for you, doesn't it?

LEN Get out of here! Go on, get! I don't want to see or hear or experience your largesse for the rest of my life!

BOB (Goes to the exit, turns back.) Don't worry. You won't. (Exits.)

(Lights out)

Scene Three

(The next morning. Len is asleep on the floor. Bob enters fully dressed, looks at Len, makes himself a cup of tea with a teabag.)

(Bob watches Len on the floor. Len tosses, but doesn't wake up. Finally Bob stands over him and drops the wet teabag on his head.)

LEN (Startled) Hey! What's that? (Jumps up.)

BOB Good morning.

LEN Oh, it's you. God, I didn't know what that was.

BOB Just a teabag.

LEN . . . I guess I deserve it after last night.

BOB You did get wound up.

LEN I didn't mean any of those things I said.

BOB (No reply.)

LEN I got carried away. I guess hell hath no fury like. . .

BOB A fairy scorned?

LEN I'll make it up to you.

BOB Will you? That should be interesting to watch.

LEN I'll . . . I'll . . .

BOB That's okay. You don't have to say anything. You've said quite enough already.

LEN Would you accept an apology?

BOB I've never understood the theory of the apology. "I didn't really think all those vicious things I said. I didn't really mean to spray those scorpions all over the kitchen floor. I'm sorry. I'm sorry. I'm sorry. I'm sorry. I'm sorry." What a bunch of total shit. You meant every word of it.

LEN I'm feeling better this morning. Must be from sleeping on the hard floor.

BOB You're virtue itself. Like the saints of old.

LEN Did you sleep well?

BOB (No reply.)

LEN Are you going to avoid talking to me?

BOB Uh huh.

LEN I guess I should've slept on the daybed.

BOB This tea is terrible. (Puts the cup down.)

LEN I could go out and get some more.

BOB That's all right. I've got to go to work.

LEN Want me to drive you?

BOB No. (Goes offstage to the bedroom.)

LEN I'm really sorry about last night. Really! . . . Really!

(BOB enters with a suitcase.)

LEN What's that?

BOB What does it look like?

LEN A suitcase.

BOB Very good! (Puts on his coat.)

LEN Will you be home for dinner? I'll fix it.

BOB (No reply, opens the suitcase, holds up a shirt.) This isn't yours by mistake, is it?

LEN No.

BOB Great. (Throws the shirt back into the suitcase.)

LEN I could sleep on the daybed for a while, if you like.

BOB Why bother?

LEN I thought it might ease . . . the situation until we get back to . . . normal.

BOB (Turns to Len.) I'll make arrangements about the mortgage once I find a place. I think I'll stay with Eddie from work until then. You'll be able to find somebody to share, I'm sure. This is almost a nice place.

LEN You're moving out?

BOB You have a gift from the obvious. Yes, I'm moving out.

LEN (Playfully) Just tried to add a little sex to a good thing.

BOB (No answer.)

LEN Reaching from one sleeping bag to another.

BOB (No answer.)

LEN Guess I'll never learn, will I?

BOB Apparently not.

LEN Don't leave hating me.

BOB . . . I won't.

LEN (Pleading) Why can't we make it as lovers? Why?

BOB (Almost crying) I don't know. I don't know.

LEN (Fighting the tears) Oh, god!

BOB (Fighting the tears) I've got to go.

LEN Don't go! We can be just roommates again.

BOB No, Len, we can't. We can't. You said too much.

LEN All babies cry in the dark. You've got to forgive them.

BOB (Closing the suitcase) I . . . (Goes to exit.) Bye, lover. (Leaves.)

LEN Bob? . . . Bob? (Sound of outside door closing.) (Almost weeping.) Please don't go!

(Lights out)
Intermission

ACT III
Scene One

(The same day. The accounting office where Rosa and Bob work. We see Rosa's desk and chair, perhaps a waste basket. Minimal set necessary.)

ROSA (Enter Rosa quickly, removing her coat, checking her desk, which has a pile of file folders on it. She picks some of them up irritably.) Where did these come from? Where did — (Goes to offstage door.) Linda, where did these folders come from? Linda? (No answer. Rosa returns. To herself) I will not lose control. I am in control. (Yelling) LINDA! Where the goddamn hell are you?

BOB (Entering) You called?

ROSA Oh, Bob . . . Sorry.

BOB Just passing by. Thought maybe there was a mugger or something in here.

ROSA Well, there isn't!

BOB Excuse me!

ROSA It's just that damn Linda. She's on a coffee break already. She left stuff I told her to do. I told her! And then she goes and leaves it here for me!

BOB I get in this morning and I find the Meyer accounts I worked on all last week are lost. Completely gone. I swear there's a hex on this office.

ROSA Besides, I stumbled over some stoned-out homeless person on the way in. He was pissin' in the goddamn elevator!

BOB Then Mrs. Mattingly tells me I should be wearing a tie. Where does she get off telling me how to dress! Who does she think she is, my mother? (Lights up a cigarette.)

ROSA Hey, I thought you didn't smoke.

BOB I don't. (Takes a puff.) I thought you didn't swear.

ROSA I don't. I didn't exactly sleep so hot last night.

BOB Me neither. What happened?

ROSA Oh, it's because of . . . (Not wanting to say) Oh, never mind. (Sharply) You know it's no smoking in the whole office, don't you?

BOB No, I haven't heard. (Takes another puff.)

ROSA Mattingly is gonna get your butt.

BOB Not my butt! What's wrong with this place? Didn't it use to be nice here?

ROSA Maybe it's something in the air. In the paint.

BOB Lead. You're probably right. It did the Romans in. Now it's seeping into our brains.

ROSA Is that why you didn't get no — any — sleep?

BOB Oh, it was . . . It was . . . (Not wanting to say) I envy you, Rosa. You have such a quiet domestic life.

ROSA (Lying) Yeah, I sure do.

BOB You've been married forever, haven't you?

ROSA Eighteen years.

BOB Must be great.

ROSA . . . Most of the time. Yeah, I have a great marriage.

BOB I suppose it starts with finding the right man. Is he still coming to fix the steps today?

ROSA I think so. Yeah, I know how to pick 'em. What about you? You married? We never talk much, do we? Just about work.

BOB No, I'm not married.

ROSA Funny, you seem like the married kind.

BOB What does that mean? Safe? Tame?

ROSA I don't know. I can just tell.

BOB No, I'm an absolute enigma.

ROSA (Hinting) You got a roommate, don't you?

BOB Yes, a wonderful roommate.

ROSA So why don't you ever talk about him?

BOB Because you probably don't want to hear. We weren't exactly blessed by the Pope.

ROSA The Pope doesn't tell me everything! Besides, I can put two and two together. I don't have to be no accountant.

BOB Well, maybe you could advise me. What is it you do with your man? How do you handle him?

ROSA I . . . I . . . cook. Raise the kids. Make love. I put up with a lot. I'm pleasant to be around.

BOB That's my problem. I'm not pleasant to be around.

ROSA You can learn a lot from magazines.

BOB Which ones?

ROSA You know — next to the counter when you're checkin' out.

BOB Right, I've seen those. You're the person who reads those?

ROSA Hey!

BOB Afraid they're for you people.

ROSA You people? What does that mean? You people?

BOB They're not written with me in mind, that's for sure.

ROSA . . . And not for me either, apparently, now I think about it.

BOB Oh, why do you say that?

ROSA I don't know if I want to talk about it. Maybe I talk too much. And I got lots of work to do. (Picks up the file folders.) They say people need to keep busy.

BOB Yeah, they do . . . Want a cigarette? (Lights up.)

ROSA (Throws the file folders down.) Hell, give me one. (He hands it to her.)

BOB We can't always do what's right, for fuck's sake!

ROSA (Taking a puff, makes a disgusted noise) This tastes terrible.

BOB I know, but it's all we have.

ROSA I don't think I want it after all.

BOB Yeah, I suppose I'd better be getting back too before old Mattingly writes me up. (Puts out the cigarette) Boy, I hate her. She's a fanny smeller.

ROSA She is?

BOB At the least! . . . I got to go. (About to leave, changes his mind) So what's the matter, Rosa? Come on, tell me.

ROSA No.

BOB Sure?

ROSA . . . It's my husband. He . . . Why don't you tell me about your roommate?

BOB All right, I will. He and I have lived together for over five years. He's got his own business. He's . . . I'm . . . And that's about it.

ROSA That's about it? Are you lovers?

BOB Rosa, you're blowing my cover!

ROSA Everybody knows.

BOB They do?

ROSA Something wrong at home?

BOB What make you think that?

ROSA I got a sixth sense. Is that right — sixth sense?

BOB Yeah, that's right. (After thinking about it) Everybody knows? What do you mean? I never dropped a single hairpin around here, as they used to say.

ROSA It's your aura. It's not the right color.

BOB I beg your pardon. My aura is just fine.

ROSA Now don't be grumpy. I mean today.

BOB I'm not grumpy!

ROSA You're grumpy. Trust me.

BOB All right, I'm grumpy. Cure me.

ROSA I'm grumpy myself.

BOB I'll cure you. Tell me

everything. Everything!

ROSA What is this? Are we playing doctor?

BOB (Laughs.) You don't know what that mean, do you?

ROSA It means you give advice and then you send a big bill.

BOB Not too far off.

ROSA Okay, so I'm the doctor. What's troubling you?

BOB I want to be the doctor.

ROSA No, I want to be the doctor!

BOB Let's alternate. Is that fair?

ROSA You go first.

BOB What's troubling you? (Seriously) Seriously.

ROSA . . . Well, I want a baby. And I don't want a baby.

BOB Ah, that's clear.

ROSA I just brought it up to my husband 'cause I wanted to have something to happen in our marriage. Nothin' happens anymore. He don't want to talk or . . . anything. (She's a little embarrassed at her revelations.) I thought I was doing the right thing, you know, talking about it. I really thought I was.

BOB And what happened?

ROSA I killed my marriage.

BOB (Comforting) Oh, Rosa, I don't think so.

ROSA I think so. I know so.

BOB (Absorbing her seriousness) That's terrible.

ROSA I know!

BOB It's probably not too late.

ROSA Believe me, it's too late, Bob.

You can have too much communication. I've learned that much. And not from no dumb magazine!

BOB (Relating to his own situation) Yeah, I know what you mean.

ROSA What happened? . . . Come on now! I told *you.*

BOB I had a chance to revive . . . the one love I've ever had in my life.

ROSA Really?

BOB One of those rare moments in anyone's lifetime, and I blew it. Absolutely blew it. And I'm supposed to be smart.

ROSA That's awful.

BOB Thanks for your comforting words.

ROSA It's not too late.

BOB Believe me, it's too late.

ROSA I didn't know you people . . . stayed together. I mean, for a long time.

BOB Rosa!

ROSA What?

BOB Don't spoil this.

ROSA What'd I say?

BOB Never mind.

ROSA Don't be hurt. I'm sorry!

BOB Okay, so we were a little promiscuous. Let me rephrase that — we were a little non-monogamous. It didn't mean we didn't care for each other. Jesus!

ROSA I happen to think fidelity is very important.

BOB No wonder straight men walk out then.

ROSA Bob!

BOB It's the truth. I get so tired of all this hand-wringing you people do over a little sex here or there. Get over it!

ROSA You're not exactly an expert on keeping your "marriage" together. You get over it!

BOB I thought we were having a nice talk.

ROSA You didn't exactly sympathize with my problem — calling me "you people," for God's sake. You don't think my problems are important.

BOB Excuse me. Kick me. For a few seconds there I wasn't — so help me God — the sensitive, understanding homo of your dreams!

ROSA No, excuse me for not being the sensitive, understanding woman of yours!

BOB I suffer ten times more than you do!

ROSA What? You don't have no clue about what I have to put up with!

BOB You're the ones who make such a big deal out of being the normal ones, the only ones, the ones with all the problems right out there in the magazines!

ROSA Well, we've got children. We've got bills —

BOB I've got bills! I have had a major catastrophe in my life. I've lost my home, my lover, my best friend, and probably my job for smoking in this stupid place, and then I have to work all day and be cheerful on top of it all and never let on! You think my life is easy?

ROSA My marriage is over. My kids are American brats. I don't earn enough, and I have to come to work in this stupid place all day, and always be so goddamn cheerful on top of it and comfort everybody else! You think my life is easy?

BOB Do you have any idea what it feels like to be considered a pervert? For all your problems, you can always expect the whole world to listen to yours. I have to be constantly on guard who hears about mine. They can get me.

ROSA You can just walk away from your problems. I got kids! I got responsibilities! Those get me!

BOB Then you shouldn't have had them! And you're dead wrong that we can walk away as if we don't have feelings!

ROSA That's why people come together — to have kids!

BOB Yeah, the grunts of the world do. That's not the only reason and you know it! Lots of straights have all the sex they want without having any kids, and nobody says boo to them!

ROSA You calling me a grunt?

BOB I'm just saying I'm fed up with you straights — your kids this, your kids that. You people are obsessed!

ROSA And how do you suppose the world keeps on without kids? We supply them.

BOB Yeah, and we supply everything else!

ROSA Bullshit!

BOB We're supposed to be the selfish ones. But you're the selfish ones. You're not doing it for the world. You're doing it for yourself, and we're expected to jump up and down and cheer because you're so goddamn self-less. It's about as far from selfless as anybody can get. You want to impose your goddamn genes on the rest of us!

ROSA And I'm suppose to jump up and down and cry 'cause you're all dying from diseases , when it's your own damn fault! If you didn't fuck so much, you wouldn't be so dead!

BOB (Shocked) Rosa!

ROSA I'm not sorry.

BOB Well, I'm not sorry either.

(Pause, as both smolder)

BOB (Quietly) I know what men want, what they must have.

ROSA And I don't?

BOB Not as much as I do.

ROSA (Quietly) I know what men want. I just don't want to give it to them anymore.

(Another pause. Both are still angry. Eventually, Bob lights another cigarette, sits on the edge of Rosa's desk)

BOB (After taking a few puffs, relenting) Even when you give it to them, after a while men don't want it. Have you noticed?

ROSA . . . Now that's really horrible.

BOB Well, it's the truth. Men are beasts.

ROSA Have you noticed that too?

BOB But we can't do without them, can we? Only lesbians can do without them.

ROSA I can do without them.

(Bob gives her a look.)

ROSA I can!

BOB . . . Well, I can't.

ROSA . . . I can't either. . . . I'm not a lesbian.

BOB Me neither.

ROSA Sometimes I wish I was.

BOB Sometimes I wish I was straight.

ROSA/
BOB (Together) No, you don't!

(They laugh)

BOB What do you think will really happen to your marriage?

ROSA Oh, Fernando might stay with me and start drinking or something.

BOB And you'd stumble on, trying to hold it together.

ROSA Right. Everything gettin' uglier and uglier. What about you?

BOB Oh, Len and I might pick up, at least the friendship part, and always be sort of polite and stiff with each other —

for the rest of our lives.

ROSA Not promising for either of us, is it?

BOB But you gotta hope.

ROSA Yeah, hope is good.

BOB (Putting out his cigarette) Well, it's great that we finally got to talk, Rosa. Isn't it?

ROSA Yeah . . . If only . . .

BOB What?

ROSA Never mind.

BOB (Having his own might-have-been moment.) If only . . .

ROSA What?

BOB If only I could have "talked" to Len like I'm talking to you.

ROSA And me to Fernando.

BOB Can I give you a hug?

ROSA Sure.

(They hug each other)

BOB (Moving away) Thanks. (Pats her hand.)

ROSA Thank you! (Pats his hand.)

BOB Watch those magazines.

ROSA Watch those hairpins.

BOB God, I feel better.

ROSA Me too.

BOB See you.

ROSA See you.

(Bob goes to the door, stops, turns back.)

BOB So, Rosa, if one of your kids turned out gay, you'd be more . . . comfortable with it now, right?

ROSA (Doesn't answer.)

BOB Rosa?

ROSA . . . I'd kill him!

(They laugh.)

(Bob looks uncertain, then downright pained about how little has really changed between them.)

(Lights fade)

Scene Two

(Len and Bob's kitchen, the same day. The sound of hammering offstage. Radio on in the kitchen.)

LEN (Taking the rhubarb pie out of the oven or off a hotplate, putting it on the table to cool, calling.) How's it going? (Turns off the radio.)

FERNANDO (In between banging noises) No sweat!

LEN How long's it going to take to fix 'em?

FERNANDO Not much longer!

LEN Want some pie? It's rhubarb! (The banging stops) You deserve a break.

(Door slams. Fernando enters, putting the hammer in the tool holder around his waist.)

FERNANDO Thanks, Mr. Nolan.

LEN Call me Len.

FERNANDO Fernando.

(They start to shake hands but hold back)

LEN You want to sit?

FERNANDO No, I can stand.

LEN Suit yourself.

(Len busies himself cutting the pie, getting a plate, fork, etc.)

FERNANDO It's a good thing you called me 'bout them steps. They coulda broke and somebody coulda sued you for everything you got! (Grins.)

LEN I'm afraid they wouldn't get much.

FERNANDO You own this place or just rent?

LEN I'm making the payments, shall we say?

FERNANDO I'm thinkin' 'bout buyin'. We're just rentin' now.

LEN (Nodding at the hammer, with a strong sexual overture.) Well, you should be able to save on repairs.

FERNANDO (Picking up and

returning the sexual overture, but with some aloofness) Yeah, I'm pretty handy. (After a pause) You gay?

LEN (Looking up, somewhat afraid) You doing a survey?

FERNANDO I work for a lot of gays, that's all.

LEN You're not gay, I take it?

FERNANDO (With some contempt) Who me?

LEN You married?

FERNANDO Sure. Nice girl. She's from Guatemala.

LEN Are you?

FERNANDO Grew up in Cuba.

LEN Kids?

FERNANDO Yeah. Two.

LEN (Handing him a piece of pie on a plate, adds a fork, but Fernando removes the fork, puts it back on the table.) Did you learn repair work down in Cuba?

FERNANDO (Eating) Naw, I escaped. When I was a kid.

LEN That sounds interesting.

(Crosses to kitchen sink.)

FERNANDO The troops came to my little school and beat me up 'cause I had some holy cards. I was Catholic then. I guess I still am. Just don't go to church no more. Went to Miami and then come up here.

LEN And somewhere along

	the way you learned to be a carpenter, right?
FERNANDO	In the army.
LEN	I wish I could fix things, but I can't.

(Shows something broken, such as the door at the bottom of the sink.)

FERNANDO	Yeah, I'm real good around the house. You're not, huh?
LEN	Oh, I get by. I'm too busy at the moment.
FERNANDO	What do you do for a living?
LEN	I distribute — (Opening refrigerator door with a flourish, revealing a doorful of cans) — soft drinks!
FERNANDO	(Shrugs.)
LEN	(Seeing Fernando's

sticky fingers) How about a napkin?

FERNANDO Naw, I don't need it. (Licks his fingers.)

(There is a look between them, sexual tension as Fernando licks several fingers one by one.)

FERNANDO Yeah, I've always worked physical. Feels good. (Slaps his hammer.)

LEN (To make conversation, busying himself) Where were you in the army?

FERNANDO Germany mostly. You been in the army?

LEN Almost. But no.

FERNANDO Yeah, I had a real good time in Germany — not from the Germans, though. They considered me a nigger — oops, I mean a "person of color." But I fucked a lot.

LEN — Did you?

FERNANDO — Some nice ass there.

LEN — (Closer) Well, I'm glad. For your sake.

FERNANDO — You gotta beer by any chance, man? I been workin' up a thirst.

LEN — Let me check the refrigerator.(Goes to it, finds a bottle of beer. While his back is turned, Fernando removes his tee-shirt, turns his back to Len, does a basketball hook shot with it onto the daybed.)

LEN — (Turning with the beer, noticing the hook shot, the nice body.)
This okay?

FERNANDO — (Referring to his naked

chest) I was gettin' hot.

LEN — No problem.(Offers the beer.) Here's your beer.

FERNANDO — (Checking the label, mockingly) A Lite, huh? Well, I guess a beer's a beer. Thanks. (Takes a swallow.)

LEN — (Striking a macho pose) Well, when you've got a real thirst!

FERNANDO — (Ignoring the mockery) You live here alone?

LEN — I have a friend I . . . share with.

FERNANDO — A guy?

LEN — Yes. . . . He's working today.

FERNANDO — What's he do?

LEN — He's an accountant.

FERNANDO — Yeah? (Smirks but

	takes a swallow to cover it.) Oh, yeah. I forgot. He works with my wife. (About the beer.) Ahhhh! That's great! Join me?
LEN	I'm afraid that's the last one.
FERNANDO	Take a swig of mine then! (Holds out the beer bottle, almost thrusting it into Len's mouth.) Come on, come on! I don't have no germs.
LEN	(Backing away) I had some tea before you arrived, so I'm really not thirsty.
FERNANDO	(Walks over toward the exit, where he entered.) Well, I'm gonna have to cut you some new steps. Got some wood out in the truck that might do.

LEN That sounds fine.

(Fernando stops and looks at a picture of a woman on a calendar, takes a swig.)

FERNANDO (Insinuatingly) So you share with this guy, huh? (He takes another swig, then brings the bottle down to his crotch invitingly. Len looks down, but raises his head, folds his arms, as if to say he is not accepting the invitation.)

(Slow Fade)

Scene Three

(The same, a few day later; radio on. Len has changed into a plaid shirt. He is doing a few dishes. Then there is a knocking offstage. He turns off the radio, exits.)

FERNANDO (Entering quickly) God, it's cold out there today! (He's wearing an open jacket over a shirt similar to Len's.)

LEN (Entering after Fernando) Well, you're certainly dressed a lot warmer than you were the other day.

FERNANDO I got it on sale. (Taking off his coat, looking down at shirt) You like it?

LEN Very nice.

FERNANDO (Noticing that his shirt looks like Len's) You don't think it makes me look like a faggot, do you?

LEN (Taking the coat, hanging it up on a hook.) What does a faggot look like?

FERNANDO (Half gesturing toward Len) Oh, you know.

LEN	(Half amused) Are you very afraid of looking like a faggot?
FERNANDO	(Sharply) I'm not afraid of nothin', man!
LEN	Good! . . . I asked you to come back today because I thought you did a good job on those steps. (Points at the shelves over the sink.) And I was wondering if you could take out these old shelves and put in a couple of cabinets — and could you paint them cornbread yellow?
FERNANDO	(Sneering) Cornbread yellow? What's that?
LEN	(Absorbing the mockery) I'll get you a sample.
FERNANDO	Whatever you say, man. (Picking up a kitchen chair and moving it

	with one hand to the shelves, not taking his eyes off Len. With heavy irony) You're the boss! (Hauls himself up on the sink to look at the old shelves, as Len cleans things away hurriedly) (As an afterthought, rude) Oh, is it okay if I stand on this?
LEN	(Since Fernando is already standing on it) Be my guest!
FERNANDO	(Checking) Hey, it's pretty dusty up here.
LEN	Yeah, I don't clean very well.
FERNANDO	(Surprised) You don't like to clean?
LEN	Nobody likes to clean, do they?
FERNANDO	(Sneeringly) Sorry, I

	just thought maybe you . . .
LEN	(Looking up) No, I'm afraid I'm not into cleaning.
FERNANDO	(Looking down) My wife, she cleans all the time.
LEN	Does she?
FERNANDO	She's real sweet.
LEN	Is she?
FERNANDO	(with a double meaning) Your friend, he does the cleaning?
LEN	(Emphasizing the words) We take turns.
FERNANDO	No kidding?
LEN	No kidding.
FERNANDO	(Breaks the tension by starting to get back down off the sink.)

LEN	(Offers his hand like a knight) Need any help?
FERNANDO	No, I can do it! (Gets down slowly.)

(Fernando struts away, then looks back over his shoulder, catches Len looking at him.)

LEN	(Quickly) Well, I guess we'd better start emptying these shelves.
FERNANDO	Do you mind doing that yourself, man? I gotta get some more tools from the truck.
LEN	(Who has been removing teacups from the shelf, placing them on the table.) No, I don't mind.
FERNANDO	(Starting to leave, noticing a teacup, picks it up) Hey, these are real cute! (Pretends to drink with his pinkie

extended.) Got flowers on 'em, huh?

LEN You don't like flowers?

FERNANDO Yeah, I like flowers. I just don't like 'em too much on cups.

LEN (Coming over, picking up a cup) These cups are pretty tough, flowers and all.

FERNANDO Is that right?

LEN Have a special glaze. You can throw one on the floor and it won't even break.

(He brings the teacup down as if to throw it hard, but he doesn't.)

FERNANDO Hey, I thought you was gonna throw it!

LEN Well, it might have broken — and ruined my point. (Puts the cup

	and saucer together as he ends this sentence.)
FERNANDO	(With a double meaning) And then you would've had to bend over to pick it up too.
LEN	Would I?
FERNANDO	Could be dangerous. You could hurt your back or somethin'.
LEN	Could I? I guess I have to be careful how I bend over then, don't I?
FERNANDO	I guess so.
LEN	You have to be pretty careful yourself, I suppose.
FERNANDO	I don't bend over.
LEN	You let your wife do it, is that it?
FERNANDO	You leave my wife out

of this.

(Len breaks the tension by getting more items from the shelves.)

FERNANDO	(Changing the tone) You know what — my Aunt Maria collects china dishes. Got all kinds.
LEN	Does she?
FERNANDO	Yeah, she's real old now, but as far back as I can remember she's collected these china dishes. Even back in Cuba.
LEN	And here I thought they didn't have any fun there. (Coming back, putting both fists on the table) Is your aunt a faggot?
FERNANDO	Huh? Laughs.) What made you say that?
LEN	Because she collects

	china. That's a sure sign.
FERNANDO	Not in a *mujer*. (Cocks his head) You've got a sense of humor.
LEN	We always do! (Goes back for more items to remove, gets up on the chair. Fernando watches his butt.) (Starting to turn back.) I — (Catches Fernando watching him. Fernando looks away fast.)
LEN	I'm afraid I didn't buy any more beer.
FERNANDO	(Looking at the pie, which is still out) You don't have some more of that pie by any chance, do you?
LEN	(Getting it, removing the cover) Yeah, there's quite a bit of it left. My roommate and I are on a diet, as of . . .

(Thinks of Bob sadly)

FERNANDO Looks good!

(Len recovers and brings it to the table, to cut. Fernando follows)

LEN You want it on a plate? (Does mocking parallel gesture to Fernando's basketball hook shot earlier) Or should I just hand it to you?

(Fernando extends his hand, daring Len to put the pie there. Len cuts the piece, the dumps it into Fernando's hand.)

FERNANDO (Eating) Excuse my manners.

LEN You're excused.

FERNANDO This is delicious! Did you make this yourself?

LEN (Lying, lifting his hands in self-mockery) I did!

FERNANDO You make a real good

pie. It's even better cold.

LEN (Moving a little closer) We can warm it up if you like.

FERNANDO (Picking up on the double meaning) How you gonna warm it up?

LEN The usual way. How would you warm it up?

FERNANDO Oh, there must be some way. . .

(Len almost reaches out, but decides not to. Instead, he turns and picks up the rest of the pie and returns it to where it was.)

FERNANDO Well, I guess I'd better get a crowbar out of my truck and start on them cabinets!

(Wiggles his sticky fingers.)

LEN (Assuming familiarity) our fingers are sticky.

As usual.

FERNANDO	(Moving them) Guess they need . . . cleaning.

(Len offers a dish towel. Fernando considers it, but wipes his fingers on his shirt.)

LEN	Do I make you nervous?
FERNANDO	Me? Why should you make me nervous?
LEN	(Throwing the dish towel on the table) Just an idea that crossed my mind.
FERNANDO	No, you seem like a nice guy.
LEN	Thanks for the compliment.
FERNANDO	(Embarrassed) Was that a compliment?(Brushes past Len, almost elbowing him out of the

	way) I didn't mean nothin' by it.
LEN	(Bowing ironically.) Thank you.
FERNANDO	I mean . . . I mean, I don't compliment guys.
LEN	You don't!
FERNANDO	I mean, I wouldn't know if what I sad was a compliment.
LEN	(Angry) It's all right. No permanent damage done by giving a compliment.
FERNANDO	(Angrier) What do you mean by that? (Threatening)
LEN	Not a thing . . . Not a thing!
	(Blackout)

Scene Four

(The same, a few minutes later. Len is reading a magazine on the daybed, looking up to see what Fernando is up to. Fernando enters with a crowbar, puts it on the table, leaves for something else, returns with a hammer, puts it on the table. It's obvious that he's restless.)

LEN (When Fernando, who wants to talk but is hiding it, stops) Yes?

FERNANDO How come I never see your roommate? (Plays with his work gloves.)

LEN Happened to miss him each time. He's . . . on vacation.

FERNANDO Oh . . . (Still hangs around.)

LEN (Gesturing at chair.) You want to sit down for a minute?

FERNANDO Oh, I don't know. I

guess I should get to work.

LEN Suit yourself. (Goes back to reading, but still watches.)

(Fernando continues to stand there, hands in pockets.)

LEN Something bothering you?

FERNANDO Oh, I don't know. (Raps his knuckles on the table.)

LEN You want to borrow my magazine, or something? (Holds it out.)

FERNANDO No, I don't read too much.

LEN Men don't.

FERNANDO (Spots a stuffed frog above Len's head, used as a wall decoration.)

	Hey, what's the frog for?
LEN	(Reaching up, tickling its crotch.) For fun! Don't you have one in your house?
FERNANDO	A frog?
LEN	No? (Reaches up, takes down the frog, works it like a puppet.) I was in a play and this was a prop.
FERNANDO	You let it stay on the wall?
LEN	Why not?
FERNANDO	It's sort of weird, isn't it?
LEN	Not if you're into frogs.
FERNANDO	I guess I'm not into frogs.
LEN	(Playing with the frog)

No? . . . You mean to tell me you've never fucked a frog?

FERNANDO Not once!

LEN (Shifting the cards.) How about the other way? Ever been. . .?

FERNANDO (Almost laughing, uncomfortable) Fucked by a frog? Definitely not.

LEN You should try it sometime.

FERNANDO Hey, we're talkin' kinda weird!

LEN (Tossing the frog to him.) Are we?

FERNANDO (Catching, holding the frog.) You got a lotta things like this?

LEN You mean in the rest of the house?

FERNANDO	Yeah . . .
LEN	A few in the bedroom. Go take a look if you want . . .
FERNANDO	That's okay. (Tosses the frog back to Len.)
LEN	What do you have in your bedroom?
FERNANDO	My wife most of the time! (Snorts.)
LEN	Bragging or complaining?
FERNANDO	She's got bit tits.
LEN	Is that one word?
FERNANDO	She does, believe me.
LEN	(Very obviously doesn't reply.)
FERNANDO	(Laughs.) What's the matter? You don't like big tits?

LEN I can take 'em or leave 'em alone. (Tosses the frog on the floor.)

FERNANDO See these hands. (Holds them out.) These hands shouldn't be workin' so much. These hands should be full of tits all the time! (Pantomimes grabbing handfuls.)

LEN (Putting his hands behind his head.) You're quite the stud, aren't you?

FERNANDO No complaints yet!

LEN I wonder what it's like to be able to brag about your sex drive like that. You never have to worry what the other guys will say, do you?

FERNANDO Huh?

LEN	If it moves, you'll fuck it, is that it?
FERNANDO	All it's got to do is lay there. Don't have to move.
LEN	(Putting his legs to the side of the daybed.) Yes, I know the type.
FERNANDO	(Moving away.) Got anything else to eat? Got any whiskey?
LEN	(Pretending to be feminine again.) Why, I must be forgetting my manners! (Goes to take more packages from the shelves.) By the way, you never told me if your wife likes to cook. I bet she does, doesn't she?
FERNANDO	(Standing by the table, watching Len bringing packages over.) Yeah, man, she does.

LEN	A real little woman, huh?
FERNANDO	Something wrong with that?
LEN	(Shaking a cake mix.) Does she bake cakes?
FERNANDO	Hey, I like women to act like women —
LEN	— And men to act like men, right?
FERNANDO	That's right.
LEN	And what does that mean exactly?
FERNANDO	Huh?
LEN	Describe being a man to me. (Fernando looks suspicious.) Go ahead. I'm interested.
FERNANDO	(Uncomfortable having to speak, but he moves away thinking, then

comes back.) Okay, okay. A man is boss, and he knows his own mind.

LEN Very interesting. Go on.

FERNANDO And a man don't take no shit from nobody, and he fights when he has to —

LEN — And even when he doesn't have to!

FERNANDO — Like when I was in the army.

LEN Sounds admirable.

FERNANDO And if he acts right, he gets treated like a man. Me, I've always been treated like a man.

LEN (Takes a chair in a "butch" way, twirling it around, sits in it backwards.) And if a man acts "wrong," what happens to him?

FERNANDO (Stuck for an answer.) He gets . . . (Moves away.)

LEN (Still sitting, not looking at Fernando.) He gets what?

FERNANDO (Unable to say.)

LEN He gets what? (After a beat, insinuatingly) . . . What do you suppose it's like? (Gets up, looks at Fernando, whose back is turned to him.) You're curious, aren't you? You're more than curious.

FERNANDO (Softly) I'm not curious . . .

LEN Not even a little bit?

FERNANDO No . . .

(Len hesitates, remembering Bob's rejection. Finally he moves closer to Fernando and holds his arm above Fernando's shoulder. After a few seconds, he brings his hand down and Fernando slowly turns his head to look at it. Then Len slides his hand down the other's arm as if to take Fernando's hand, but Fernando balks and jerks his hand away.)

LEN	(After a pause) You want to go into the bedroom?
FERNANDO	(Takes a step toward the bedroom, then stops.)
LEN	How about on the daybed?
FERNANDO	(After a considerable pause, he sits on the daybed and starts to remove his shirt.)
LEN	(Coming nearer, then touching Fernando's shoulder. Fernando flinches a little.) Have you done this before?
FERNANDO	(Softly) I used to do it to my cousin, about ten years ago.

(Both start to unbutton their shirts, but Fernando looks up with a start when Len pulls his own shirttails out.)

LEN Changing your mind?

FERNANDO (Shakes his head no.)

(They finish removing their shirts, separately.)

LEN (Touching him again. This time no flinching.) Don't be afraid. (Moves behind him, touching both shoulders.) I think I know what you need . . . I have something we can use . . .

(Gestures, meaning he has a condom,)

FERNANDO (Nods, then sadly.) A guy who gets fucked ain't a real man.

LEN It's up to you.

FERNANDO (Whispering) I'm afraid. There's no goin'

	back once it's . . .
LEN	(Both hands on Fern-ando's shoulders.) Maybe it's a victory, not a loss. (Fernando looks at him.) Your eyes are very beautiful . . . Do you want to leave?
FERNANDO	(Very slowly shakes his head no.)
LEN	You're sure? (Gets up and flips the light switch to low, returns.)

(Fernando leans back part way against Len's body.)

LEN	Relax . . . (Moves Fernando's hand over to Fernando's zipper. Relax . . .

(Fernando begins to unzip his own trousers.)

LEN	(Moving Fernando so that he is leaning

toward the pillow on the daybed) Is it all right? (Touches Fernando's waist.) Is it?

FERNANDO (Quietly) Yes . . .

LEN (Undoing his top button, unzipping his fly.) I'm going to enter you with all the tenderness I'm capable of. Don't be afraid. (Moves one hand down inside Fernando's trousers, touching a spot between the buttocks.) I can feel you . . . opening . . .

FERNANDO (After a moment) Yes, yes . . . (Sighs.)

LEN Welcome to the other side, Fernando.

(Tableau. Slow Fade)

End of Play

For royalty quotes, please contact
curzon@pacbell.net

Reviews of "Last Call"

"The best-written, and most profess-
sionally produced, is "Last Call," by
Daniel Curzon, directed by Ed
Decker."— *San Francisco Chronicle*

"Between Curzon's play and . . . you
can have a fun evening of theater . . ."
— *Coming Up*

"The play, though short, is like spun
gold."—KQED-FM

"The most vivid of these brief theatre-
pieces . . . has to be Daniel Curzon's
Last Call, performed under the auspices
of One Act's Playwright's Theatre with
the capable direction of Ed Decker.
—*The San Francisco Paper*

". . . permits jarring truths to be
presented in a palatable, highly
entertaining perspective."
—*Bay Area Reporter*

Performed as part of National
Endowment for the Arts Grant
—KPFA-FM

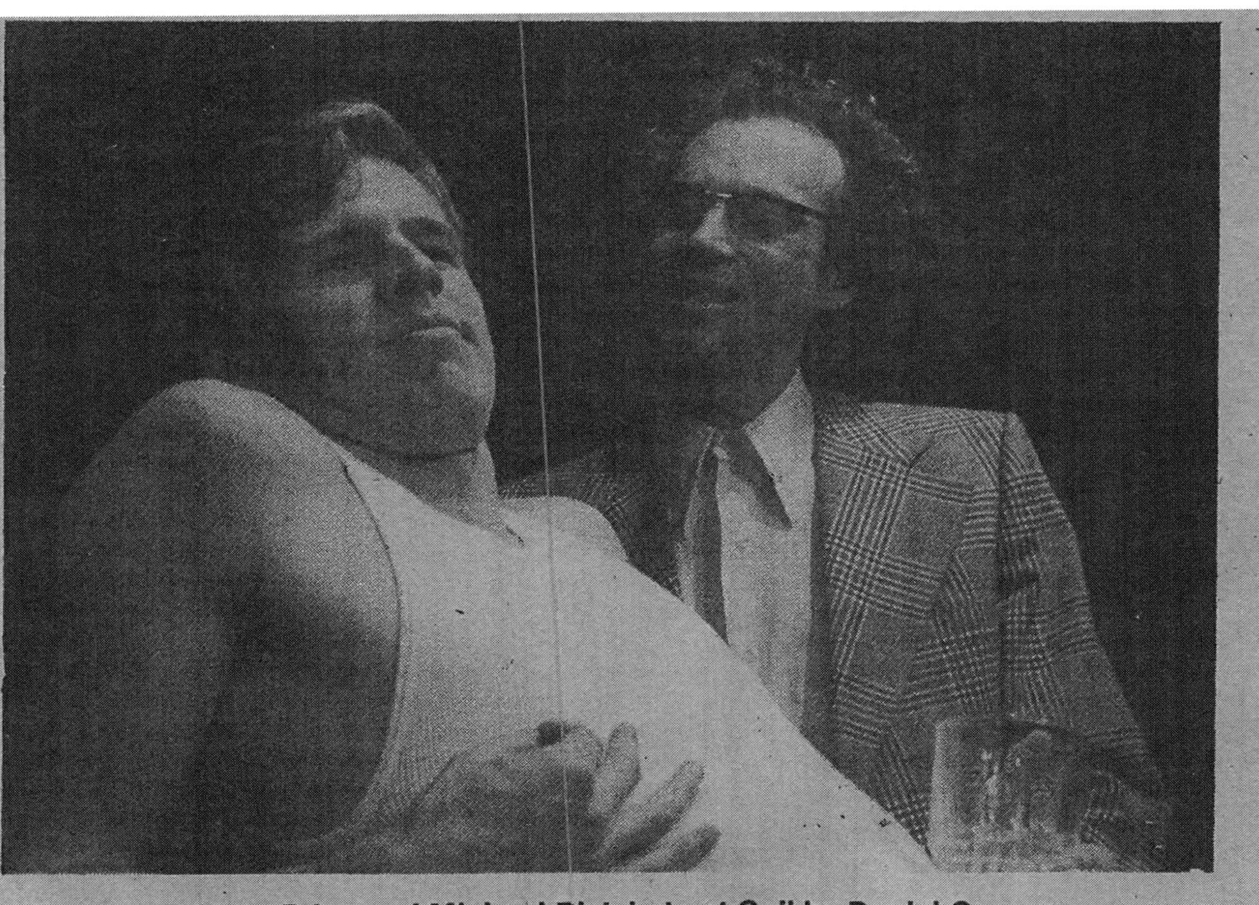

Photo Pamela Clarke, © 1981

Steve Price and Michael Risk in Last Call by Daniel Curzon

LAST CALL

CHARACTERS:
- BARTENDER, male, fairly good-looking.
- HERB, an older man, or an odd-looking man
- DAVID, an attractive younger man.
- 3 BAR PATRONS, possibly cut-outs

SETTING: A gay bar, 1:30 A.M. on a weeknight. The bar counter itself should have two sections, more or less at right angles. A pinball machine on the side.

(As the play begins, Herb is sitting on a barstool with a Bloody Mary in his hand. He is somewhat drunk. David enters and, with an air of self-confidence, says to the Bartender:

DAVID A beer, please!

HERB (To audience) Give me a beer please, and make it free. I'm so handsome I shouldn't be expected to pay.

(David pays for his beer, sits at a section of the bar so that he and Herb face each other.)

DAVID (To Bartender) Slow night, huh?

BAR'ER (Washing some glasses) Yeah.

HERB (To audience) What do you mean slow? I'm here! But, Jesus, who'd want that one over there with (The actor should insert some unattractive detail about himself.) God, what a toad he is!

DAVID (To audience) Don't see anybody I know. The beer's good, though. Wonder if that guy's cruising me. Not exactly my type.

HERB (Not hearing the previous remark) I don't suppose anybody's his type. Certainly not us trolls! But I can't help being unattractive. Don't you love that word? Unattractive, it's so much nicer sounding than repulsive.

DAVID He doesn't seem to do anything to make himself look better. He could lose some weight or go to the gym or at least grow some facial hair.

HERB All gay men care about is appearance, you must realize. They're hung up on looks, looks, looks! Physicality — thy name is homosexual! Does he care that I'm a clarinetist of some note. Did you get the pun? Clarinetist! Note! Wouldn't you want to have sex with someone as clever as me? No? If I were straight, I'd have tons of women after me. I know that for a fact. Women — good-looking women — come up all the time and want to make love to me, because I'm such a fucking good clarinetist! But, alas, I like men. Well, I don't really *like* men. But I want to participate in their flesh, shall we say. But, sigh, very few of them want to participate in mine. Isn't that enough to break your heart?

DAVID Wonder if he's got an interesting personality. Sometimes homely guys do. Of course if I speak first, he'll think I want to make it with him. So I'd better not say anything. Maybe he'll leave soon.

HERB (Not hearing DAVID, of course) I'm not leaving. I was here first. Perhaps I ought to mark my spot. If I'm a dog, I might as well act like one. (Lifts his leg.) This is mine. Do not approach. Do not cross. I'm staying here until I catch me a trick for the night. I've made up my mind!

DAVID I must say drunks really turn me off. I can't figure them out. I think I'd work twice as hard at developing my best qualities instead of sitting in a bar pouring drinks into myself, getting sloshed, loud, and obnoxious on top of everything else.

HERB Barkeep! Another Mickey Finn, please! (As the drink is being fixed) I'm feeling good! How are you feeling?

BAR'ER (Dully) Great. Here's your Bloody Mary.

HERB (Toasting) To charm! Here's a tip. (Takes out some change.) Here's a tip for talking to me all night long in my deep loneliness.

BAR'ER Sure, thanks.

HERB Think nothing of it, as I'm sure you will. Hey, send my friend over there a drink, too. (Indicates David.) But don't tell him who sent it.

BAR'ER (placing the beer in front of David.) From a secret admirer.

DAVID Hey, thanks!

HERB (To audience) I just want everyone in this bar to be happy. There is so little happiness in bars. Laughter, yes, but little happiness. Have you noticed? Well, I've noticed. Perhaps that's because I'm more perceptive than you. It couldn't possibly be because I'm more unhappy, could it?

DAVID I wonder who sent me this.

HERB (To the audience) Yoo-hoo, guess who sent you that!

DAVID It's really nice of whoever did it.

HERB Me, me, me! Look over here! Our eyes will lock and we'll go home together!

DAVID (Looking around, but not at Herb) Maybe it was that cute guy in the back there, leaning against the wall. I think I caught his eye a few times.

HERB Me, me, me! But — stop! —
I don't want you to go home
with me just because I bought
you a drink. Not even two
drinks — never! I want you
to go home with me because I
turn you on. I couldn't, of
course, touch you unless it
was absolutely mutual!

DAVID (Goes to pinball machine.)
Oh, I hope it wasn't that guy
at the bar. I don't want to hurt
his feelings. Really I don't,
but he seems like a loser.

HERB I bet he's got a brain this
small, though.(Gestures.)
Maybe even this small.
(Makes tiny gesture.)
Someone that good-looking
obviously has neglected his
intelligence. Just look at him,
I bet he doesn't even know
Mahler's Fifth! (Hums.)
You don't know Mahler's
Fifth, do you? See, what did
I tell you! I bet you don't
even know Mahler's First!

DAVID I think they rig these things so

the balls race right through. (Bangs on pinball machine.) Magnets — they've got magnets to make the games go faster!

HERB What did I tell you! A pinball jock! I think that's immoral. All that energy wasted on a toy! He could be using his hands on something else, like my — How about a little action there, big boy? It doesn't have to be love. What do you say?

DAVID Hey, I got a free game!

HERB Wow! You put some steel balls in those little holes! Why, it ought to be in the sports pages!

DAVID Hey, this machine's great!

HERB Some people have athletic ability. You deserve no credit for it. It's hereditary. The same goes for looks, by the way. You either have 'em or you don't. You happen to have 'em. I don't. But you didn't earn them! I suppose my musical ability is hereditary too. But I have practiced — for hours and hours! Have you practiced being handsome? Huh? Have you?

DAVID (To audience) God, I'm having a good time tonight! This is the fourth bar I've been to. It's what I needed — to relax. I though I'd never get through the day at the bank. Everybody was crabby today. And the construction work outside gave me a splitting headache. And that damn construction is scheduled to go on for five more months!

(He returns to his stool.)

HERB He's turned his back on me. But do I care? I'm strong, I'm mature. But you, Hot Stuff, you're . . . (Fumbles for words.)

DAVID (Looking around) Uh-oh, that

guy's still looking at me.
Usually I like [ ] men, but
he's . . . he's . . .

HERB (Still to audience) Youth, and beauty, that's all they care about! Shallow! Shallow! Shallow!

DAVID (Looking at Herb again) I wonder if I know him from somewhere is that why he keeps staring over here?

HERB He's looking at me! He's looking at me! Oh, my god, maybe he's interested after all! I knew he was a nice guy I could tell right off. Didn't I say that! (Still to audience.) Hi, my name's Herb (David turns away for some other reason.) Hey, don't look away! (David looks back, not hearing him, uncertain whether he knows Herb.) Maybe he'd go home with me if he thought I was special. What can I be? Something pitiful? That's it! Something pitiful, but not downright revolting. How about it if I were . . .blind? That's it! (Herb gets up, pretends to be blind, walks into the pinball machine.) Excuse me, sir. (Feels the machine.) I don't see . . . you see.

DAVID I bet he's on drugs.

HERB Is he cruising me yet? (Looks out the corner of his eye) Must be hell to cruise when you're blind. (David stops paying attention.) Maybe if I were lame. That turns some people on, you know. (Starts to limp past David.)

DAVID I guess that guy's leg went to sleep.

HERB (Trying to be sexy as he limps around) Come and get it, buddy. It's all yours! You like my style?

DAVID I wonder if he picks up much in here. If I were him, I'd try some other method of meeting people — join a club or something. Maybe he's got a lover and doesn't need to meet people. I wish I had one. I admit it! I cannot find a lover.

HERB — I bet he's got a hot lover. I know the type, Greedy. A hot lover and all the tricks he wants. But I don't begrudge him anything. He deserves what he gets because he's so gorgeous. Got any leftovers?

DAVID — (Tiring of the pinball machine) This thing is no fun! (Looks around deciding whether to stay.)

HERB — Don't go! We've only just met!

DAVID — (Looks around) Where did that cute guy go?

HERB — I wonder if he'd take money. Some people don't mind paying — they even get off on it. Me, I mind. Makes me feel terrible.

DAVID Tonight doesn't really seem to be my night. Maybe I should try some other bar. (Looks at his watch.) Although it's almost closing time.

HERB If you leave this bar, I swear I'll never talk to you again! (David goes toward exit, carrying his beer, looking as if he might leave.) I mean it! You're not walking out on me again! What does our relationship mean to you if you come and go anytime you please! Do you ever consider my feelings? Of course not! You can't even stay and have a drink with me, can you? Have to be gallivanting somewhere else! What is it? Do I bore you? Is that it? Are we getting tired of each other after all this time? Go on, tell me. I want to hear you say it. No, don't tell me! I know — I've become predictable. We've known each other all this time and now there's nothing I do or say that you don't already know. I knew it had to end this way. Goodbye! (Turns away.)

DAVID I'd really just sort of like to talk to somebody nice tonight. Just cuddle. I'm not very horny.

HERB I bet you're cutting out on me, aren't you? I've smelled lubricant on your breath. And it wasn't ours! How do you explain that, wise guy? Don't say a word to me, you crud!

DAVID Maybe I should have one more drink here. Who knows. Something might happen with that cute number back there.

(Signals to Bartender.)

HERB Oh, so you've come back, huh? What makes you think I'll take you back? I'm not easy! Don't you ever think you can just sneak back any old time you feel like it!

Don't you forget that I've got
feelings too!

DAVID (To Bartender) Thanks.

BAR'ER Sure thing.

HERB Are you drinking again? I
thought you were over that.
Me — I haven't touched
a drop in months. (Takes a
drink of his Bloody Mary.)
But you, you're incorrigible.
No wonder I left you!

DAVID (To audience) My problem is
that people always relate to
me physically. It's not that I
expect powerful human
interaction every time I meet
somebody. I mean, I am
beyond that kind of utopian
bullshit. But it might be nice
if, just once, somebody didn't
check out my crotch before
they looked in my eyes.

HERB Bartender! Another drink for
a thirsty man, if you would be
so kind!

DAVID Like that guy over there, for instance. What do you want from me, pal? Let me guess. Right? Right! I'm not being vain about it. It just is. But I'm very tired of it. And then you get mad at me because I don't fall all over you because you want me!

HERB (Toasting) To alcohol!

DAVID And if I say something about your attitude, then I'm called egotistical. I'm too concerned with my looks. No, friend, it's *you* who are too concerned with my looks!

HERB Would I like to dance? No, thank you. I'm sitting this one out. Don't bother me. We hunks only go with other hunks.

DAVID People put too much emphasis on sex. It doesn't matter that much. Really. It's a habit. Like drinking. We all have far more sex than we need.

HERB No, no. I don't want you to buy me a drink either! I want to be aloof!

DAVID (Pretending to be Herb) "Hiya, pal? Whatcha doing here tonight? I was noticing you from across the room. You're just what the MD ordered! You live near here? My car's right outside."

HERB (Still turned away from David.) Don't try to make up with me. I've had it with you!

DAVID "What do you mean you don't want to go? My car's right outside! I think you're a doll. Why don't you want to come home with me? How about your place then? I've got some good grass on me. How about a Quaalude? We'll both look better after one or two of these, don't you think? Come on! Come on! What more do you want? Do you think I'm ugly or something? Well, you're not so hot yourself, fuckface!"

HERB (Turning around, but speaking so that David can't hear.) You really are wonderful to look at, do you know that? Beauty is so rare in this world, no wonder we worship it.

DAVID (Being himself, to audience.) Sorry if I sound bitter. But I've been through that so many times I . . . it's flattering the first few hundred times. Then it gets old. Real old.

HERB I wonder if you ever had plastic surgery? Did you? I haven't had it. You find that hard to believe, don't you? Well, it's true. This face is exactly the way God made it.

DAVID Maybe I ought to go home and listen to records. I have a new Beethoven that's a knockout.

HERB I wonder if you would rush over here and kiss me if I had something done to my face.

A tuck here, a tuck there.
Here a tuck. There a tuck.
Everywhere a tuck-tuck. Oh,
fuck!

DAVID Sometimes I think I ought to disfigure myself. At least then I'd know if people liked me, not just the outside of me. Maybe I should put some scars . . . here and here . . . and here. A twisted lip perhaps?

HERB I wonder how much a body overhaul costs. I hear there are these magician-surgeons who tighten and trim and redesign your entire body from scratch. And when they're finished, you are irresistible. Irresistible!

DAVID Maybe if I had some loathsome skin disease. You know, it's not really very satisfying to know that my body inspires — orgasms! I mean, what does that amount to when you actually think about it?

HERB Are my arms too long? I'll have them shortened at once. Well, how do they look now? Oh, you liked them longer?

DAVID All I really want is one person I can love and that loves me!

HERB All I really want is one trick that doesn't throw up when I kiss him!

DAVID I'm going to stop working out at the gym. I've got to take part of the blame for the way I'm treated. I've worked too hard on — (Indicates a part of his body.)

HERB I've always been ugly of course. Ever since I was a child. I remember my mother's first words to my father: "Let's send it back, dear." But I was a stubborn child. I wouldn't go back. I snarled at them and they ran out of the nursery. And naturally I never saw them again. I vowed then that I would not be like most people. If I was ugly okay, I would be the ugliest ugly person in the whole world!

DAVID (Takes a card out of his wallet.) Here is the root of most of my problems — The Hunky Gym and Workout Room.

(Tears up the card.)

HERB And because I was unfit for human intercourse, so to speak, I devoted my energies to my clarinet. It was obviously phallic, but did I care? I practiced in the bathtub. I practiced with the other orphans. I practiced alone . . . a lot. Every time I didn't have sex I got better at my clarinet. Soon I was in demand all over the country. "Play for us!" they cried. And play I did — madly, passionately. "Oh, don't stop!" they yelled. "Don't ever, ever stop!"

DAVID Time I took control of my life

and made it into what I want
— not what others want!

HERB And now I have the most musical fingers of all the clarinetists of all the symphony orchestras of all the nations of all the planets of all the solar systems in the universe! And am I happy? Damn right, I'm happy!

DAVID There must be more to life than sex! Four out of five tricks end in divorce!

HERB (Loudly) I play like an angel because I can't get laid!

DAVID (Loudly) Isn't there anybody here that I can love?

BAR'ER (Louder still) Last call!

HERB Is it really? I only just got here!

BAR'ER Afraid so.

HERB Well, one more Bloody Mary then! What the hell! And

another beer for my friend
over there.

BAR'ER (As he serves the drinks) Another one from your secret admirer.

DAVID Thanks, but I think I've had enough. Why don't you have it? (Bartender shrugs, pours beer into a glass, takes a sip.)

HERB My gift spurned? Given away? Doesn't bother me. I have other things to think about! For instance, I haven't played the pinball machine all night! The Mafia that owns it will be incensed. (Goes to it.) Look at those lines. Feel that wood, that plastic. I could go for you, baby!

DAVID (To bartender) That guy's pretty drunk, isn't he?

BAR'ER Yeah, I guess. He's been in here a few times before. Business is slow tonight or I would have thrown him out.

DAVID Oh, he's not hurting anybody.

BAR'ER (To Herb, who is hugging the pinball machine) Hey, buddy, you have to pay for any damage to the machine!

HERB (Looking at him) I wouldn't hurt this machine. I love this machine. And this machine is . . . taken with me. (Softer) It doesn't hurt anything to love it . . . (To Bartender) We're inseparable.

BAR'ER (Under his breath) You're insufferable.

HERB (To the machine) Do you come here often? Oh, you're a regular? Funny, I've never noticed you before. But then I don't come here that often. Do you live nearby? I live j just a dozen blocks away. You're from out of town, huh? Staying in a hotel? That can be pretty expensive. I know, because I travel. I play in a symphony. Yes, that's right. Do you like classical music? You do! Isn't that a coincidence! Well, it looks like we have something in common.

BAR'ER (Calling to Herb) We close in ten minutes!

HERB (To machine) You hear that doll? We'd better be on our way before they kick us out. But, no, you probably don't go out with customers, do you? Could you make an exception for little old me? What do you say? Pretty please. I couldn't help noticing your pretty lights. And your balls are terrific! I could really go for you. (Starts to hump the pinball machine.) Oh, baby! Hey, you've got it!

BAR'ER (Noticing Herb) Christ! (He goes over and pulls the plug on the pinball machine. The lights go out.) Night's over, buddy! Better head on home.

HERB (Still hugging the machine) But this machine and I have fallen for each other. I am asking for its hand in marriage.

BAR'ER Yeah, yeah. Closing up, pal. Finish up your drink now.

HERB Can I take this machine home with me.

BAR'ER (Patronizing him) Yeah, yeah.

(He starts to clean up, turns on the bar lights.)

HERB (Tries to lift machine.) We're going home together! Don't try to stop us! We know it's against the law, but we defy you!

BAR'ER Want some coffee, pal?

HERB I do not! I want this machine! How much will you take for it?

BAR'ER It's not for sale.

HERB Please!

BAR'ER Hey, buddy!

HERB Okay, okay! I get your message. (Looks at the machine again, tenderly.) Well, I guess this is goodbye . . . Will you wait for me? I'll come back, I promise. I do promise! (Kisses machine.) Thank you for a wonderful, wonderful time . . . Good night. (Walks away, looking back longingly, his voice breaking.) I love you!

DAVID (Finishing his beer, getting up as Herb goes past him, to the bartender) Well, I guess I better call it a night.

(Leaves a tip on the bar.)

BAR'ER Thanks!

HERB (To machine) Goodbye! (Bumps into David.) Excuse me.

DAVID Sure thing. (They are finally

standing face to face; they look directly at each other for the very first time.)

HERB (Suddenly grabbing David's arm) I like you! I want you to come home with me.

DAVID Hey! Hey! (Tries to pull free.) Let go of my arm!

HERB I'm not going to let go until you come with me!

DAVID Hey, you're drunk!

HERB You have a gift for the obvious.

DAVID Would you mind letting go of my arm?

HERB Why don't you come home with me?

DAVID I'm trying to be polite now!

HERB You think I'm ugly, don't you? Just because you're good-looking you think you can get anybody you want

and the rest of us can go
home alone!

DAVID (Angrily) Let go of my arm!

HERB (Letting go) Take your
fucking arm. I don't want it!

DAVID (Rubs his arm.) Goddamn!

HERB Show a little interest in someone and this is what you get.

DAVID You've no right to touch me.

HERB It's the only affection I've
had all night.

DAVID I'm sorry about your
problems. But you can't take
them out on me.

HERB You think you're hot shit,
don't you?

DAVID Hey, I don't need this. I've
got my own problems.

BAR'ER (Noticing) You better be
leaving, pal.

HERB I'll leave when I'm good and ready. I've been kicked out of better places than this!

BAR'ER (Moving towards Herb) Good night, buddy!

HERB Wait! I have one thing to say. And only one thing. (Turns to the Bartender.) How about you? Do you want to come home with me?

BAR'ER Come on, pal! Come on! (As he escorts Herb to the door, he calls out to the room in general) Okay, everybody! We're closing!

HERB (Turning back to David) I hate handsome men!

DAVID You ugly guys make me sick! You only want the good-looking ones, too! If you're so frustrated, why don't you have sex with people who look like *you*!

HERB (Obviously hurt by the remark) That wasn't nice.

BAR'ER (Forcing him out the door) Goodnight, buddy!

HERB That wasn't nice at all. (Herb exits.)

BAR'ER (Calling after Herb) And don't come back here either! You're 86ed!

(Pause.)

DAVID Why do things have to be like that?

BAR'ER I have stuff like that all the time.

DAVID How do you put up with it?

BAR'ER That's the way it is.

DAVID I felt sorry for him. . . I didn't just want to make it with him. Maybe if he could get someone to massage his back . . . to hold him, he'd be . . .

BAR'ER Yeah, I suppose. (Bartender and David look at each other.) Live around here?

DAVID Not too far. How about you?

BAR'ER I live upstairs.

DAVID Pretty close, huh?

BAR'ER I got a new stereo. Great sound.

DAVID You live alone?

BAR'ER At the moment, yes. How about you?

DAVID The same.

BAR'ER Got plans for the rest of the night?

DAVID Not really.

BAR'ER How would you like to see my new stereo? I've got the new [name of the latest pop singer] album.

DAVID That sounds interesting. (David smiles.)

BAR'ER (Smiles too, leans over and kisses David.) I'll try to

make it interesting . . .
(He takes David's beer
bottle; their hands touch
briefly. The Bartender goes
around to make sure
everyone has left.) Okay,
everybody! Out! Out! Out!
(He comes back, straightens
out the bar stools, gives the
bar a final wipe.

(David is waiting for him near the exit. The Bartender gives a last look around, turns back to David, eyeing him.)

You're very attractive, you
know that?

DAVID (Sort of sadly) Yeah . . . so
I've been told.

(The Bartender turns off the lights.)

Slow Fade.

COMEBACK
— a musical

[Book by Daniel Curzon, music by Dan Turner, lyrics by Curzon and Turner , this show was begun in 1978 and had a staged reading
at the Berkeley Stage Company in 1980 and at the Noe Valley Ministry in San Francisco in 1987.]

ACT I

Scene 1

CHARACTERS:
ROSALIND, 30-60, a cabaret singer who used to be a man
GEORGE, 30-60, the earlier male self
ALEX, same age range, Rosalind's unsuspecting fiancé
ASSISTANT, any age, versatile male to play many extra parts

SETTING: A dressing room with one bare light, backstage at a cabaret. There is a dressing table, a chaise lounge, and various posters of past performers, including one of GEORGE SMITH. There is a door that leads to the stage. In center stage is a full-length "mirror" that acts as an entranceway and exit for visitors from the past and future.

AT RISE: The door opens and a woman (ROSALIND) enters quickly, carrying a dress and a cosmetics case. She looks around as if unsure of herself, then sets the cosmetics case on the dressing table and hangs the dress on a Chinese screen. She examines the framed star posters of those who have entertained at the club in the past. As she takes the picture of GEORGE — his former self — in her hands she says:

ROSALIND Goodbye, George.

(Dim applause begins to build, surprising her. We hear "A Guy I Know.")

(ROSALIND grows cold and nervous and puts the picture back on the wall. She goes to her cosmetic case, takes items out, starting to get ready for a performance. But she can't ignore the poster or the song and returns to the picture and turns it around. Again she goes to the dressing table. Finally she returns to the poster of GEORGE and removes it from the wall and starts to throw it away — but once more she can't. She goes back to the dressing table. Finally at the end of the song she takes GEORGE'S picture and throws it into a trash container and wipes her hands.)

GEORGE (singing, perhaps partly visible on stage)

A GUY I KNOW

THERE'S A GUY I KNOW,
GOT A BRAIN LIKE A DYNAMO.
THERE'S NO DOUBT!
SHOUT IT OUT!
THERE'S A GUY WHO'S TOUGH.
WHEN HE FIGHTS YOU DON'T SEE HIM PUFF.
THERE'S NO DOUBT! SHOUT IT OUT! LOUD!
HE'S GOT A JAW THAT ISN'T GLASS.
SO DON'T YOU GIVE HIM ANY SASS.
'CAUSE IF YOU DO, HE'LL WHIP YOUR ASS!

Comeback

YOU'LL LIKE THIS GUY 'CAUSE
HE NEVER WAILS.
YOU'LL LIKE THIS GUY 'CAUSE
HE'S TOUGH AS NAILS.
SOME FOLKS HATE HIM.
THEY'RE NOT HIS BEST FAN.
HE'S NO SISSY.
HE'S JUST ALL MAN!
SOME FOLKS TELL HIM
HE SHOULD BE MODEST.
HOW CAN HE BE?
HE KNOWS HE'S BEST!
I KNOW A GUY — GUESS WHO?
WORKING HARD'S WHAT HE
LIKES TO DO.
DO YOU HEAR?
IS IT CLEAR WHO?
HE'S GOT A JAW THAT ISN'T
GLASS.
SO DON'T YOU GIVE HIM ANY
SASS.
'CAUSE IF YOU DO, HE'LL WHIP
YOUR ASS!
HE ISN'T RICH,
BUT HE'S GOT HIS PRIDE.
HE DIGS A DITCH,
BUT HE'S GOT HIS PRIDE.
YES, LIFE'S A BITCH,
BUT HE'S GOT HIS PRIDE!

(Suddenly the dressing room door opens and ALEX — the fiancé — enters with a newspaper.)

ROSALIND Alex! I'm so glad you made it! I'm late! I'm so nervous! Have you seen the crowd out there? They're putting in extra chairs. Did your sister come? (closer to him) You've been so patient with me. (putting an arm around him) Thank you for making this a wonderful debut!

ALEX (pulling away) Don't you mean "comeback"?

(He waves the tabloid newspaper.)

ROSALIND What is it?

ALEX (Doesn't answer.)

ROSALIND Alex?

ALEX You know what's in here.

ROSALIND	Is it about the show? . . . (realizing what he knows) Oh, no! They put it in the newspaper? They didn't!
ALEX	You can imagine my surprise. Why didn't you tell me, Rosalind?
ROSALIND	(speechless, paralyzed)
ALEX	Why didn't you tell me who you used to be?
ROSALIND	. . . I couldn't.
ALEX	(flabbergasted) You don't think I'd be interested that you used to be a man? You lied to me. . . . You lied.
ROSALIND	I didn't lie. I just didn't say anything.
ALEX	You don't consider that a lie?
ROSALIND	Do you want me to

make excuses? I didn't tell you because . . . because — I don't know the reason.

ALEX Bullshit! You didn't tell me because you didn't want to lose me.

ROSALIND I didn't tell you because I didn't want to hurt you.

ALEX Don't you think I'm hurting now? What am I supposed to do — ignore this? (Holds up the newspaper.) Is it true? What does it make me?

ROSALIND Yes . . . it's true. Are you afraid of what people may think? Isn't that it? What the folks back home will talk about at the neighbor-hood picnic?

ALEX This news about you

was rather sudden, Rosalind! (Throws the newspaper down.) Did you plan this? I can't think of a better publicity stunt!

ROSALIND — No. I didn't want this. I wanted to keep it a secret.

ALEX — Well, it's not a secret anymore. Why do you think you have such a big crowd out there? (Points offstage.) What do you suppose they've come to see? What do you suppose?

ROSALIND — Oh, God! (touching her mouth anxiously)

ALEX — Okay — from them maybe I can understand, but how could you want to keep it a secret from me?

ROSALIND — It was so romantic, Alex.

I just couldn't tell you. I wanted to enjoy the moment. I started to tell you that first time you kissed me. I didn't. Then the moment turned into months and —

ALEX — And the months have turned into now!

(The ASSISTANT enters as the STAGE MANAGER.)

STAGE MANAGER — (knocking as he enters) Ten minutes, Ms. Smith! (He sees that something is amiss and backs out.)

ALEX — Well, what am I supposed to do next — just forget about it? I can't, Rosalind! We've got to settle this.

ROSALIND — Don't drive me crazy before I have to go out there! (gently) If I had told you, would you have accepted my past?

ALEX — I don't know . . .

ROSALIND — Is it because I didn't tell you or because of *what* I didn't tell?

ALEX — Of course I don't know about that either.

ROSALIND — (hurt) I see . . .

ALEX — You have to grant me the right to be at least shaken up over all this. I'm a simple guy, Rosalind, that's all. I don't mean to put you down — honest. I don't know . . . I just don't know about all this sex stuff. And now, here I am right in the middle of it. And you didn't even tell me?

ROSALIND — Will you give me time to explain?

ALEX	You have a show to do. I'd better go. (Starts to leave.)
ROSALIND	Will you come back later, after the show?
ALEX	(at the door) I don't know how to answer that. Excuse me, but I just don't know! (He exits too quickly.)
ROSALIND	(She follows him to the door.) Alex! Damn! . . . I think you've answered it.

(She stands in the middle of the room looking at herself in the full-length mirror, then lies the chaise lounge, dejected. She touches her throbbing head.) What am I going to do?

<u>Scene 2</u>

(The dressing room mirror lights come up as GEORGE walks through the mirror frame from the dark side. He is carrying a bouquet of flowers. ROSALIND, aware of his presence, slowly sits up on the couch.)

ROSALIND George, is that you?

GEORGE (checking the trash) You threw away my picture, Rosalind. How could you?

ROSALIND What are you doing here?

GEORGE I've brought flowers for your opening.

ROSALIND I won't accept flowers from the grave.

GEORGE (sets the flowers on the dressing table, primps in the mirror) You know you couldn't go on without me.

ROSALIND I thought I killed you.

GEORGE Any bets on that?

ROSALIND Leave me alone,

	George. You don't exist!
GEORGE	The cat's out of the bag, Ms. Smith. That crowd out there? They haven't come to see a woman. They've come to see what's left of me. (Holds up the newspaper) "Ex-Singing Star Is Ex-Man!"
ROSALIND	I got rid of you before. I can do it again. Get out!
GEORGE	You've got to expect them to be curious. What if [male star] came back as [female star]?
ROSALIND	Go away!
GEORGE	For now! (GEORGE shrugs and passes through the mirror.) See you!
ROSALIND	(singing)

I USED TO BE A STAR

WHAT AM I GOING TO SAY?
HOW AM I GOING TO SAY
HELLO, REMEMBER ME?
HELLO, REMEMBER ME?
I USED TO BE A STAR!
HOW DO YOU LIKE IT SO FAR?
AREN'T YOU THRILLED THAT I'M
HERE?
SHOULD I BRAG ABOUT WHAT I
USED TO BE?
OR WILL THAT MAKE THEM HATE
ME?
WILL THEY DESPISE ME FOR
MAKING A CHANGE,
OR WILL THEY LIKE WHAT THEY
SEE?
WHAT ARE THEY GOING TO SAY?
WHAT ARE THEY GOING TO
THINK?
WILL THEY SAY "FABULOUS"?
OR WILL THEY SAY "YOU STINK"?
WHAT IS ALEX GOING TO SAY?
WHAT IS ALEX GOING TO FEEL?
WILL HE LOVE ME AS HE DID?
OR WILL HE THINK THAT I'M NOT
REAL?
HELLO, REMEMBER ME?
HELLO, REMEMBER ME?
I USED TO BE A STAR!

SHOULD I FORGET ABOUT A
CAREER,
OR DO IT NO MATTER WHAT
ANYONE SAYS?
WHO THE HELL ARE THEY?
WHAT DO THEY KNOW?
WHAT THE HELL DO I KNOW?
I MUSTN'T BE TOO BOLD.
I MUSTN'T BE TOO SHY.
AND IF THEY DON'T WANT ME,
ALL I WILL DO IS DIE.
IT'S ONLY BEEN FOUR YEARS
SINCE I COULD FILL A HALL.
IT'S ONLY BEEN FOUR YEARS.
THEY'VE COME TO SNICKER
WHEN I FALL.
HAVE I GOT IT ANYMORE?
DID I EVER REALLY HAVE IT?
SHOULD I GIVE THEM
EVERYTHING I'VE GOT?
OR SHOULD I MAKE THEM BEG
FOR IT?
WHAT DO YOU DO WHEN NO ONE
BEGS FOR IT?
DO YOU FADE AWAY AND DIE?
OR GIVE IT ONE MORE TRY?
ALEX, REMEMBER ME?
DO YOU ALL REMEMBER ME?
I USED TO BE A STAR!

(At the end of the song, she turns to the mirror.)

ROSALIND George? Are you there?

GEORGE (appearing) Y- e - s- s?

ROSALIND What am I going to do?

GEORGE Are you asking me to stay?

ROSALIND Only for a moment. And then you have to leave — permanently.

GEORGE Has it ever crossed your mind that maybe, just maybe, our little operation was a mistake?

ROSALIND It wasn't a mistake.

GEORGE Naturally you'd say that. All that pain we went through, mental and otherwise, has to mean something, doesn't it?

ROSALIND It was your idea!

GEORGE My idea! All I was doing was standing in front of the mirror — bored — looking at my body, thinking I needed to lose a pound or two. At most a face-lift!

GEORGE (singing)

CHANGE

OH, I NEED A CHANGE! I'M TIRED
OF BEING SO BANAL AND TAME.
I NEED A CHANGE! I'M BORED TO
TEARS ALWAYS STAYING THE
SAME.
AND SO — I'LL TAKE OFF
THESE CLOTHES — MAYBE THIS
NOSE —
EVERYTHING GOES!
OH, I NEED A CHANGE! I'M SICK
AS CAN BE OF THIS DREADFUL
ENNUI.
I NEED A CHANGE! FED UP TO
HERE WITH THIS PERSON CALLED
ME.

AND SO, I'LL DO AS I PLEASE!
REFURBISH THESE [meaning hips],
EVEN MY KNEES!
OH, I NEED A
CHANGE! ALTHOUGH FILLED
WITH DREAD I WILL EAT
NO MORE BREAD!
I NEED A CHANGE! THIS IS THE
END OF ALL SNACKS IN MY BED.
OH YEAH, EVERYBODY NEEDS A
CHANGE! IT'S SO NICE TO RE-
ARRANGE!
NO — IT'S NOT A PHASE!
THERE'LL BE LOTS OF PRAISE!
BUT NO
MAYONNAISE!
OH, FAT WILL DISAPPEAR, IF I
PERSEVERE! WHO THE HELL
NEEDS BEER!
EVERYBODY NEEDS A CHANGE!

ROSALIND (dancing a tango with GEORGE) George!

GEORGE What?

ROSALIND I'm thinking about doing something.

GEORGE (playing along, in sing-song) I know!

ROSALIND What do you think of the idea?

GEORGE Don't ask and you won't be disappointed!

ROSALIND I want to be born.

GEORGE Pardon me. I don't want to die.

ROSALIND I've been inside you for years, screaming to get out.

GEORGE Maybe there's another me inside *you* screaming to get out!

ROSALIND Be serious about this!

(Tries to stop dancing.)

GEORGE Keep dancing! If we get serious, I may start to cry.

ROSALIND (stopping) It's what I've always secretly wanted. I've been miserable for so long. You know that,

George. All the ways I've tried for ail these years to drown out these feelings. You know — you know what I mean!

GEORGE — Do you have any idea what you're asking of me? They're going to —

ROSALIND — Please, George, please!

GEORGE — Talk about a castrating woman!

ROSALIND — No, it will be wonderful! (singing second verse)

CHANGE

OH, I'LL HAVE A CHANGE! I'VE MADE UP MY MIND THAT IT'S TIME TO BEGIN.
I'LL HAVE A CHANGE. UP WITH MY CHIN, AND I'LL BE FEMININE.
AND SO, I'LL KNOW WHO I'LL BE!
HELLO TO ME! THANKS, DEAR M.D.

OH, I'LL HAVE A CHANGE!
I THINK IT'S BIZARRE NOT TO
KNOW WHO YOU ARE.
I'LL HAVE A CHANGE! NO ONE
CAN TELL ME I'M GOING TOO
FAR!
AND SO, IF I MODERNIZE, I'LL
SCANDALIZE, NO COMPROMISE!
OH, I'LL HAVE A CHANGE! I'LL
TURN BACK THE CLOCKS.
OH, I'LL BE SUCH A FOX. I'LL
HAVE A CHANGE.
WHY SHOULD WE ALL HAVE TO
BE ORTHODOX?
OH YEAH, EVERYBODY NEEDS A
CHANGE!
IT'S SO NICE TO RE-ARRANGE!
OH, HE'LL FIX THESE BREASTS!
WHO WANTS SECOND-BESTS!
THEY'LL PASS ALL THE TESTS!
OH, I CAN GET THE KNACK.
THERE'S NO TURNING BACK!
HOPE HE'S NOT A QUACK!
EVERYBODY NEEDS A CHANGE!
OLE!

GEORGE (gesturing at his body) Well, apparently you won that round, didn't you?

ROSALIND Don't be a sore loser, George. Scars, wounds — they all pass with time.

GEORGE Do you know what you are?

ROSALIND I have a feeling you're going to tell me.

GEORGE You, my dear, are a conventional, role-playing, unliberated capon!

ROSALIND That kind of remark is why I don't want you around. You're pushy and intrusive — and suffer from far too much testosterone!

GEORGE Go on! Even a bad review — as long as you spell my name right! G-E-O-R —

ROSALIND Let me spell the ways — you're insensitive, demanding, jealous —

and besides you're
horny ail the time!

GEORGE — You've forgotten ruthless, stubborn, loud, to say nothing of talented!

ROSALIND — I don't want to argue or compete with you, George. You've had your years — your turn. Now I want my chance.

GEORGE — But what do they want? (pointing to offstage audience)

(ROSALIND starts to get dressed.)

ROSALIND — (singing)

JUST AS I AM

NO MATTER HOW PEOPLE TALK,
NO MATTER HOW GREAT THE PROBLEM,
OR WHO MAY DISAGREE,
ALL I AM IS JUST ME.

Comeback

I DON'T KNOW WHAT I SHOULD
SAY.
I DON'T KNOW WHAT I CAN
PROMISE.
WILL THEY LIKE WHAT THEY
SEE?
ALL I AM IS JUST ME.
AND IF I SHOULD ASK YOU
IF YOU COULD LOVE ME,
OH PLEASE GOD, DON'T ANSWER
THAT YOU'RE SO SORRY.
FORGIVE ME IF I'M TOO PLAIN.
FORGIVE ME IF I'M NOT
CAUTIOUS.
THAT'S THE WAY I MUST BE.
ALL I AM IS JUST ME.
I'M NOT AS BRAVE AS I SEEM.
I'M NOT SURE WHICH WAY IS
FORWARD.
BUT I HOPE TO BE FREE.
ALL I AM IS JUST ME.
AND IF I SHOULD ASK YOU
IF YOU COULD LOVE ME,
OH PLEASE GOD, DON'T ANSWER
THAT YOU'RE SO SORRY.
PLEASE LOVE ME JUST AS I AM!
DON'T DESERT ME!
PLEASE LOVE ME JUST AS I AM!
AND DON'T HURT ME!
PLEASE LOVE ME JUST AS I AM.
FOR WITHOUT YOU I'M DAMNED!

GEORGE (Yawns.) Oh, is it finished? (Yawns again.)

ROSALIND Oh god, that might happen! Is there anything worse than offering yourself like some package of cookies on a shelf, and they put you back, and they put you back — shiny wrapper and all! (referring to her dress)

GEORGE (referring to his new body) It'll take more than a shiny new wrapper, cookie! Maybe if you stick with my hits, they'll pay attention. (sings)

THERE'S A GUY I KNOW!
GOT A BRAIN LIKE A DYNAMO!

ROSALIND That's not my style anymore, George.

GEORGE	It worked before. What's wrong with it?
ROSALIND	It's vulgar.
GEORGE	Me vulgar?
ROSALIND	An audience likes something new. Something artistic.
GEORGE	Don't deceive yourself! (singing)

HOW TO SELL A SONG

IF YOU WANT TO SELL A SONG,
IF YOU WANT TO BE A HIT,
THERE'S ONE RULE YOU HAVE TO FOLLOW,
AND YOU'RE LOOKING RIGHT AT IT!
PUT AWAY THOSE STUFFY ART THINGS.
GIVE 'EM LOTS OF SUDS.
DO A NUMBER ON THEIR HEART-STRINGS.
EVERYBODY DOES.
IF YOU WANT TO BE A SMASH,
IF YOU WANT TO MAKE IT STICK,

GET YOURSELF SOME GREAT
ARRANGEMENTS,
AND BE SURE TO MAKE 'EM
SLICK.
GIVE 'EM CHRISTMAS. THROW IN
NEW YEAR'S.
EVEN KISS THEIR KIDS.
HOWDY-DO'S AND HALLELUJAHS
—
THAT'S THE WAY IT IS!

ROSALIND (singing)

TRUTH, WHY CAN'T THERE BE
TRUTH?
IS IT ALL ILLUSIONS?
(I NEED SOME VERMOUTH.)
WHY CAN'T MY SONG JUST BE
SMALL
IF THAT SIZE TELLS IT ALL?
CRASS, WHY MUST IT BE CRASS?
WILL EVERYTHING SHATTER
IF NOT MADE OF BRASS?
I'M SURE THEY WON'T HEAR A
NOTE
WHEN YOU'VE DONE IT BY ROTE,
'CAUSE PEOPLE WON'T BELIEVE
IN YOU!

GEORGE (singing)

LISTEN, SWEETIE! GET IT STRAIGHT.
FOLKS WON'T PAY FOR WHAT THEY HATE.
IF YOU WANT TO MAKE THE BUCKS,
GIVE 'EM GLITZ ALTHOUGH IT SUCKS.

ROSALIND (singing)

HE WHO SELLS COUNTERFEITS
ALWAYS A CRIME COMMITS.
MUST WE BE BOISTEROUS AND BRASH?
IT'S ONLY MERCHANDISE
WHEN IT'S BEEN MADE OF LIES.
CONNOSIEURS MIGHT CALL IT TRASH.

GEORGE (singing)

GET IT THROUGH YOUR LITTLE SKULL:
DRACHMAS DON'T COME IF YOU'RE DULL.
BOSSES DON'T CARE IF IT STINKS,
JUST AS LONG AS IT SELLS DRINKS.

ROSALIND (singing)

SINGERS IN CABARETS
WHO ACT LIKE SALOMES,
SERVING UP SONGS TILL YOU'RE DEAD,
FLAUNTING IN ALL THEIR SETS
SHOULD REALLY VEIL THEIR THREATS —
OR BE BEHEADED INSTEAD!

GEORGE (singing)

SELL IT HARD OR THEY WILL SNORE.

ROSALIND (singing)

MUST I SELL IT LIKE A WHORE?
I KNOW HOW TO SPILL MY GUTS.

GEORGE (singing)

BABE, YOU GOT TO GRAB THEIR NUTS!

ROSALIND (singing)

I KNOW JUST WHAT YOU MEAN.
YOU WANT IT PHILISTINE.
I WANT IT POLISHED AND FINE!

GEORGE (singing)

SINGERS WHO PACK THEIR
SHOWS
KNOW HOW TO ACT LIKE PRO'S.

ROSALIND (singing)

THE WAY TO DO IT IS MINE!

GEORGE (singing)

THE WAY TO DO IT IS MINE!

BOTH (harmonizing)

THE WAY TO DO IT IS MINE!

(They laugh together as the song ends, showing a little camaraderie.)

GEORGE I've got the solution!
Why don't we do a duo!

ROSALIND Good try, George. But
no thanks.

GEORGE But I'm unemployed
now — thanks to you.
Give a guy a break!

ROSALIND No, George!

GEORGE — (in mock agony) Please!

ROSALIND — I can't! Alex has you on his mind already — you bother him. You need to disappear once and for all.

GEORGE — But I have insights where men are concerned! Really! If you want to keep your lover, you'd better listen to old George.

ROSALIND — I'm afraid from now on, on and offstage, it's a one-woman show!

GEORGE — (pause) So — what's it like?

ROSALIND — What's what like?

GEORGE — Being a woman.

ROSALIND — Well, for one thing, people don't listen to you as much as they do when you're a man. (pointedly) For

	instance, they don't leave when you ask them to.
GEORGE	Is that a hint? You need me around, to remind you of things.
ROSALIND	Like what?
GEORGE	Well, it wasn't so long ago when some person of your description, as I recall, absent-mindedly found herself standing in front of a urinal in the men's room of a fashionable downtown restaurant.
ROSALIND	(brushing his hair) Á little slip. I'd had a little too much wine, that's all.
GEORGE	You don't really mind if I stay, do you? I won't be any trouble.
ROSALIND	You already are trouble.

GEORGE — Don't patronize me! I've asked you nicely.

ROSALIND — No.

GEORGE — Okay, Rosalind, if I can't make this comeback with you, you're not going to make it either!

ROSALIND — What are you talking about? You can't stop me.

GEORGE — Watch me! There's someone I'd like you to meet. (calling at the mirror) Ronnie?

Scene 3

(The ASSISTANT enters through the mirror as RONNIE.)

ROSALIND — (surprised) Ronnie! How are you?

RONNIE — Hello, dad. I heard you're going to be in show business again.

ROSALIND	Yes. (pause) I'm thinking about it.
RONNIE	I suppose you want me to sit in the audience and say, "Hey, that's my mommy up there! *People* magazine might pick it up! Maybe you'll make the cover of *Time* — "Man of the Year"!
ROSALIND	Do you dislike me that much?
RONNIE	It isn't pleasant being rejected — as you'll soon find out on stage.
ROSALIND	I didn't reject you! When your mother died, I took you on the road with me. But you —
RONNIE	But I what?
ROSALIND	You became such a problem I couldn't take you anywhere, so I . . . so I —

RONNIE	So you hired a keeper for the poor little monster. If you'd cared about me, you'd have gotten another kind of job and stayed home like a normal person. But why should I have expected anything from you? I'm only your only child!
ROSALIND	When I did see you, you wouldn't let me touch you. I gave you pets and you mistreated them.
RONNIE	Yeah, at least that was fun!
ROSALIND	You would have driven me insane. We simply didn't get along.
RONNIE	Parents are supposed to like their kids. It's considered a package deal! But your great "career" in plush beer joints — excuse me,

champagne joints — was more important than me!

ROSALIND Sometimes we have to choose.

RONNIE I didn't have a choice. I didn't have a mother or a father. But lucky me — no, I have both! Hello — you mother-father! You think being a great performer is more important than any number of ordinary children.

ROSALIND That's not true. I'm not so sure I'm a great performer.

RONNIE Don't be so sure I'm so ordinary!

ROSALIND (gently) I never even thought it.

RONNIE Okay, okay, so it was the way I thought about myself, being compared to such a famous father.

ROSALIND	We wanted things from each other we couldn't get — or give.
RONNIE	Is that the most you can say?
ROSALIND	(hurting) I hating to say it, but parents don't always love their children.
RONNIE	Children don't always love their parents either!
ROSALIND	(moving toward him) Ronnie, maybe I can . . .
GEORGE	It's too late. He's grown up. You think you can make up for the past with a few motherly hugs now?
ROSALIND	(singing)

TWO LULLABIES

WHEN YOU HUG ME IN THE DARK
AND TELL ME YOU'RE NOT
SCARED,

WHEN I TUCK YOU IN TO BED
WITH STORIES WE HAVE SHARED,
WHEN YOU SLEEP UPON MY LAP,
I ROCK YOU TO AND FRO,
WHEN YOUR FINGERS CLING TO
MINE, THEN MOMMY LOVES YOU
SO.
BUT THERE ARE THOSE OTHER
TIMES,
THOUGH I LOVE YOU LOTS,
I TRY HARD TO KEEP THEM STILL,
BUT I HAVE OTHER THOUGHTS.

GEORGE (singing)

I DON'T MISS YOU AT ALL. I
DON'T MISS YOU A TAT.
YOU ARE LAZY, DEFICIENT, A
DUMPY LITTLE BRAT.
YOU WON'T EAT YOUR VEGIES.
YOUR HAIR IS LANK AND LIMP.
TAKEN ALL TOGETHER, DEAR,
YOU'RE SOMETHING OF A WIMP,
WHO'S GIVEN HIS FATHER JUST
NOTHING BUT PAIN.
YOU NEED PSYCHOANALYSIS
AND CRUTCHES FOR YOUR
BRAIN.

ROSALIND (singing)

THEN YOU KISS ME ON THE
CHEEK AND DRIVE AWAY THE
ACHE.
THEN I REALIZE THAT KIDS CAN
GIVE AND NOT JUST TAKE.
WHEN YOU LAUGH AND TICKLE
ME AND SAY YOU THINK I'M FUN.
WHEN YOU SAY YOU LOVE ME
TOO, I MELT 'CAUSE YOU'RE MY
SON.
BUT THERE ARE THOSE OTHER
TIMES,
THOUGH I LOVE YOU LOTS.
I TRY HARD TO KEEP THEM STILL,
BUT I HAVE OTHER THOUGHTS.

GEORGE (singing)

I DON'T MISS YOU AT ALL. I
DON'T MISS YOU ONE BIT.
YOU ARE GROUCHY,
DEMANDING, AND ALWAYS IN A
SNIT.
AND NO ONE CAN TELL YOU THE
WAY YOU SHOULD BEHAVE.
YOU ARE UNHOUSEBREAKABLE
AND SHOULD LIVE IN A CAVE,
WAY UP IN THE MOUNTAINS OR
ELSE DOWN IN A HOLE.

TELL ME WHY MY DARLING
CUPIE DOLL TURNED INTO SUCH
A TROLL.

BOTH (singing)

SWEET AND SOUR'S WHAT YOU
WERE,
THAT WE ALWAYS KNEW.

ROSALIND (singing)

FOR THE SWEET I GIVE YOU
THANKS —

GEORGE (singing)

AND HOPE YOU HAVE KIDS TOO!

ROSALIND Now that you're grown up, Ron, can't we at least be friends?

RON You don't seem to realize. I don't approve of what you're doing. (angry) I don't approve! People know I'm George Smith's son. How do you think I'll feel when my father appears prancing around on the stage in a dress?

ROSALIND What am I supposed to say?

RON You don't have to say anything! Just let me say something. If you go out on that stage tonight, I'll never speak to you again! (Exiting through the mirror) Kisses on your opening, Rosalind!

GEORGE (with a double meaning) Yeah, kisses on your opening, Rosalind! Aren't you glad you became a "mother"?

(ROSALIND stands looking after her son)

Ros, what's wrong? We're all sure you did the right thing!

ROSALIND (with desperation)
Alex! Alex! Where are you?

Scene 4

(ALEX appears through the lighted mirror. ROSALIND reaches for him. He reaches for her.)

GEORGE (stepping between them before their hands touch) (to ALEX)

(singing)

HELLO, REMEMBER ME?
HELLO, REMEMBER ME?

ALEX Yes. You're George Smith. We met.

GEORGE He remembers me, Rosalind!

ROSALIND He remembers who you *were*.

GEORGE I loved you, a long time ago.

ALEX (uncomfortable because it's a man) You did?

GEORGE From afar. Didn't you notice?

ALEX Well, I don't know if . . .

ROSALIND But now I've changed. Utterly.

GEORGE No I haven't!

ALEX (confused) I see.

ROSALIND Do you think you could love me now?

GEORGE He remembers *me*, Rosalind, and he always will!

ROSALIND No! Alex, dance with me! Please.

ALEX Dance with you?

ROSALIND Let's try. Please. I want to be held.

(ALEX hesitantly takes her in his arms; they begin to dance.)

ROSALIND That's not me anymore!

GEORGE Ah, that could have been me. If only . . . If only . . .

GEORGE (singing)

I MADE A FOOL OF MYSELF FOR LOVE

I MADE A FOOL OF MYSELF FOR LOVE.
I WANTED SOMEONE WHO DIDN'T WANT ME.
NO QUARRELS OF COURSE. NO CHANCE FOR DIVORCE.
SOMETHING THAT DOESN'T START CAN'T FALL APART.
I MADE A FOOL OF MYSELF FOR LOVE.
I YEARNED FOR SOMEONE WHO DIDN'T NEED ME.
THE LITTLE TOY BOAT I SAILED WOULDN'T FLOAT.
I GUESS THOSE HOLIDAYS WERE JUST A PHASE.

EVERY NOW AND THEN I PAUSE
AND THINK ABOUT THE CAUSE,
AND WONDER IF YOU WONDER
WHAT'S BECOME OF ME.

(GEORGE cuts in on ROSALIND, asking ALEX to dance. ALEX feels awkward, looks at ROSALIND, refuses, and disappears through the mirror.)

ROSALIND Don't go!

(singing second verse)

I MADE A FOOL OF MYSELF FOR LOVE.
I CRIED FOR SOMEONE WHO WOULDN'T TOUCH ME.
INSIDE THERE'S A BRUISE. HOW COULD YOU REFUSE?
HOW ODD THAT I SHOULD FEEL WHAT WASN'T REAL.
I MADE A FOOL OF MYSELF FOR LOVE.
I WANTED SOMEONE WHO DIDN'T WANT ME.
I HOPED WE WOULD DANCE,
HAVE WINE AND ROMANCE.
THE WINE WAS LEMONADE. NO MUSIC PLAYED.
EVERY NOW AND THEN I PAUSE

AND PUT ASIDE APPLAUSE,
AND WONDER IF YOU WONDER
WHAT WILL COME TO BE.
I MADE A FOOL OF MYSELF FOR
LOVE —
NOW NOBODY FOOLS WITH ME.

GEORGE (gesturing after ALEX) And you made such a sweet couple too.

ROSALIND He'll come back. This is just a sad dream!

GEORGE Maybe he won't. I don't hear him pounding down your door. (referring to the real dressing room entrance) What can be keeping him?

ROSALIND I think I need a drink.

GEORGE A pick-me-up? I thought that was my song. I guess you can take the man out of the girl, but you can't take the drink out of the drunk!

ROSALIND	Come to think of it, I'd better not.
GEORGE	How about a tranquilizer?
ROSALIND	How about a tranquilizer gun? I understand it works on elephants. It might even work on you!
GEORGE	Roz, how unkind. No drinkee-poo?
ROSALIND	I don't need that anymore!
GEORGE	Right! You only needed booze and pills when you didn't know who you were. But now your sexual crisis is over — salvation through surgery. Goddamn, this gal's on the cutting edge of society — so to speak!
ROSALIND	(shivering) Stop!

GEORGE Hey, somebody bring the lady a drink!

Scene 5

(The ASSISTANT enters through the lighted mirror as the PUSHER.)

PUSHER I'm wanted?

ROSALIND No thank you, Mr. Nice Guy.

PUSHER What's the matter? Chicken?

ROSALIND (for GEORGE'S benefit) No, capon, remember? (to PUSHER) I don't want one. Thanks.

GEORGE I don't want one either — I want a dozen!

ROSALIND (trying to move away, but the PUSHER blocks her path) Excuse me!

PUSHER Want to forget your problems?

ROSALIND Yes . . .

PUSHER Well then, maybe I can be of service! (Opens his coat and reveals an array of drugs.)

ROSALIND No.

GEORGE Want a sniff?

PUSHER Want a snort?

GEORGE An upper?

PUSHER A downer?

GEORGE Some hash?

PUSHER Some smack?

GEORGE Some dreams — nice dreams?

PUSHER We have self-service here!

ROSALIND (tempted) . . . No! I've changed!

(GEORGE and the PUSHER offer alcohol and drugs as they sing with growing intensity:)

GEORGE AND PUSHER (singing)

WHIRLWIND

WHEN YOU'RE DEPRESSED, YOU
CAN GET WIRED, (PUSHER)
WHEN YOU'RE ALONE, YOU'LL
FEEL ADMIRED, (GEORGE)
IF YOU'RE AT WORK, YOU WON'T
FEEL TIRED, (PUSHER)
IF YOU'RE IN LOVE, YOU'LL BE
DESIRED! (GEORGE)
(LAUGH)
WHY DON'T YOU DO IT, HUH?
WHY DON'T YOU TRY SOME
NOW! (BOTH)
WHY DON'T YOU DO IT, HUH?
WHY DON'T YOU BUY SOME
NOW!
WHEN YOU'RE AROUND,
THERE'LL BE A FUROR,
(GEORGE)
WHEN YOU'RE AFRAID, YOU'LL
FEEL SECURER, (PUSHER)
IF YOU ARE WEAK, YOU'LL FEEL
MUCH SURER, (GEORGE)

IF YOU ARE SOILED, YOU WILL
FEEL PURER! (PUSHER)
(LAUGH)
WHY DON'T YOU DO IT, HUH?
WHY DON'T YOU TRY SOME
NOW! (BOTH)
WHY DON'T YOU DO IT, HUH?
WHY DON'T YOU BUY SOME
NOW!
WHEN YOU HAVE FOES, THEY'LL
BE REFUTED, (GEORGE)
WHEN YOU HAVE FRIENDS,
YOU'LL BE SALUTED,
(GEORGE)
WHEN YOU'VE A HORN, IT WILL
BE TOOTED, (PUSHER)
IF YOU ARE — (PUSHER)
OH, DON'T BE A PRUDE, LIKE
SOME UGLY OLD MAIDEN AUNT.

(GEORGE)
DON'T BE A PRIG WITH A FACE
THAT IS GLUM AND GAUNT.
(GEORGE)
DON'T BE A SQUARE. BE A REAL
SWINGING BON VIVANT!
(BOTH)

(ROSALIND joins the other two, singing.)

WHEN YOU ARE DAMP, YOU'LL
BE IGNITED,
WHEN YOU ARE BORED, YOU'LL
BE EXCITED.
IF YOU'RE DISMAYED, YOU'LL BE
DELIGHTED,
IF THERE IS FUN, YOU'LL BE
INVITED! (LAUGH)

(They fall dizzily to the floor laughing. Then ROSALIND's laugh turns into near-tears.)

PUSHER (offering drugs) What'll it be, lady?

ROSALIND (waving him away) Go away! Go away!

(The PUSHER looks at GEORGE, then slinks off through the mirror.)

GEORGE (offering his hand) Want some help?

ROSALIND (from the floor) I can make it. (out of breath) I'm stronger now.

GEORGE (sensitively) Just trying to help . . .

ROSALIND (quietly) You're ruining my life, George.

GEORGE No, you're ruining mine. I've gone from reviews in *The New York Times* to exposes in trashy tabloids.

ROSALIND It won't always be that way! I can be as big a star as you were, George. I'll make them forget you.

GEORGE I can see it now. The silver limousine arrives at Carnegie Hall. The star makes his way to the stage door surrounded by cheering throngs. Suddenly a break in the crowd — lights, camera, the eyes of the world are on you —

(Immediately the ASSISTANT enters through the mirror as a REPORTER.)

Scene 6

REPORTER	Tell me, Ms. Smith, how does it feel to be back in the entertainment world?
ROSALIND	(bravely) It's marvelous!
REPORTER	We certainly missed you.
ROSALIND	Thank you.
REPORTER	The industry loves a new . . . face.
ROSALIND	I'm hoping.
REPORTER	(fawning) You're my favorite entertainer. I saw you in Vegas when I was a teenager.
ROSALIND	(looking at GEORGE, who points to himself) How nice.
GEORGE	Yes, yes, but how is your . . . health?

ROSALIND I feel like a million dollars!

GEORGE But then money isn't what it used to be, is it?

REPORTER Do you feel you have as much to offer the public as you used to?

GEORGE She gave up a lot for her new career!

ROSALIND Oh, George, it wasn't that big!

GEORGE (getting back at her) I've always thought it rather pitiful the way some performers will go to any extreme to get back into the public eye, don't you?

(The REPORTER is taking notes.)

ROSALIND George always says the right thing!

GEORGE How kind of you to notice, Roz. I take it all

back. It's not pitiful at all. It's cute!

ROSALIND Cute?

GEORGE Yes, has-been ladies prancing about the stage, croaking out the latest teenybopper fad. So dignified, don't you think? And now that we have a lady who used to be a gentleman, well, it's the best thing to happen since . . . since —

ROSALIND Barnum and Bailey? (aside) I can't go through with this.

REPORTER Tell us, Ms. Smith, is it true you started your career as a bearded lady in a freak show?

ROSALIND No, but I did do a little American television.

REPORTER	Isn't it true that you performed in carnivals in Singapore?
GEORGE	And didn't you entertain the troops in the Franco-Prussian War?
ROSALIND	And I thought they'd forgotten me!
REPORTER	Ms. Smith, we'd like a few details about your —
GEORGE	Yes, every single morsel!
ROSALIND	(backing off) Well, I'm not sure that —
REPORTER	Now don't be coy. Just a few intimate — very intimate — questions?
GEORGE	Of course! Ms. Smith is the epitome of graciousness. Just how old are you?

REPORTER	How many times have you been wed?
GEORGE	How many lovers have walked out your door?
ROSALIND	Please! I feel faint.
REPORTER	Do you sleep by yourself in a great big bed?
GEORGE	Do you like consenting sex, or do you prefer to be forced?
REPORTER	How much money do you make?
GEORGE	Are those eyelashes also fake?
REPORTER	Do you have habits that might be considered exotic?
ROSALIND	Please!
GEORGE	(waving a tabloid) The public wants to know!

REPORTER (waving his notepad) The public has its rights!

GEORGE How many nervous breakdowns have you had?

REPORTER Do you have fits?

ROSALIND Wait!

GEORGE What brand of silicone are your tits?

ROSALIND What!

GEORGE (waving the tabloid) Answer the questions!

REPORTER (waving the notepad) Answer the questions!

GEORGE/ REPORTER Answer the questions!

ROSALIND I'm getting ill —

REPORTER Do you read Charles Dickens?

GEORGE	(to REPORTER) Now you're going too far!
REPORTER	Do you think you're as beautiful as Venus?
GEORGE	Is it true that you still have your p —
ROSALIND	Stop!
REPORTER/ GEORGE	Do you —
ROSALIND	(running away) No — no — no!
REPORTER/ GEORGE	(following her relentlessly, speaking alternately) Do you? Do you? Do you? Do you? (together, disgusted) . . . You *do*?

(The scandalized reporter leaves through the mirror.)

GEORGE	(gently) The public has its rights.

ROSALIND The public thinks it owns you, but what do they know? What do they see in the spotlight? An image. Do they know me personally? My friends! Of course! They'll stand by me.

(She holds out his arm to the mirror, anticipating a warm welcome.)

<u>Scene 7</u>

ROSALIND Hello!

(The ASSISTANT as the FRIEND enters through the mirror, then walks right past ROSALIND, who was prepared to hug him.)

FRIEND (to GEORGE) Good to see you, buddy! (holds out his hand to shake)

GEORGE (pointing to ROSALIND) I'm over there.

FRIEND (startled) What?

ROSALIND I've changed.

FRIEND My goodness, what have you done to yourself!

GEORGE It's a little surprise! Like what you see?

(The FRIEND makes some inarticulate noises, speechless.)

GEORGE (to ROSALIND) He's speechless, Rosalind.

ROSALIND (to FRIEND) Well, how have *you* been?

FRIEND George, could I have a word with you? (confidentially) Did you really have to go that far? I mean, it's one thing to wear new fashions, or even change your hair style. But if you ask me, changing your whole body seems like showing off. For god's sake, why?

ROSALIND	My reasons were personal.
FRIEND	Believe me, I wasn't asking to hear the gory details! (to GEORGE) I'm sorry, I've got to get out of here. I hope you understand, George. (Starts to leave.)
GEORGE	I understand completely.
FRIEND	(coming back) There are a couple of things, if you don't mind.
GEORGE	Yes?
FRIEND	(to ROSALIND) Well, did they take your .. you know, and put it where your . . . you know is?
ROSALIND	(patient) . . . I really can't remember.

FRIEND	My god! Wait till I tell 'em this! (He leaves, shaking his head, trying to stifle his snickers.)
ROSALIND	Do you think he wants me to break a leg tonight?
GEORGE	Both legs.
ROSALIND	Who needs 'em!
ROSALIND	(singing)

FRIENDS

I'VE HAD SOME FRIENDS, BUT
I'VE ALWAYS HAD TO BUY 'EM.
I'VE HAD SOME FRIENDS, BUT
NOBODY I COULD TRUST.
I NEEDED THEM, BUT WHAT DID
THEY CARE.
THEY CAME AROUND IF THE
WEATHER WAS FAIR.
I TAKE IT BACK — THEY LIKED
ME WHEN I DID FAVORS.
I TAKE IT BACK — THEY LOVED
ME WHEN I HAD CASH.
I FELT THE WARMTH IN OTHERS,
YOU SEE.

I THOUGHT WE HAD A SPECIAL
ESPRIT.
WHO GIVES A DAMN! KNOW WHO
I AM!
SO NOW I'M COUNTING, I'M
COUNTING ON ME!

NOW I'M NOT SO DUMB! I'M MY
ONLY CHUM! NOT SOME OTHER
CRUMB!
FRIENDS — THEY CAN MAKE YOU
CRAWL! THEY CAN BE SO SMALL!
YOU CAN HAVE 'EM ALL!

I'VE HAD SOME FRIENDS! YEAH,
I'VE HAD JUST ONE TOO MANY!
I'VE HAD SOME FRIENDS! YEAH,
I'VE HAD 'EM UP TO HERE!
I'LL LOVE MYSELF INSTEAD OF
THOSE CREEPS.
I'LL LOVE MYSELF. THEN I'LL
KNOW IT'S FOR KEEPS.
I'LL GET ALONG AND WON'T
HAVE TO COUNT ON NO ONE.
I'VE GET ALONG AND WON'T
HAVE TO GIVE A DAMN.
ALL THAT YOU GET FROM
PEOPLE IS PAIN.
THEY LIKE YOU BEST WHEN YOU
OPEN A VEIN.
WHO CAN I TELL TO GO TO HELL?

PEOPLE JUST DRIVE ME, THEY DRIVE ME INSANE!

NOW I'M NOT SO DUMB! I'M MY ONLY CHUM! NOT SOME OTHER CRUMB!
FRIENDS — THEY CAN MAKE YOU CRAWL! THEY CAN BE SO SMALL.
YOU CAN HAVE 'EM! YOU CAN HAVE 'EM! YOU CAN HAVE 'EM ALL!

GEORGE (at the end of her outburst) Feel better?

ROSALIND No.

GEORGE Take me with you. It'll be easier. We'll make new friends. We'll get a new lover. Forget Alex. We'll get somebody who likes three-ways!

ROSALIND Maybe it's too late to start over again. Maybe I'm too old. Maybe I should just quit. I think I've lost Alex. And I'm a joke to most people, including you.

GEORGE — That's why you need a pal in your hour of need. Walk through that storm! Climb every mountain — that kind of stuff!

ROSALIND — And you want to help me out of the goodness of your heart, right?

GEORGE — Ros, of course! What else? I'm thinking only of you!

ROSALIND — You are so full of —

GEORGE — (breaking in) (singing)

COMEBACK

(GEORGE) BREAK A LEG!
(ROSALIND) (I'LL BREAË MY NECK!
(GEORGE) BUT YOU'LL COME BACK! YEAH, YOU'LL COME BACK!
(GEORGE) YOU'LL BE GREAT!
(ROSALIND) I'LÌ BE DRECK!

(GEORGE) NO, YOU'LL COME
BACK! (ROSALIND) SHOULD I
COME BACK?
(ROSALIND) WHAT SHOULD I DO
TO FIND MY NICHE?
IT'S AWFULY HARD TO MAKE A
SWITCH!
(GEORGE) GO FOR BROKE!
(ROSALIND) GO AWAY!
(GEORGE) BUT I'LL COME BACK!
YEAH, I'LL COME BACK! YOU'RE
THE BEST!
(ROSALIND) YOU'RE PASSE!
(GEORGE) NO, I'LL COME BACK!
(ROSALIND) SHOULD HE COME
BACK?
(ROSALIND) HOW CAN I TELL
WHICH ROAD TO TAKE?
WHAT IF IT'S ALL A BIG
MISTAKE!
(GEORGE) HEY THERE! BE THE
LUCKY ONE, DEAR!
HEY THERE! WHY NOT HAVE
SOME FUN, DEAR!
(ROSALIND) BAD THINGS GATHER
LIKE CLOUDS IN BAD WEATHER.
(GEORGE) GOOD THINGS HAPPEN
WHEN YOU GO AND GRAB 'EM!
WE CAN WIN, HIT THE TOP!
YEAH, WE'LL COME BACK! GOD,
WE'LL COME BACK!

(ROSALIND) SHUT YOUR MOUTH!
WE'RE A FLOP!
SHOULD I COME BACK? SHOULD I
COME BACK?
(GEORGE) WHAT I HAVE TOLD
YOU MUST SUFFICE.
IF YOU ARE WISE TAKE MY
ADVICE.
(ROSALIND) YOU ARE RIGHT! I'M
MYSELF!
SO I'LL COME BACK! YEAH, I'LL
COME BACK!
(GEORGE) YOU'D BE WRONG BY
YOURELF.
LET ME COME BACK!
(ROSALIND) NO, I'LL COME BACK!
I'LL TAKE THE WORLD
AND MAKE IT TWIRL! NOBODY
HERE CAN STOP THIS GIRL!
HEY THERE! I'M THE LUCKY ONE,
DEAR!
HEY THERE! I'LL BE HAVING FUN,
DEAR!
(GEORGE) BAD THINGS GATHER
LIKE CLOUDS IN BAD WEATHER.
(ROSALIND) GOOD THING HAPPEN
WHEN YOU GO AND GRAB 'EM!
(GEORGE) YOU'LL COME BACK —
CRYING!
(ROSALIND) NO, I'LL COME BACK
— SMILING AND PROUD!

GEORGE Rosalind, how can I put it so you'll understand? (emphasizing each word) They don't want you!

(The ASSISTANT enters as the STAGE MANAGER.)

ASSISTANT (at door, with telegram) Telegram, Ms. Smith!

(ROSALIND grabs it and tears it open.)

GEORGE Well?

ROSALIND It's from my agent. (reads) "Best wishes . . ." They want me in New York . . . if tonight goes all right.

GEORGE (Leading her) And if it doesn't?

ROSALIND He has another offer.

GEORGE Did he say where?

ROSALIND I didn't look.

GEORGE (forcing) Where?

ROSALIND (looking at the telegram) It's a . . . It's called . . . the Club Sideshow.

GEORGE (chuckling) A nice place?

ROSALIND Maybe I won't have to take it.

GEORGE I've played some pretty bad places in my day. I wouldn't mind.

ROSALIND I would! I'm not playing in some dive, where they gawk at me and keep calling me George all night long!

GEORGE You'll take it and you'll be grateful. You got me into this — with you whacking away at my body — no, my soul! But it's not too late. I'm still alive. You haven't cut me out of your life entirely yet!

ROSALIND I'm going out there alone, George.

GEORGE No you're not!

ROSALIND Alone. It's over, George. It's over! It's over!

GEORGE No, Rosalind, it's not over. Those people out there are always going to wonder what happened to George! (passing back through the mirror) (in a whisper) Always! Always! (Exits.)

(ROSALIND is left alone, uncertain, as the lights fade.)

END OF ACT I

Intermission

ACT II

Scene 1

(ROSALIND is discovered in the same position as at the end of Act I. GEORGE is gone. The ASSISTANT enters through the dressing room door as the STAGE MANAGER.)

STAGE MANAGER   Five minutes, Ms. Smith! Do you need some help?

ROSALIND   No, thank you. I'll be fine.

(The STAGE MANAGER nods and leaves.)

ROSALIND   (to herself) What if it doesn't go well tonight? Can anyone ever really change, fundamentally? Or is it just a desperate wish?

ROSALIND   (singing)

DON'T BE AFRAID OF YOURSELF

DON'T BE AFRAID OF YOURSELF.
DON'T BE AFRAID TO BE YOU.
DON'T BE FRIGHTENED OF
TRYING. DON'T BE SCARED OF
THE NEW.
IF YOU FIND IT HARD FLYING,
JUST REMEMBER THAT VIEW!
DON'T BE AFRAID OF YOURSELF.
DON'T BE AFRAID OF THE PAST.
DON'T BE FRIGHTENED OF
LIVING. DON'T BE SCARED YOU
WON'T
LAST.
CAN'T SPEND LIFE IN MISGIVING,
FOR YOUR FUTURE IS VAST!
PEOPLE MAY WANT TO MOCK.
YOU MAY BE TEMPTED TO QUIT.
YOU'LL BE A LAUGHING STOCK
—
IF YOU SHOULD BOW YOUR HEAD
AND SUBMIT!
DON'T BE AFRAID OF YOURSELF.
DON'T BR AFRAID TO BE GREAT.
THE BEST IS WHAT WE CREATE!
SO DON'T WAIT — DON'T LIMIT
YOUR SCOPE!
I AM SURE YOU CAN COPE.
NO ONE CAN LIVE — AND LIVE
WITHOUT HOPE!

(At the end of the song ROSALIND hears interior bar sounds, raucous laughter. The noise grows louder.)

(Reluctantly ROSALIND approaches the mirror since the lights have begun to pulsate and chase each other like those at the entrance to a night club.)

ROSALIND — Is anyone there? Hello? Can you tell me the name of this club?

(The ASSISTANT immediately stumbles through the mirror as a drunk, scaring ROSALIND.)

DRUNK — Club Sideshow, baby. Want a little side action? (He grabs her arm.)

ROSALIND — Let go, please!

DRUNK — What's wrong? You don't like me?

ROSALIND — Let go.

DRUNK — I asked if you liked me!

ROSALIND Please!

GEORGE (unseen, over loudspeaker) Need any help, my womanly friend?

ROSALIND No!

(She manages to break free of the DRUNK, who lunges for her. As she steps to the side, he falls back through the mirror.)

GEORGE (over loudspeaker) All you have to do is ask, and I'll come running!

ROSALIND (singing to herself to build up her courage)

DON'T BE AFRAID OF
YOURSELF!
DON'T BE AFRAID TO BE
YOU!

(She walks boldly up to the mirror.)

Hello? I'm here!

(The lights flash like those of a theater marquee.)

GEORGE	(popping out of the mirror as a sleazy producer in a carny coat and derby) Hi, toots! (The lights stop flashing.)
ROSALIND	Is this the Club Sideshow? I'm supposed to sing here.
GEORGE	You the broad what's had the change?
ROSALIND	(nervous) Ah . . . ah . . .
GEORGE	Okay, okay, let's see your . . . vocal arrangements. (pause) Your legs! Your legs!
ROSALIND	(smiling) What key are my legs in?
GEORGE	You don't still got hair on 'em, do you? Ha, ha, ha! (Checking her out, touching her.)

You take all your clothes off at the end of your act and strike a pose, right?

ROSALIND I don't undress, I'm afraid.

GEORGE Never? You sleep in your clothes? Ha, ha, ha! You expect our customers to pay good money just to hear you sing?

ROSALIND Well, I thought that —

GEORGE Come on! I ain't got all day. Let's see what you got to offer. And it better be commercial! Okay, Max!

(A spotlight his ROSALIND. Nervously she begins to sing her new song in the harsh light, without accompaniment.)

ROSALIND (timidly) "Á butterfly can fly at night. Her dazzling wings will give her light. And when it's time she'll take her flight. She'll do it! She'll do it!"

GEORGE (simultaneously, like a barker) Ladies and gents, feast your eyes on this! Is it a man? Is it a woman? Is it a human being? Hurry, hurry, hurry! She walks. She talks. She does the Hawaiian hula!

(ROSALIND attempts a timid hula.)

Is that it? You call *that* an act?

ROSALIND Well . . .

GEORGE Listen good! If you've got something people want to see, they'll pay big money to catch a gander. And if I'm any judge of character — and I am — I think you've got poten-tial. With your natural equipment, or whatever, you could go to the very top!

ROSALIND I could?

GEORGE And when you get there —

(ALEX enters through the mirror in a tuxedo and sings with GEORGE, both centering their attention on ROSALIND.)

GEORGE (singing)

SUCCESS

THERE'S NOTHING LIKE SUCCESS,
AND I MEAN NOTHING LESS.
THE FAME, THE FORTUNE I MUST CONFESS
HAVE MADE YOU EVERYTHING
YOU ARE RIGHT NOW.

ALEX (singing)

NO SHYNESS WHEN YOU START.
PUT GLAMOUR IN THE PART.
THE FEARS, THE THROBBING WITHIN YOUR HEART
CAN TURN TO MAGIC WHEN YOU SHOW 'EM HOW.

GEORGE (singing)

NICE TO STRUT AND NICE TO
LAUGH AND NICE TO TRAVEL
FAR.
NICE TO SIGN YOUR AUTOGRAPH
— I MEAN WHEN YOU'RE A STAR.

ALEX (singing)

YOUR LIMOUSINE'S NOT COLD,
NOR IS YOUR CHAUFFEUR OLD.
THE ROYAL CARPET HAS BEEN
UNROLLED,

GEORGE (singing)

AND WHEN IT COMES TO
TROUBLES YOU HAVE NONE.

ALEX (singing)

NO MATTER WHAT YOUR AGE,
WE'LL SEE YOU ON THE STAGE.
YOUR SEXY AURA IS ALL THE
RAGE.

GEORGE (singing)

AND YOU KNOW YOU ARE
CLEARLY NUMBER ONE.

BOTH (singing)

THOUGH YOU MAY THINK YOU
ARE CRAZY, ACTING RATHER
BOLD,
WHAT'S THE USE IN BEING LAZY
WHEN YOU'RE GROWING OLD!

ALEX (singing)

NOT AN HOUR AND NOT A DAY
AND NOT A YEAR GOES BY

GEORGE (singing)

THAT SOME HUNKY GUY WON'T
SAY I'LL LOVE YOU TILL I DIE!
SO LET THE MUSIC PLAY. BE
AVANT GARDE, RISQUE.
THE JOY, THE SPARKLE ARE HERE
TO STAY.

ALEX (singing)

YOU'VE COME TO PACK THE
HOUSE AND MAKE THEM CHEER.
WE KNOW IT'S SURE BEEN
ROUGH, WITH TEARS AND ALL
THAT STUFF.

GEORGE (singing)

BUT ONCE YOU'VE MADE IT THEY
KISS YOUR DUFF!
THE WAY TO DO IT IS TO BE
SINCERE.

BOTH (singing)

THOUGH YOU HAVE TO KNOCK A
FEW RIGHT ON THEIR DERRIERS,
TALENT JUST COMES PUSHING
THROUGH AND KICKS THEM
DOWN THE
STAIRS.

GEORGE (singing)

THERE'S NOT A THING TO LOSE.

ALEX (singing)

YOU'LL NEVER GET THE BLUES.
GEORGE (singing)
YOU'RE MUCH TOO BUSY WITH
INTERVIEWS.

ALEX (singing)

YES, ALL OF THIS CAN GIVE
YOUR LIFE SOME ZING.

SO BE A STAR TODAY. GET ON
THAT GREAT WHITE WAY.

GEORGE (singing)

AND MAKE THEM HAPY THEY
HAD TO PAY.

ALEX (singing)

YES, MAKE THEM GLAD THEY
CAME TO HEAR YOU SING.

BOTH (singing)

THOUGH YOU THINK YOUR
GREAT ROMANCES CANNOT BE
OUTDONE,
FIDDLING WITH YOUR FINANCES
GUARANTEES MORE FUN.

ROSALIND (caught up, joining in)

WOULD I DO IT ALL AGAIN JUST
TO ATTAIN SUCCESS?
LET ME SAY IT WITH A GRIN. THE
ANSWER'S YES, YES, YES!

GEORGE (singing)

THERE'S NOTHING LIKE SUCCESS,
TO BRING AROUND THE PRESS,
AND FAME AND FORTUNE DONE
TO EXCESS
CAN MAKE YOU PLEASED YOU
TURNED OUT JUST LIKE ME!
SO PUT YOUR BEST FACE ON.
REMEMBER, LIFE'S A CON.

ROSALIND (singing)

BESIDES, NEXT CENTURY WE'LL
ALL BE GONE!

ALEX (singing)

LET'S ALL BE EVERYTHING WE
WANT TO BE!

ALL THREE (singing)

LET'S ALL BE EVERYTHING WE
WANT TO BE! SUCCESS!

ROSALIND It sounds fantastic!

GEORGE Maybe I can squeeze you in. You like animals?

ROSALIND What?

GEORGE	I've got a donkey that just may like your type. He's very personable, for a donkey. In time you'll grow to like him too!
ROSALIND	Ha! Ha! Ha! (She imitates his laugh.) You *are* kidding, aren't you?
GEORGE	You a troublemaker?
ROSALIND	(to herself) No, it won't be like this! I won't let it.
GEORGE	(as himself) Cross your heart and hope to die?
ROSALIND	Yes! Yes! (She crosses her heart.)
GEORGE	Sorry, it's out of your hands! They don't allow criminals to appear in that club.
ROSALIND	Criminal?

(GEORGE forcibly moves ROSALIND with her back to the dressing room door. He puts her arms behind her back as if putting on handcuffs and then puts a blindfold on her.)

<u>Scene 2</u>

(The ASSISTANT as the WITNESS enters through the mirror and marches downstage opposite ROSALIND.)

ROSALIND (blindfolded) George?

GEORGE Company, ready!

(The WITNESS stands at attention.)

ROSALIND George!

GEORGE Does the convict wish to say a few words before we proceed?

ROSALIND Convict? I didn't even get a trial?

GEORGE Formalities! Formalities!

ROSALIND Can't I at least know what I'm accused of?

GEORGE The damsel in distress wants to know what she's accused of! Step forward!

WITNESS (as the son) She neglected her only child! (Steps back.)

GEORGE She was a drunk — and a druggie! (Steps back.)

GEORGE Step forward!

WITNESS She deeply embarrassed her friends! (Steps back.)

GEORGE Step forward! (He steps back and then forward again quickly.)

GEORGE She couldn't keep her lover! (Steps back.)

ROSALIND But Alex loves me! He'll come back!

GEORGE	Will he? He can't love you unless he loves me as well.
ROSALIND	I'll make him forget you. I killed you! I killed you!
GEORGE	Ah, hah! You've heard it from her own mouth. (Steps forward.) She murdered George Smith!
ROSALIND	I won't listen!
GEORGE	Of course you won't! It's the truth!
ROSALIND	It's not the whole truth! Won't anybody speak up for me? (Silence.) Nobody?
GEORGE	There *is* one character witness.
ROSALIND	Who is it?
GEORGE	Me.

ROSALIND I don't think I want to hear anything more you have to say.

GEORGE Ladies and gentlemen of the Firing Squad, what do you see before you? Exhibit A — one Rosalind Smith. All woman! Now I ask you — is this all-woman all bad? Of course she isn't! Just because she destroyed my career and my life and now wants to eradicate every trace of my existence, should we be angry with her? Of course not! She knows what she's doing! She's always known, hasn't she? Her whole life has been one long mess, and now she thinks she's going to solve everything by running away from it. I rest my case! Ready, aim . . . (Drum roll.)

ROSALIND (tearing off the blindfold) No!

GEORGE Any last words?

ROSALIND I won't die for you, George! When you accuse me, you accuse yourself! I won't be guilty of *your* crimes! I won't let my life end! Man or woman, I don't want to be the kind of person you are!

GEORGE There was nothing wrong with the way I was! Don't you try to shift the blame to me.

ROSALIND Can't you see yourself? You don't even need this (meaning the blindfold) in order not to see. You're so stubborn and unsubtle. It's always attack, attack. You were the one who hated your son! You were the one who drank and drugged

yourself so that no
one could stand to be
around you! Why don't
you put yourself in front
of the firing squad?
Why not? Aren't you
man enough for that?

GEORGE But I'm not like that . . .
I'm not like . . .

ROSALIND You're not? Just what
are you, George?

GEORGE (singing)

WHAT MEMORY KNOWS

I WISH I COULD, I WISH I COULD
JUST TELL MYSELF SOME LIES.
I WAS A SAINT, I WAS SO GOOD, I
SHOULD HAVE WON A PRIZE.
THE FUN, THE FUN, BUT NOT THE
BLUES.
THE PICK-ME-UPS, BUT NOT THE
BOOZE.
ONLY THE BEST! DISCARD THE
REST!
I WISH I COULD, I WISH I COULD
JUST TELL MYSELF SOME LIES.

I WAS A SAINT, I WAS SO GOOD,
NO NEED FOR ALIBIS.
THE UPS, THE UPS, AND ALL THE
THRILLS.
THE PARTIES, YES, BUT NOT THE
PILLS.
OH, CAN'T YOU SEE THAT
WASN'T ME!
HOW CAN WE WARM WHAT
MEMORY CHILLS?

I THINK THERE MUST — THERE
MUST HAVE BEEN SOME GOOD
AMONG
THE BAD.
I'M SURE THERE WAS, THERE
HAD TO BE, SO WHY DO I FEEL
SAD?
THE HEIGHTS, THE HEIGHTS, BUT
NOT THE DOUBTS.
THE WINDFALLS, YES, BUT NOT
THE DROUGHTS.
WHAT I REGRET I MUST FORGET!
I THINK THERE MUST, THERE
MUST HAVE BEEN SOME GOOD
AMONG THE
BAD.
I''M SURE THERE WAS, THERE
HAD TO BE, SO WHY DON'T I
FEEL GLAD?

I MUST, I MUST REMEMBER
THOSE, THE SUMMERS, YES, BUT
NOT THE
SNOWS.
THE GOOD — THAT'S ALL I MUST
RECALL!
HOW CAN WE SOOTHE WHAT
MEMORY KNOWS?

ROSALIND (bringing ALEX from the mirror) George, there's someone here who wants to talk with you.

GEORGE (subdued) Oh?

ALEX Hello.

GEORGE Hello.

ALEX I feel sort of awkward.

GEORGE So do I.

ALEX I just wanted to say that I love Rosalind very much. Very much. (Looks at her.) I'd never been as happy with anyone as I was with her, until I read that story in the newspaper. I couldn't believe it. I didn't want to believe it! I won't lie. It does make a difference. A tremendous difference. When I kiss her, when we make love, I can't help remembering who she was. . . So I guess I just want to say that I understand. You don't want to die. It's perfectly under-standable. I think you belong more to her than I do, and so I'm . . . so I'm giving you to each other. Be happy together! Goodbye. . . . Goodbye, Rosalind.

(ALEX kisses her quickly and leaves through the mirror.)

GEORGE Are you trying to make me noble, Rosalind?

ROSALIND What do you mean?

GEORGE Aren't I supposed to be magnanimous now and call Alex back and give up my place to him? Because he loves you more than I do, I should surrender, and let you two be happy. I know what your ploy is, and yet the funny thing is . . . I'm considering it. Out with the old, in with the new. Love instead of . . . whatever it is I am.

ROSALIND Would you, George? Would you?

GEORGE I may do it. But I want you to ask yourself something first? Are you willing?

ROSALIND I'm willing . . .

GEORGE What if, once I'm gone, completely gone, and you're completely you,

it's still *not* enough?
What then?

ROSALIND — That won't happen.

GEORGE — (softly) Yes, it might.
And you know it.

ROSALIND — George, why must you always . . . (softly) Yes, it might. And I know it. My life might fall apart. No audiences, or insulting ones. Alex rejecting me. And then even you'll be gone. With me alone, growing older and older. Oh, it could happen! I know that.

(She takes GEORGE's hand. Together they sing:)

THE DAY THAT WE DIE

ROSALIND — (singing)

SOMEDAY THERE MUST COME
THE MOMENT
WHEN WE ASK THE QUESTION

AND WE STARE AT THE SKY,
FOR WE WONDER WHAT DAY IT
WILL BE,
THE DAY THAT WE DIE.

GEORGE (singing)

SOMETIME WE BEGIN TO NOTICE
AS THE YEARS REMAKE US,
AND WE MUST PONDER WHY,
AND WE WORRY ABOUT WHERE
WE'LL BE,
THE DAY THAT WE DIE.

ROSALIND (singing)

WILL WE SIT AROUND GROWN
USELESS,
PARALYZED AND HOPELESS,
JUST TOO TRAMPLED TO TRY.

GEORGE (singing)

WITH OUR FUTURE NOW LOST IN
THE PAST,
THE DAY THAT WE DIE.

ROSALIND (singing)

WHAT DO WE KNOW? WHERE DO
WE GO?

IF IT GETS WORSE, WHO SHOULD
WE CURSE?

GEORGE (singing)

WILL YOU BE YOU? WILL I BE ME?
I GUESS WE'LL SEE.

ROSALIND (singing)

DO WE ALWAYS WIND UP
LONELY?
IF YOU KNOW DON'T TELL ME.
I PREFER THAT YOU LIE.
ARE WE HUGGED BY SOME
VISITING NURSE,
THE DAY THAT WE DIE?

GEORGE (singing)

NO ONE GETS ALL THAT HE
WANTED.
ONLY DISAPPOINTED.
WAS HE AIMING TOO HIGH?
MUST WE LIVE WITH A FISTFUL
OF DUST,
THE DAY THAT WE DIE?

ROSALIND (singing)

SHOULD WE FIGHT IT OR
SURRENDER?
SHOULD WE TRY TO LINGER?
SHOULD WE COWER AND CRY?

GEORGE (singing)

OR PERHAPS WE MUST LIVE WITH
THE TRUTH,
THE DAY THAT WE DIE.

ROSALIND (singing)

WHAT DO WE KNOW? WHERE DO
WE GO?

GEORGE (singing)

HOW DO WE END?

ROSALIND (singing)

COULD BE WE BLEND.

GEORGE (singing)

WILL I BE YOU?

ROSALIND (singing)

WILL YOU BE ME?

BOTH (harmonizing)

I GUESS WE'LL SEE.

ROSALIND How about a compromise?

GEORGE What do you have in mind?

ROSALIND It may mean losing Alex, but I'll accept you — if you'll accept me.

GEORGE But I accept you!

ROSALIND No you don't. No you *don't*!

GEORGE What do I have to do?

ROSALIND I'm probably asking the impossible.

GEORGE Oh no, not another sex change?

ROSALIND Do you know you always use jokes to get out of things?

GEORGE	Sorry, hereafter I'll try to be somber.
ROSALIND	Not somber . . .
GEORGE	What then?
ROSALIND	I want you to . . . like me, George.
GEORGE	Like you? How do I like thee? Let me count the ways! (realizing he is joking his way out of the situation again) Sorry! Let me re-phrase that. Ah. . . (Can't think of anything.)
ROSALIND	That's what I've felt ail along. You're saying that you don't like what you've become.
GEORGE	How do I answer that? What am I going to do now? Go back? There's no going back. We both know that. It's

all done. The only question is . . . to be Rosalind or not to be . . . sorry.

ROSALIND (realizing it more fully) You *really* don't like me, do you?

GEORGE (examining her face seriously) It's just a *question*, Rosalind. I recall a very unhappy boy named George, who lived in a place far, far away from here. And this George was unhappy because he felt like a changeling — a child taken from its rightful place and left with a family that's not really his. And so he decided to make everything . . . change. He would find where he belonged. No matter how difficult, no matter how far. And when this boy reached his destination, what did he find? (touching her face) Himself? Or had he passed into the wrong country? Maybe even into enemy territory? . . . I just want to be sure that the country I'm going to live in for the rest of my life is better than the one I left behind.

ROSALIND It's better, George. It's better.

GEORGE Is it? (searching her eyes, then kissing her deeply) . . . I guess I'm Rosalind.

ROSALIND (kissing him) I guess I'm George.

(The ASSISTANT knocks at the dressing room door as the STAGE MANAGER.)

STAGE MANAGER	One minute, Ms. Smith!
ROSALIND	It's time to go. (Gives final touches to herself.)
GEORGE	(also primping) Am I fabulous?
ROSALIND	How do I look?
GEORGE	(adding finishing touches to ROSALIND'S makeup) Let's hope!

(ALEX enters through the dressing room door.)

ALEX	Rosalind? (seeing that she is about to go on stage) I can come back later.
ROSALIND	It can wait. (Afraid to bring up the subject) How are you?

ALEX	Better. I'm sorry I ran out before. It knocked the wind out of me, that's all.
ROSALIND	What do you think will happen to us?
ALEX	I was going to ask you the same thing.
ROSALIND	George isn't going to go away, not completely.
GEORGE	I won't be around that much! Just a teeny weenie bit — I promise!
ALEX	(to ROSALIND) Maybe we should take some time and get to know each other – again.
ROSALIND	Maybe so. For the first time.
ALEX	I like playing Scrabble, and tossing a Frisbee around the yard, and reading the Sunday

	paper on this small bench I have in my back garden.
ROSALIND	Do you? I like long walks and listening to old records. But then you know that, don't you?
ALEX	Yeah, I know that . . .
ROSALIND	Do you want to talk later?
ALEX	I'm afraid, Rosalind.
ROSALIND	Of what?
ALEX	Of other things you may not have told me . . .
ROSALIND	We'll have to talk, and say everything, everything!
ALEX	I do love you — I think it was you.
ROSALIND	Will you promise to come back afterwards?

ALEX	That's not too much to ask. I'm come back, and we'll talk . . . we'll talk . . .
ROSALIND	Wish me . . .
ALEX	Of course . . . (He exits through the dressing room door.)
STAGE MANAGER	(entering) You're on, Ms. Smith!

(GEORGE hears the message, hurries to the door and begins to exit.)

ROSALIND	(stopping him) George!
GEORGE	Sorry!

(GEORGE steps back, gesturing for her to pass in front of him. We see bright light streaming in, hear the audience clapping rhythmically, to encourage ROSALIND to enter.)

(ROSALIND walks toward the door and then through. GEORGE starts to follow her, then stops, goes back and retrieves his picture from the trash, puts it back on the wall, and hurries after ROSALIND as the lights fade to black.)

(The ANNOUNCER is played by the ASSISTANT over a loudspeaker.)

ANNOUNCER Ladies and gentlemen, The [name of the actual theater] is proud to present Ms. Rosalind Smith!

ROSALIND (in a spotlight, surrounded by black) It's good to be b— (Starts to say 'back' but doesn't.) . . . to be here. I'd like to dedicate my first song to someone special, someone who will always be a part of my life — Mr. George Smith! (Looks over her shoulder.) Wherever he is.

ROSALIND (singing)

GO DO IT

A BUTTERFLY CAN FLY AT
NIGHT.
HER DAZZLING WINGS WILL GIVE
HER LIGHT.
AND WHEN IT'S TIME SHE'LL
TAKE HER FLIGHT.
SHE'LL DO IT! SHE'LL DO IT!
A HUMMINGBIRD CAN LEARN TO
SING.
THERE'S MORE TO LIFE THAN
WANDERING.
AND THERE'S NO NEED TO WAIT
TILL SPRING.
SHE'LL DO IT! SHE'LL DO IT!

EVERYONE WILL ANALYZE IT.
EVERYONE WILL BE SURPRISED.
EVERYONE WILL EMPHASIZE IT
—
SHE WAS DISGUISED.

A LITTLE DOE'S SUPPOSED TO
RUN

WHEN ANY HUNTER LIFTS HIS
GUN,

BUT FIGHTING BACK JUST MIGHT
BE FUN.
GO DO IT! GO DO IT!
A UNICORN CANNOT EXIST.
AND IF IT'S BORN IT MUST INSIST.

AND SO TO GROW IT MUST
INSIST.
GO DO IT! GO DO IT!

EVERYONE WILL REALIZE IT.
EVERYONE WILL BE QUITE
DAZED.
EVERYONE WILL RECOGNIZE IT.
AND WON'T THEY BE AMAZED!

BLACKOUT
FINI

PLAYS by DANIEL CURZON AVAILABLE FOR PRODUCTION

(all scripts are copyrighted)

FULL-LENGTHS

1. **A PINT AT THE PREGNANT PRIEST,** *or a Pint at the Queen's Arse* — Set in a modern-day country Irish pub, Old Ireland and New Ireland meet in a black romp that is both touching and comic. An American tourist encounters a grouchy pub owner as well as Mad Mary, who lives in a cardboard box, to say nothing of Father Finnessey, who is a pregnant Catholic priest.
Mood: Comedy, with touching moments
Characters: (4) American Tourist, Pub Owner, Mad Mary, Father Finnessey
Playing Time: About 1 ½ hours, with one intermission

2. **GOD ARRIVES** — God finally arrives, bringing mankind, in the form of homeless Stoogey and Piddle, various spiritual, worldly, and mental "answers" to life's riddles, while the sinister clown

Bozo interferes, presented in a comic, absurdist manner that is a comment on the theater as much as on human existence. Original script with entirely new content.
Mood: Absurdist Comedy
Characters: (4) Stoogey, Piddle, God, Bozo
Playing Time: About 1 ½ hours + intermission
WINNER: NATIONAL NEW PLAY CONTEST (Southwest Theatre Assoc., 1999)
Also: Performed at the Edinburgh Fringe Festival, Edinburgh, Scotland, California Travel Troupe, 2000.

3. **1001 NIGHTS AT THE HOUSE OF PANCAKES** — a series of vignettes that capture fragments of people's lives as overheard in a restaurant — from the sad to the comic to the odd, with an emphasis on realistic drama/comedy: a grandparent who has had to reject a grandchild forced on her, an Asian military bride who, as her English gets better, realizes who she has actually married, a militant smoker who won't leave the restaurant, and two lovesick teens who think they've invented Love. Most roles can be

played by either males or females, and some of the pieces could be done twice in each performance, to show how the dynamics change when the sex of the person changes. The vignettes can be done in almost any order, even with different casting for every performance, to give different texture to each evening.
Mood: Realistic comedy and drama
Characters: (6) (men and women, mixed) Multiple parts, of all types.
Playing Time: Varies — from half an hour to two hours, depending on the number of pieces used. Probably around 1 hour and 10 minutes with no intermission would be best

4. **A HISTORY OF REALLY, REALLY BAD IDEAS** — A series of sketches that take a comic look at the silly ideas that have ruled the world — from sex to voicemail, from the Oracle at Delphi to dating O.J. Simpson.
Mood: Satirical, from light to harsh
Characters: (5 or 6) (three men, two or three women) They play multiple parts
Playing Time: From five minutes to one and a half hours, depending on number of sketches used
First Performed: B.A.I.T. Fringe Festival, San Francisco, 1996.

5. **SIMPSON AGONISTES: The Truth and Nothing But, or the O.J. Simpson Trial**
— A satire on the trial of the century, giving all the unsaid subtext of those involved, whether it be Marcia Clark, Dr. Robin Cotton, or Rosa Lopez.
Mood: Satirical, from light to bitter
Characters: (6-8) to play multiple parts, can be done with scripts in hand at microphones
Playing Time: Half an hour to two hours, depending on amount used. Not all scenes necessary. Select as needed

6. **THE BLASPHEMER** — What happens when the leaders of Islam place a price on the head of a former Muslim who has written a book questioning the validity and sanctity of the religious faith in which he was raised. What happens to the marriage of such a writer, who is married to an American. Western and Muslim cultural conflict at issue.
Mood: Docu-drama, with some humor
Characters: (7): The novelist, his wife, plus three men and two women for multiple parts.
Playing time: 2 hours (+ intermission)

7. **MY UNKNOWN SON** — A man who has donated his sperm to a lesbian couple at the same time he is writing a history of the theater encounters various versions of the son he wants and doesn't want, from Greek tragedy to Shakespearean comedy to Oscar Wilde high farce to Sam Shepard, aided and resisted by a feisty Midwife.
Mood: Basically a comedy, with some powerful and touching scenes
Characters (3): The Father, the Son, the Midwife (all major roles)
Playing time: 1 hour, 18 minutes (no intermission)
Produced by Martin Kaufman, off-Broadway Equity production at the Kaufman Theater in Theater Row, NYC, October, 1988.
Also staged at the Circle Rep Lab, NYC, October, 1987.
First performed at Marin Theater Co, summer, 1987, Marin, California.
Published by Dialogus Play Service (out of print).Published by Lodestar Literary Site, 2003

8. **WHEN BERTHA WAS A PRETTY NAME** — Several couples and family members are down for the weekend. The hosts, two male lovers,

are worried about *Ma Mere*, who does not approve of their love. Suzette is not happy with her wooden-legged stuffy lover, and — drawing-room comedy like those by Coward and Maugham, set in the present with modern issues.
Mood: High Comedy; some farce
Characters: (8) Two Male Lovers; the Homophobic Mother Ogre; the sister, Suzette; her Stuffy Lover; a Sex-Crazed Ex-lover of the Host; an English Butler; a Woman Publisher
Playing Time: 2 hours (+ intermission)
Work-shopped: West Coast Playwrights, Marin County, Ca, 1988.
Published by Dialogus (out of print).

9. **STUCK** — A modern-day white male heterosexual liberal Prometheus, in the form of a part-time college teacher, finds himself caught between Affirm-ative Action, neo-conservatism, and a student's sexual harassment accusation.
Mood: Comedy / Drama.
Characters: (5) Joe, in his thirties; Ionia, his feminist office mate; Herm, his gay conservative colleague; Leo Sues, the corrupt chairman of the Humanities Department; Boris Zilch, dumb student
Playing Time: 2 hours (+ intermission)
Finalist: National New Play Contest, '03

10. **MARGARET AND ERNIE VS. THE WORLD** — A retired woman school teacher, now blind, is introduced to a retired construction worker who has had a slight stroke; they encounter social and personal pressures to be a couple. How many plays are about the loves of the elderly?
Mood: Touching drama with laughs
Characters: (6) Margaret, Ernie should be at least in their sixties — star parts; a fussy male Social Worker; a Junkie Thief; a Guard, a female Usher
Playing Time: Three acts, under 2 hours (+ intermission)
First produced: The One-Act Theatre Company, San Francisco, 1981.

11. **THE THIRD PART OF HENRY THE FOURTH** — Hal, now king, is challenged by his choleric brother, the Duke of Lancaster. Indeed he has to fear being thought a "playboy" monarch because he has sneaked Falstaff and his cronies into the castle for some high jinks and hilarity.
Mood: Authentic neo-Shakespearean play, not a parody, a sequel to *Henry IV, Parts I, II*
Characters: (15-19) King Hal; Falstaff; Duke of Lancaster; Frederick (a

pompous emissary); Mistress Quickly; Doll Tearsheet; Duchess of Lancaster; assorted roles
Playing Time: approximately 3 hours (+ intermission)
Agent Jeffrey Simmons, London: "I really am mightily impressed with HENRY IV Part Three, and I do not use words lightly. It is quite remarkably good and at times quite splendid."

12. **CINDERELLA II** — What happens after you live happily ever after? Cinderella finds Prince Charming too "perfect." She's is falling in love with his less-than-charming brother, Prince Moe, and she's even homesick for her awful stepsisters. Meanwhile, the evil court jester is plotting to overthrow the prince.
Mood: Musical Comedy (Music by Dan Turner. Book and Lyrics by Curzon)
Characters: (15-16) Cinderella, Prince Charming, Prince Moe, the Fairy Godmother; Tickle, the jester; two stepsisters (Gargola/Odia); Father; Mother; assorted smaller roles
Playing Time: 2 hours and 5 minutes. (+ intermission)
First produced by the Angels of Light (Offshoot of the Cockettes), S.F., 1984.

WINNER: 3 Bay Area Theater Critics Circle Awards) (Tape of music available).

13. **OLIVER CROMWELL AND THE BOYS (No Mince Pies)** — Oliver Cromwell and the Puritans are on the rampage, because they've been persecuted. King Charles I of England is a bit of fop and rather cruel and loses his head to them. The Puritans, once in power, turn out to be cruel taskmasters themselves, trying to legislate morality according to their code, punishing adultery and even Christmas celebrations. Judith, the daughter of a Puritan family, yearns to perform in the theater in a time when women are not allowed to.
Mood: Musical Comedy — with parallels to contemporary religious fundamentalists, but with entertainment the priority. (Music by Dan Turner, Book and Lyrics by Curzon)
Characters: (15) Judith; her Mother; her Father; her Brother; Cromwell; Charles I (singing roles); Heretic; Counselors, etc.
Playing Time: 2 hours (+ intermission) (Tape of music available.)
Workshop Production at City College of San Francisco, summer, 1986).

14. **PIXIES IN PERIL**— A parody of fairy tales. A Wimp sets off against his will on a quest for the dragon's gold, with pixies, a meddling magician, kinky spiders, hillbilly gremlins, an Imp Princess who changes clothes every fifteen minutes, etc.
Mood: Broad Comedy
Characters: (12-15, with doubling) Robin Goodfellow — the Wimp; Pixies; Glorioso, a magician; Affectionette, the Imp Queen; Ogress; Spiders; assorted Monsters and Villains; the Dragon
Playing Time: 2 hours (+ intermission)
Published by Dialogus Play Service (out of print).

15. **DON'T RUB ME THE WRONG WAY** — Four bisexuals answer an ad by mistake when a man advertises his furniture as "a good bi" when he wants to move. There is also a dangerous genie released from a magic lantern after a thousand years, and he's not happy with the human race he is forced to serve and determines to do something about it.
Mood: A comedy with satirical bite.
Characters: (6) Sam, the non-bisexual main character; a "Liberated" Lady; a Reluctant Swinger; a comically Creepy Guy; a Man who Speaks No Known

Language; the Genie; a dog for a walk-on part
Playing Time: 2 hours (+ intermission)
Staged Reading: Gay Performance Company, New York, Spring, 1991.
Staged Reading: Phoenix Theater, San Francisco, 1996.
Published by Dialogus Play Service (out of print).

16. **I'M GLAD I'M ME AND NOT YOU, or Avatars** — Four people appear in various versions of themselves from 1893 to 1953 to 1973 to 1993 to 2093, revealing the way sexual taboos change and re-assert themselves in expansive and repressive times.
Mood: Serious comedy
Characters: (4) Adrian, who's gay; Matilda, who's prudish; Alice, who's liberal; Henry, who's "good old Henry"
Playing Time: 2 hours (+ intermission)

17. **BEER AND RHUBARB PIE** — A sexy, homophobic, macho Cuban repairman, having marital problems, encounters a gentlemanly gay man, who is also having sexual problems with his ex-lover — now his roommate. Sexual tensions.
Mood: Drama with some humor

Characters: (4) the Cuban Repairman; Cuban's wife; Gay Man; Ex-lover, now Roommate
Playing Time: (3 acts) 1 hour 45 minutes (+ intermission). (Videotape of one-act version available)
Produced twice at Theater Rhinoceros, San Francisco, 1980, 1981. (one-act)
Staged reading; Gay Performances Co, May, 1990, NYC (three-act version)
Published by Dialogus Play Service (one-act version) (out of print).

18. **THE BIRTHDAY GIRL**— A woman drug addict of the middle class hates life. Her long-suffering husband watches and reluctantly begins to be sucked in as he discovers that he is addicted to his wife's addiction.
Mood: Serious drama
Characters: (6) the Addict; her Husband; Teenage Sister; Mother; Father; Doctor
Playing Time: (2 acts) About 2 hours (+ intermission)
First performed as one-act at One Act Theater Co, San Francisco, 1982.

THE BIRTHDAY BOY— gay version of *The Birthday Girl*, with two men instead of a husband and wife. (same as above)

Published by Dialogus Play Service (out of print).

PLEASE, NOT TO US — the lesbian version of *The Birthday Boy.*

19. **BENEATH THE SURFACE** — Representative members of various prevailing minorities, from the handicapped to Native American, are trapped together in a subway train that is losing its air; their real feelings for each other come out. Unsentimental view of self-interest and bigotry in minorities.
Mood: Biting satirical comedy.
Characters: (12) Asian; Gay; Lesbian; Black Woman; Black Man; White Woman; White Man; Foreigner, etc. (can be played in masks)
Playing Time: 1 hour and fifteen minutes (no intermission)
First performed in shorter version, Earnest Players, San Francisco, 1979.

20. **SEX SHOW** — 15 satirical skits on various aspects of sex, from the ways men are allowed to touch to a man having a dialogue with his penis about whether to masturbate.
Mood: Comedy

Characters: (5) People (all men?) who can play multiple roles
Playing Time: under 2 hrs (intermission)
First performed: Gay Community Center, San Francisco, 1977.
Also Leavenworth YMCA , San Francisco, 1977.
Also Produced at the Mabuhay Gardens, San Francisco, 1977.
Nominated for Best Script by San Francisco Bay Area Theater Critics Circle, 1977.

21. **DEMONS** — A gay man is visited by the spirits of three women in his life: a grade school nun; his mother; his ex-wife.
Mood: Drama with laughs
Characters: (4) the Man; the Nun; the Mother; the Ex-Wife
Playing Time: 2 hours (+ intermission)
Staged reading: Julian Theater, San Francisco, 1983.
Published by Dialogus Play Service (out of print).

22. **COMEBACK (a musical)** —A male cabaret singer is making a come-back as a female after a sex change. Personal and career challenges follow.
Mood: Musical Drama. (Music by Dan

Turner, Lyrics by Curzon)
Characters: (4) The Male Self; the Female Self; the Lover; Person to play various smaller roles
Playing Time: 2 hours (one intermission) (Tape of music available)
Staged Reading: Berkeley Stage Co., 1980; Noe Valley Ministry, 1987.
Published by Dialogus Play Service (out of print).

23. **VERY NASTY INDEED** — A thriller set in an English manor house, where two sisters, a husband, and a gardener plot and counterplot clever murders against each other.
Mood: Thriller with comic overtones. Keeps the audience on pins and needles wondering who will win.
Characters: (4) The older sisters (in her 40s); the younger sister (in her 30s); the husband (30s); the feeble-minded gardener (in his 20s)
Playing Time: 2 hours (one intermission)

24. **HUGELY ENTERTAINING** — A group of "seminarians" is taking a theatre course in London. They ought to get along since they have a common interest, but someone's purse has been

stolen, another asks really dumb questions of their British theatre guests, one is a transsexual studying to be a clairvoyant, another is an old Shake-spearean actor going blind, another a woman director with enrollment prob-lems, a bed-wetting, blithe countess, and then some really interesting characters are there too . . .
Mood: Realistic comedy drama
Characters: (10) Each is a mixture of the comic and the sad, like most people: a witty, suicidal lesbian, with lover troubles, has a play to market, fortyish; an old British actor going blind, Shakespeare idolater, over sixty; the British Guest (multiple parts played by a man over thirty — actor, director, always the same person with different names, sometimes a mustache or other slight changes; the self-reliant, im-patient, falsely compassionate director of the program, heard it all, once killed someone in a car accident, over thirty-five; a poorly self-educated, badly dressed social outcast male, any age; a would-be clairvoyant, sensitive, also a transsexual, played by a man, over forty, but not a "drag" role; something of a male gold-digger but not too good at it, who is also a scholarship actor, thirties,

handsome, under thirty-five; a young actress, opinionated, aloof, optimistic, overindulged, may have potential, under twenty; a nice woman who tells people what they want to hear, others try to guess her secret and gossip about her, over forty; the Countess De La Rue, streetwise, self-assured, bed-wetting nobility whom others always want to wait on, changes her plans often, exerts natural superiority, unfazed by her own foibles, over thirty-five
Playing Time: (3 acts, about three hours)

25. **HOW TO MURDER YOUR VERY BEST FRIENDS (a**vailable in a three-act version) See information below under one-acts.

26. **HEAVEN — THE MUSICAL** — A hot new dance Club has just opened. Besides the hot dancing and the "refreshments," there are rumors that sex and other Unmentionables Things of all types (straight, bi, gay) take place in secret "closets" spread throughout the building. People are outside clamoring to get in; they'll even pay — whatever is asked. But you can't get in — not unless the Doorman picks you. And he's *very fussy and arbitrary* about who these

Special People are. Even some famous people have been turned away. An engaged young couple is out on the town just before they are to go back home to the Midwest to be married. They've decided to have a Bachelor Party in the big city before the big day — only together. *Aww*, how sweet! They see the commotion outside the new Club and stop to see what's going on. They shouldn't have.
Characters: (10-20) An impulsive young woman from the Midwest, in her twenties; her fiancé, a conservative young man, also in his twenties; has a twin brother who died; a brother and a sister in their forties, with the sister very butch and the brother fem, also trying to get into the Club; the Doorman, any age, a dynamic, contradictory sexy Mephistopheles in leather; the Delightfools, a group of versatile actor-singer-dancers who play all other parts.
Mood: Musical Drama
Playing Time: (2 acts, three hours)

ONE-ACTS

1. **"A Streetcar Named Viagra"** — It's 1946 and a playwright named Tennessee en- counters a drag queen named Desiree in auditions for the out-of-town workshop of his Broadway-bound play, inspiring him to make alterations in the role of the original "Lance" DuBois.
Mood: Comedy/Satire
Characters: (3) The Director (male) any age, The Playwright (male in his thirties), Desiree (male, any age, drag role)
Playing Time: around 30 minutes

2. **"A Celebrity Stalking"** — A self-important writer on a flight to collect a famous prize encounters a sympathetic ear and a dead body.
Mood: Comedy
Characters: (3) The Writer, male or female, any age, should be eccentric; Dale, male or female, gracious, any age but over fifty might be better; Voice of flight attendant, male or female
Playing Time: about 10 minutes

3. **"A Tale of Terror"** — "Al" Queada himself has been captured by a bounty hunter and is being brought back on a

plane for a sex change. (three chairs)
Mood: Comedy
Characters: (4) Bubba, a man between 25-50, macho, in Western clothes; Al, a man, almost any age, wearing Islamic women's traditional garb (the all-encompassing *burqa*); Skippy, a man, between 25-60, nerdy, in a nice business suit and tie; Airplane Voice, male or female (can be pre-recorded)
Playing Time: about 12 minutes

4. **"Don't Open This Box Whatever You Do"** — A young man discovers a box left for him by his dead father containing information he may not want to know.
Mood: Serious Fantasy
Characters: (2) Narrator, any age; the Son (or Daughter), early twenties
Playing Time: 20 minutes
Produced by the California Travel Troupe, Edinburgh Festival, 2001.

5. **"Modern Beast Fables"** — A collection of 20+ beast fables in the tradition of Aesop but with new examples and new morals (the Cat and the Hummingbird, The Monkeys and the Gun, the Anaconda and the Opossum, the Wildebeest and the Lioness, etc.)

Mood: Comedy; some biting comedy
Characters: Narrator plus one, two, or three beasts (minimal costuming required)
Playing Time: They vary from one minute to five minutes each

6. **"Batman and Robin: Cute Meat"** — Batman and Robin meet on an airplane and develop a rapport. (Just two chairs required)
Mood: Comedy
Characters: (3) Batman, Robin, Flight Attendant (Also available as "Batperson and Robbie")
Playing Time: 10-12 minutes
Staged Reading: Actors Theatre of Santa Cruz, April, 2002. (Runner-Up in contest)
Also Staged Reading at First Stage, Los Angeles, June, 2002.

7. **"Nun of the Above"** — A Catholic nun encounters a representative of the Devil, who knows a terrible secret she is carrying. (Just two chairs needed)
Mood: Dark Comedy
Characters: (3) Sister Romina, any age; Man, a sinister man over 25; Voice
Playing Time: 10 minutes

8. **"A Fool's Audition"** — A man is auditioning for the job of Fool at the court of a king who beheads those who don't get the job.
Mood: Comedy
Characters: (3) The Fool, any age; the King, any age; the Advisor, any age.
Playing Time: 15 minutes
PRIZE WINNER: Produced at the Great Platte River Playwrights' Festival, U of Nebraska — Kearney, Summer, 2001.

9. **"Peni"** — Two guys (played by women with three-foot-long penises) have big needs.
Mood: Biting satire of feminist dislike of the male sex drive
Characters: (2) Zack, played by a woman, any age; Jack, played by a woman, any age
All that is needed are two three-foot-long "penises," preferably made of Styrofoam, that can be strapped on.
Playing Time: About 20 minutes

10. **"Air Rage"** — A high school teacher on an airplane encounters a former student to whom he once gave a D. There are resentments on both sides. (Just two chairs needed)
Mood: Realistic Comedy

Characters: (3) Mr. Brown, a high school teacher, any age between 40-70, Jeremy, the less-than-stellar former student, between 20-35; Flight Attendant, any age or sex (a few lines)
Playing Time: 12-15 minutes

11. **"So Middle Class"** — An answer to "Zoo Story," wherein a middle-class man who merely wants to read a book on a park bench winds up having a tension-filled afternoon with a "home-less" person and a lot gets said and done that has been bottled for too long.
Mood: Serious drama
Characters: (2) Thomas, who is middle-class, between thirty-five and seventy years old; Tobey, who is of any age, disheveled, annoying, some dignity tool.
Playing Time: 35 minutes
FIRST PRIZE, WINNER in ATTIC THEATRE ONE-ACT CONTEST
Produced: Attic Theatre, L.A., 1998.
Produced: California Travel Troupe, San Francisco, February, 2001.
Also performed at The Marsh, San Francisco, 1994.

12. **"The Hit"**— Four producer- writers have their bill of short plays picked up by an outside producer, at which time

the power plays (to say nothing of the slashing and burning) begin.
Mood: Satirical comedy
Characters: (4) Don, who's needy, sour; Patty, who's overly enthusiastic; Bea, who's very sociable but changeable; Neil, who's temperamental and crabby.
Playing Time: 20 minutes
WINNER: ATTIC THEATRE PLAY CONTEST (one of 12 selected).
Produced: Attic Theatre, Los Angeles, Feb.- March, 1997.

13. **How to Murder Your Very Best Friends,** Also called **The Murder of Gonzago — a Comedy** (one-act version) — A group of eccentric playwrights meets for its regular play reading session. Only this time a woman playwright, although she has connived to win their support, goes berserk when critiqued and reveals "horrible" secrets about the others. Backstage dirt and a play within a play within a play!
Mood: Comedy.
Characters: (4): Annabelle, the neurotic lead; a Maternal Female; Macho Stud; Gay Man.
Playing Time: 45 minutes
Produced by Theatre Rhinoceros, 1986.
Produced by Above Board Theatre, San

Francisco, 1993.
Published by Dialogus Play Service (out of print).

14. "**Your Town**" — Through life with a typical couple, from courtship to marriage to kids to caring for aging parents to old age, all in 18 minutes.
Mood: Biting satire on traditional "family" values.
Characters: (5) Woman; Man; Son; Daughter; Narrator.
Playing Time: 18 minutes
Produced by Earnest Players, in bill of one-acts called *Gaymes*, S. F., 1978.

15. "**Last Call**" — A handsome man and an un-handsome man cruise but barely speak in a gay bar, though what they're thinking becomes clear in its ironies and disappointments.
Mood: Amusing and touching.
Characters: (3) The Good-Looking Man; the Less Attractive Man; Bartender.
Playing Time: 20 minutes.
First produced: The One-Act Theater Co., San Francisco, 1981.Radio adaptation, NEA grant, 1982. Broadcast KQED, June, 1989 and KPFA radio.
Published by Dialogus Play Service in *Homosexual Acts* (out of print).

16. "**One Man's Opinion**" — A killer of homosexuals explains himself in hate-filled terms.
Mood: Drama.
Characters: (1, 2 or 3) the Killer; Police Officer or two (non-speaking part(s).
Playing Time: 12 minutes
Performed as part of *Homosexual Acts*, Theater Off Square, New York, 1991.
Published by Dialogus Play Service (in *Homosexual Acts*) (out of print).

17. "**Immortality**" — A gay man meets with his lesbian friend to discuss the baby they are planning, only to learn she has changed her mind about him as a donor because of AIDS.
Mood: Drama.
Characters: (2) Gay Man; Lesbian.
Playing Time: 11 minutes
Produced in bill of one-acts by Theater Rhinoceros, 1986.
Published by Dialogus Play Service (in *Homosexual Acts*) (out of print).

18. "**Rev. What's His Name**" — A Christian minister, full of Christian love, teaches a Bible study class of children about AIDS as a punishment from God.
Mood: Satirical comedy.
Characters: (1 to 6) the Reverend (as

monologue) speaking to unseen kids in Bible class.
Playing Time: 5 minutes
First performed as part of *The AIDS Show*, Theater Rhinoceros, SF, 1984. Also national tour of the United States. Performed in acting class of American Conservatory Theater, SF, 1986. Winner of special award from Bay Area Theater Critics Circle, 1984).
Published in *West Coast Plays* as part of *The AIDS Show,* 1985.

19. "**Sour Grapes**" — Members of a critics circle encounter a director-producer who has received bad reviews and hence tries to poison them, thus highlighting the eternal conflict between artist and critic. But conflicts between the critics also emerge along with interesting deathbed "confessions."
Mood: Comedy.
Characters: (6) director/producer; jaded critic; nice critic; push-over critic; hypocritical critic; foolish critic.
Playing Time: 50 minutes
One of three winners of play contest, Actors Theatre of Santa Cruz, 1997.

20. “**The Tasteful Transvestite and the Three Bullies**” — Claudette Camembert is a straight man who simply wants to wear tasteful frocks, but three bullies don’t want him to. So what is one to do but teach such bullies a lesson, no?
Mood: Comedy
Characters: (4) Claudette (a transvestite with a French accent); Three Bullies
Playing Time: 10 minutes
First produced: Absolute Theatre Company, San Francisco, 1994.
Also produced by New Conservatory Theatre, San Francisco, Spring, 1994.
Published by Dialogus Play Service (in *Homosexual Acts*) (out of print).

21. “**A Christmas Miracle at the Open Mess**” — Two gay officers, recently become lovers, risk the military’s wrath by slow dancing together in an officers club on Christmas Eve.
Mood: Touching drama
Characters: (3) Chet, who’s new to gay life; Graham, older, more cynical; Major Sullins, a coarse, drunken homophobe
Playing Time: 10 minutes
First produced by the Absolute Theatre Company, San Francisco, 1994.
Also produced by The New Conservatory Theatre, Spring, 1994.

Also produced by Frank Calo in "Men In and Out of Clothes: Four One-Act Plays," The Raw Space, NYC, Winter, 2000. — "a very fine play" (Andres J. Wrath, online review).
Published by Dialogus Play Service (in *Homosexual Acts*) (out of print).

22. "**Producing with Poppy**" — a self-aggrandizing, self-deceived woman producer maneuvers herself through a theater company.
Mood: Satirical comedy
Characters: (1) Poppy, the producer. (Could be male Popsy)
Playing Time: 15 minutes

23. "**In a Five-and-Ten-Cent Store**" — A lonely man and a sex doll.
Mood: Touching drama
Characters: (1) Claude, any age; Sweetie, the sex doll, male or female, depending on the company.
Playing Time: 10 minutes.

24. "**Body and Soul**" from *Sex Show* — a man arguing with his penis) (included in *Sexy Shorts*)
Mood: Broad sexual comedy
Characters: (2), two males, one in bed; one as the penis

Playing Time: 6 minutes
Produced by the New Conservatory Theatre, San Francisco, 1996.

25. "**Celebrities in Hell**" — with Eddie Murphy and the Pope in Hell with AIDS
Mood: Biting satire
Characters: (3) (Murphy, Pope, Guard)
Playing Time: 11 minutes
Broadcast on KPFA radio; included in *Homosexual Acts*, NYC, 1991.

26. "**I Married the Nightstalker**" – a woman wants the notorious serial murderer as her husband. Go figure.
Mood: Satire
Characters: (3) (Stalker, Wife, Minister)
Playing Time: 7 minutes

27. **"Hard to Swallow"** — Two friends have come to see the swallows at Capistrano, but they aren't there. What else isn't there?
Mood: Drama
Characters: (2) Dan, a man, any age between 50 and 75; Ann, a woman, any age between 20-70
Playing Time: 10 minutes

28. **"The Importance of Being P.C."** — One can never be too correct, in this spoof of *The Importance of Being Earnest*, with today's 'correctnesses' substituted for Victorian ones
Mood: Comedy
Characters: (2) Mrs. Berkeley, a forceful, politically correct matron; Jack Wirthliss, a suitor to her daughter
Playing Time: 10 minutes
Runner-Up, 10-Minute Play Contest, Actors' Theatre of Santa Cruz, 2004.

29. **"A-Holes Anonymous"** — You can send assholes to therapy, but can you make it stick?
Mood: Comedy
Characters: (4) Group Leader; A-Holes #1, #2, and #3
Playing Time: 10 minutes

For Production Rights: Tel: 415-585-3410 or e-mail: curzon@pacbell.net
Impulse Playwrights Agency represents *Pixies in Peril*, *How to Murder Your Very Best Friends, Very Nasty Indeed, Cinderella II: Happily Ever After?*
Tel: 866-627-4426 or 3131 S.W. Sherwood Place, Portland OR 97201

Made in the USA